Billy's *Fault Line* is going to rock your world and show you how Hollywood, the media, and college campuses have worked together to crack the foundations of our children's Christian faith. Thankfully (and thrillingly!) the foundations *can* and *are* now being repaired by a new breed of courageous Christians who have ditched the escapist "run and hide" mentality and embraced an optimistic and victorious engage-and-transform strategy. Read it carefully, and join the growing movement of vibrant, Spirit-filled Christians who are learning how to shape the next generation of life on earth to be more like it is in heaven.

—KIRK CAMERON
ACTOR AND DIRECTOR

In a country that praises the right to free speech while at the same time trying to quiet any voice that doesn't fall in line with the mainstream media, Billy's voice won't stay quiet. With this new book he offers up an encouragement to Christians to not complain but instead to get involved and be the change our world needs right now.

—MATTHEW WEST
CHRISTIAN SINGER

Billy Hallowell brings his typical conscientious professionalism to an area of great controversy and concern—the corruption of the most influential sectors of culture. But instead of writing just another lament, he also rightly points out how our side voluntarily vacated those arenas. Thankfully Billy reminds us the gospel commands us to go and not retreat for a reason.

—STEVE DEACE
NATIONALLY SYNDICATED TALK SHOW HOST

Fault Line takes readers deep into the debate over free speech in America, with Hallowell masterfully tackling how the media, Hollywood, and universities have unfortunately become echo chambers in recent years. Readers will come away educated about the problem—and inspired to make a difference by ensuring that these essential arenas include additional voices. *Fault Line* is a must-read for all Americans.

—KEVIN SORBO
ACTOR

WITHDRAWN

D1358139

America faces some serious challenges today, with religious freedom in many ways hanging in the balance. *Fault Line* is a great read for those looking to understand where we are morally and how our collective cultural values have changed. My good friend Billy Hallowell carefully breaks down how information is passed on and filtered in society. He offers a call for conservatives and Christians to engage with the culture rather than retreat. Ultimately and most importantly Billy encourages readers to adhere to truth.

—CANDACE CAMERON BURE
ACTRESS, AUTHOR, AND COHOST OF *THE VIEW*

America is ill with the disease of secular humanism. In *Fault Line* Billy Hallowell exposes the secular forces at work in our media and universities and their collective impact on our culture, specifically American youth. *Fault Line* is an indispensable resource for anyone wondering how we got so sick or looking for the cure.

—SAM SORBO
AUTHOR AND ACTRESS

This is an important book on a supremely important subject. May its message get out as far and wide as possible, and may it help correct the extraordinarily destructive trends it has so vitally revealed.

—ERIC METAXAS
NEW YORK TIMES BEST-SELLING AUTHOR OF
IF YOU CAN KEEP IT AND *BONHOEFFER*
NATIONALLY SYNDICATED RADIO HOST OF
THE ERIC METAXAS SHOW

It's pretty obvious to everyone that our culture isn't healthy. *Fault Line* examines where we stand as a society and gives us a sobering diagnosis. The only question is, will we accept the cure?

—STU BURGUIERE
COHOST OF *THE GLENN BECK PROGRAM* AND *PAT AND STU*
HOST OF *THE WONDERFUL WORLD OF STU*

FAULT LINE

BILLY HALLOWELL

FRONT
LINE

Most CHARISMA HOUSE BOOK GROUP products are available at special quantity discounts for bulk purchase for sales promotions, premiums, fund-raising, and educational needs. For details, write Charisma House Book Group, 600 Rinehart Road, Lake Mary, Florida 32746, or telephone (407) 333-0600.

FAULT LINE by Billy Hallowell
Published by FrontLine
Charisma Media/Charisma House Book Group
600 Rinehart Road
Lake Mary, Florida 32746
www.charismahouse.com

This book or parts thereof may not be reproduced in any form, stored in a retrieval system, or transmitted in any form by any means—electronic, mechanical, photocopy, recording, or otherwise—without prior written permission of the publisher, except as provided by United States of America copyright law.

Scripture quotations are taken from the Modern English Version. Copyright © 2014 by Military Bible Association. Used by permission. All rights reserved.

Billy Hallowell's reporting and interviews from *The Church Boys* are the property of TheBlaze Inc. and are used herein with permission. All such reporting is the sole property of TheBlaze Inc. All rights reserved.

Copyright © 2017 by Billy Hallowell
All rights reserved

Cover design by Vincent Pirozzi
Design Director: Justin Evans

Visit the author's website at www.billyhallowell.com.

Library of Congress Cataloging-in-Publication Data:
An application to register this book for cataloging has been submitted to the Library of Congress.
International Standard Book Number: 978-1-62998-724-8
E-book ISBN: 978-1-62998-725-5

While the author has made every effort to provide accurate telephone numbers and Internet addresses at the time of publication, neither the publisher nor the author assumes any responsibility for errors or for changes that occur after publication. Sources are provided throughout the text; some sources may contain content not appropriate for all audiences.

17 18 19 20 21 — 9 8 7 6 5 4 3 2 1
Printed in the United States of America

Train up a child in the way he should go, and
when he is old he will not depart from it.

—PROVERBS 22:6

I would like to dedicate this book to Andrea,
Ava, and Lilyana. The three of you are my world.
I thank God for you every day.

CONTENTS

Acknowledgments ix

Foreword *by Sean Hannity* xi

Introduction xiii

PART 1

Chapter 1: America's Moral Meltdown......................... 1

Chapter 2: What's Really Going On With Our Culture 10

Chapter 3: Millennials: A Complex Generation 15

Chapter 4: Millennials: Losing Their Faith and Religion 22

PART 2

Chapter 5: TV Then and Now: How the Tides Have Changed 31

Chapter 6: Scripting Culture: Driving Home an Agenda 40

Chapter 7: Movies Then and Now: The Paradigm Shift......... 50

Chapter 8: Lyrical Conundrum: Music's Devolving State........ 61

PART 3

Chapter 9: The Greatest Irony of Our Age.................... 71

Chapter 10: Campus Chaos Rages............................ 79

Chapter 11: The Rise of Colleges' All-Comers Policies.......... 86

Chapter 12: The True Impact on Academia.................... 95

PART 4

Chapter 13: The Media Paradox:
Ignorance Versus Intentionality? 107

Chapter 14: Is There Proof the Media Are Biased?............. 117

Chapter 15: How Did We Get Here? 127

PART 5

Chapter 16: Is Free Speech Under Attack?.................... 135

Chapter 17: Religious Freedom Battles Abound 145

Chapter 18: The Solution................................... 160

Notes 171

ACKNOWLEDGMENTS

I WOULD LIKE TO acknowledge and profoundly and formally thank the following individuals and institutions, as this book would not have been possible without them:

First and foremost, thank You, Lord, for continuing to amaze me by paving for me such a fascinating and rewarding path—one that continues to surprise me.

Second, thank you to Charisma House for allowing me to explore such a fundamentally fascinating topic: bias in our nation's main informational spheres. It's something I'm incredibly passionate about, and I'm so thankful for the opportunity to dive deep into it.

I would also like to specifically thank Woodley Auguste and Todd Starnes for your friendship and guidance in connecting me with the publisher and with this project. Megan Turner, I'm also immeasurably grateful for your hard work and dedication on the manuscript. You're extremely talented and a pleasure to work with.

I'm also grateful to my wife, Andrea Hallowell, who allowed me many days and hours away from her and our two young kids. She was a true partner in this project, and I couldn't have done it without her.

Last—but most certainly not least—thank you to my parents, who have always believed in me and who (though I'm far from perfect) fervently instilled in me the importance of embracing truth, sticking to my convictions, and standing for what's right.

Thank you all for making this book a reality.

FOREWORD

AMERICA IS FACING a cultural crisis. For far too long the mainstream media, Hollywood, and universities have held an anti-Christian and anti-conservative bias, with the three informational spheres coalescing to illicit a dire collective impact on society. Over time the results of the imbalanced informational dominance have been profound, with public opinion transforming and moral relativism rapidly spreading among members of every American generation.

From increasingly disconnected and confused views on religion to more permissive and apathetic perspectives on a variety of social and political issues, the effects of the dominance of secular and anti-conservative messaging have been stunning—and the problem only appears to be increasing in severity, with polls and research showing just how far we've fallen.

Millennials are more disconnected from faith than any previous generation in the modern era, though the impact extends well beyond youths. Moral confusion is running rampant, with relativism increasingly taking hold; meanwhile free speech is in peril as a bizarre obsession with political correctness profoundly transforms the landscape. These are just some of the broader narratives that Billy Hallowell addresses in *Fault Line* as he looks at the impact that a constant stream of secularized and left-of-center material has had on citizens, both young and old.

Throughout my many years working in radio and television, I have personally observed the pervasive impact that bias can have, and I've made it a point to call out incidents as I've observed them, specifically situations that show an unfair balance in the three informational arenas Hallowell discusses. While some may refute the idea that liberal or anti-Christian bias exists in media, entertainment, and university settings, the impact is undeniable. People have become afraid to speak out amid free speech attacks, while others face a barrage of controversy simply for sharing a sincerely held belief.

Fault Line will take you through some of the many examples of bias in each arena, while also exposing the statistics and facts that show the impact these messages are having on the masses. This book comes at a time in which society appears to be separating most from the values that once made America her strongest—the values of free speech and religious freedom and the ability to openly discuss and debate tough topics without unfairly maligning or shutting down ideological opponents.

From continued attacks on free speech, such as the horrific treatment that former Miss California Carrie Prejean faced for merely stating her opposition to same-sex marriage to an ever-increasingly diminished understanding of the First Amendment and religious liberty, the stakes have never been higher.

Many of the leaders and key figures in Hollywood, the media, and universities have failed miserably to create environments that foster free speech, with each sphere all too often presenting only one side of the story. These informational outlets undeniably dominate the stream of information in society, with the imbalance doing a collective disservice to viewers, students, and consumers alike. After all, how can people make educated decisions about tough topics if they've been force-fed only one perspective?

Despite the secular and overtly liberal nature of media, education, and Hollywood, each of us has a responsibility to educate ourselves about what's unfolding in society and who's truly controlling the message we consume. *Fault Line* also challenges conservatives and Christians alike not to retreat from these arenas, with Hallowell imploring readers to enter into these spheres as producers, actors, journalists, and professors to engage in the culture—or to take other steps to ensure their voices are heard amid the static.

—SEAN HANNITY

INTRODUCTION

AMERICANS SEEM CONFUSED, lost, and culturally disengaged. A higher proportion of people than ever before are losing touch with their moral center, with a biblical and ethical disconnect rapidly deepening and intensifying.

To a degree, the likely catalysts for these changing dynamics are understandable. Life is ever complicated; most of us are busy with work, kids, and the chaos of life. Perhaps we're too tied up to think about the finer things in life as deeply as we once did, though I would argue there are other far more pervasive causal factors at play. For instance, many of us are increasingly glued to our smartphones, tablets, computers, TVs, MP3 players, and other devices.

Through these avenues the messages streaming from Hollywood and the media that were once relatively benign—or at least less explicit than they are now—and were contained to a few channels and signals are now blasting at us from multiple angles. In everything from on-demand TV content and films coming from an over-sexualized Hollywood to the boundless information channels that the Internet provides, we're all on information overload.

The TV shows, movies, lyrics, and news we consume have changed dramatically over the years, with evolving content and subject matter yielding an intense flow of increasingly graphic content. Our devices and TVs have become like trash receptacles, with our minds serving as digital garbage dumps. The consumption level of this content differs based on the person, but one thing is for sure: over time our nation has collectively become desensitized, growing accustomed to the messages and themes we're viewing and hearing.

No longer are many of us shocked, revolted, or, at the least, turned off by it all; instead, many of us have simply come to expect it. We've stopped pushing back against it and have instead succumbed to the endless barrage of culturally troubling content.

The collective situation has created a fault line, and the beginnings of a cultural earthquake are most certainly afoot. From a transformation in traditional moral understandings to shifting theological alliances, society is, in many ways, at a bizarre and troubling turning point. There's unraveling of sorts, with the former bases of our culture being abandoned for a no-holds-barred mentality that places the collective moral conscience on ever-shifting ground.

Just consider that more Americans than ever before are counting themselves among the "nones"—the cohort of people who are either atheist, agnostic, or unaffiliated with a particular faith. This group of citizens has, in fact, continued to grow in recent years, with nearly one-fourth of the public and—perhaps most concerning—more than one-third of individuals born between 1981 and 1996 counting themselves among its ranks, according to the Pew Research Center.[1] To give you an idea of just how quickly the tides have changed, consider that 16 percent of Americans called themselves "nones" in 2007; by 2014 that number was up to 23 percent.[2]

But the cultural changes afoot go well beyond an evolution in religious allegiance. We're living in an era in which people are increasingly unable to firmly embrace a set of solid truths. Just consider the fact that in 2016 nearly six out of ten Americans said that "knowing what is right or wrong is a matter of personal experience"—whatever that means.[3] There's a wishy-washiness that has invaded, embedded, and taken control of our hearts and minds, and sadly many of us don't even recognize what's happening as we trade in a set of norms that have underpinned our society for a moral relativism that offers little ethical consistency and disproportionately emphasizes the self over adherence to a more profound code of ideals.

The key question surrounding all of these changes is, why? It's a complex curiosity that has increasingly sparked debate and discussion among experts, theologians, and preachers. And though there are a plethora of potential reasons, I would argue—and fervently—that there's a very specific cultural education paradigm at play that Americans, and in particular Bible believers and political conservatives, must adequately understand if they want even a fighting chance at helping stem the tide of cultural chaos.

Pause for a moment and consider where many people, particularly young adults, receive an education in contemporary society, taking into account that my definition of education is, in this instance, extended to include any avenue or venue through which people are fed potentially transformational information. Without a doubt the university classroom, the media, and Hollywood are the three main systems, outside of the church, that feed the masses with life-changing and perspective-shaping information.

Now here's the problem: There's evidence that these three main educational veins—the mainstream media, entertainment, and the university system—lean to the political Left and on a theological front typically misrepresent, underrepresent, or paint an inaccurate picture of what Christianity and faith truly encapsulate. And with some churches losing footing or, at the least, cultural reach—especially in those three educational settings—there's a clear conundrum we must confront.

First and foremost there's a free speech balance that is all too often not being struck, as these educational areas serve up content that many times runs counter to faith ideals while embracing and distributing stories, programs, and content tailored to more secular ideals. As a result, public perspectives can and have been shaped and desensitization has run rampant, leading, for example, to the mass toleration of bizarre content that wouldn't have had a place on television even a decade ago.

Rather than welcoming all perspectives, the mainstream media, entertainment industry, and the university system tend to eschew Christian and conservative values—many times doing so without even recognizing the character, intensity, or even the pervasiveness of their biases. And at the same time there are atheist and secular activist groups that are intentionally organizing like never before. Through lobbying, targeted lawsuits, and strategic campaigns these organizations are working to spread their message of nonbelief on a massive scale—all while stripping faith out of the mix.

These activists continue to permeate important sectors of influence as they become increasingly savvy at acquiring and refining the skills needed to win the culture war. Battle by battle, nativity scene by nativity scene, non-theists are ardently working toward a public square free from biblical sentiment. Does that mean that these individuals and groups are always wrong? Absolutely not, as some of their cases raise important First Amendment questions. Is the point of this book to denigrate atheists? Not in the least. The intention is to serve as a wake-up call for the masses, particularly those who have concerns about the state of free speech and expression in America.

With all of this in mind, *Fault Line* will explore how society's main educational avenues fail to deliver fair-minded content and how their biases are introducing and reinforcing negative values and stereotypes, while cutting out specific perspectives—mainly Christian and conservative ideals—that would not only offer up positive perspective if permitted into the fold, but would also enable individuals on all sides of the aisle to engage in robust and healthy conversation.

But before we get into the meat of my arguments, I should warn you: this book isn't meant to be seen merely as a treatise filled with rampant complaints and vents; it's essentially a call for Christians and conservatives to boldly step up to the plate to make their voices heard. After all, it's quite easy to complain about being cut out of the media, Hollywood, and academia, but the reality is that many of the faithful and those on the political Right have taken steps over the years toward self-alienation and abandonment, retreating from the nation's most important and impactful educational venues.

Without enough of these people in college classrooms and newsrooms and on the sets of films and TV shows, we're at risk of losing the very soul of our nation. And if that happens, it's nobody's fault but our own.

PART 1

CHAPTER 1

AMERICA'S MORAL MELTDOWN

THE **MORALS AND** standards that once stood at the core of the American conscience are rapidly eroding, giving way to an entirely looser set of parameters, standards, and norms, especially when it comes to issues of sexual ethics.

There is a moral chaos of sorts afoot—one in which many of the traditional values associated with and adhered to through faith have been slowly loosened over time, with the speed of the denigration continuing to increase. There's a growing, active, and, in many ways, intentional hostility against many of the ethics and values that previously enjoyed a prominent place in our society.

Famed Christian apologist Josh McDowell, who has authored more than 140 books on Christianity and culture during his more than fifty years in ministry, told me that we're experiencing a profound "lostness of truth," pointing to a transformative cultural movement under way in both ideology and perspective. "We've had a complete epistemological shift, which means there's been a total shift in the nature and the source of truth," McDowell said.[1]

CHANGING MORALITY

Consider the rapid change in opinion that has taken root over the past fourteen years on issues such as premarital sex, having babies out of wedlock, divorce, or even polygamy. We're in the midst of a moral meltdown as Americans have become more apathetic, complacent, and permissive on a plethora of ethical fronts.

Don't believe me? Just consider the fact that 45 percent of American respondents told Gallup in 2002 that "having a baby outside of marriage" was morally acceptable. But when the same question was asked again in 2015, that proportion jumped to 61 percent. In the same vein, moral support for premarital sex jumped from 53 percent in 2001 to 68 percent in 2015.[2]

Pause and think about that for a moment. Nearly seven in ten Americans actually believe that it is now *morally acceptable* for a man and a woman to have sex outside of marriage, leaving only a minority of the public standing on higher moral ground. And a 2015 study about Americans' changing sexual behaviors between 1972 and 2012 seemingly backs the notion that people are putting these opinions into practice.

Using the General Social Survey, the study found that adults from 2000–2012 had more sexual partners and were more likely to have had intercourse with a casual date, acquaintance, or pickup than adults in the 1970s and 1980s, according to the study's abstract. Additionally, they were more likely to accept most forms of sex outside of marriage.

"The percentage who believed premarital sex among adults was 'not wrong at all' was 29 percent in the early 1970s, 42 percent in the 1980s and 1990s, 49 percent in the 2000s, and 58 percent between 2010 and 2012," the text reads.[3]

From a purely moral and biblical standpoint, that's nothing short of troubling, but it really only represents one facet of the overarching problem.

Consider the increase in support for polyamory (romantic relationships that include more than two participants), which ticked up from just 7 percent of Americans in 2003 to 14 percent in 2016.[4] While that may not seem like an overwhelming proportion, in reality it means that more than one in ten Americans now believe that it is morally acceptable for individuals to have more than one partner or spouse.

There's also been an increase in moral support for divorce, jumping from 59 percent to 71 percent over the past few years, with the moral acceptability of homosexuality moving from 40 to 63 percent.[5] And the list goes on.

In summarizing its data back in 2015, Gallup said, "Americans are becoming more liberal on social issues"—a sentiment that is impossible to deny based on the indicators.[6] And as the dominos just keep falling, speaking out about moral truth is paramount. But beyond that there's a responsibility to protect the rights of free speech, as well as the right for people to live out their personal faith in all they do.

THE CAUSE OF OUR LACK OF MORALITY

So, how did we get here? That's the central question. While understanding the statistics and the changes in society over the past few years is certainly important, the bigger issue is pinpointing the causes, especially if there's any hope of navigating the fallout. It's clear there is a deeper willingness to suddenly embrace many behaviors that were once deemed immoral.

From a 30,000-foot view, the catalysts for where we find ourselves appear to be rooted in both tolerance and relativism. The former, which is defined as the "willingness to accept feelings, habits, or beliefs that are different from your own," is where the problem begins.[7] Certainly it is entirely appropriate and rightful to be tolerant of others and to show love for every person regardless of any moral or ideological differences. But when tolerance moves us to the acceptance phase, things can get a little bit tricky.

Relativism, on the other hand, takes tolerance and injects it with steroids, leading many people to more generally conclude that "ethical truths depend on the individuals and groups holding them" and not on a broader set of universal truths, such as the parameters outlined in the Bible.[8] When this happens en masse, the result is an apathetic populace filled with people who can no longer differentiate their personal moral truth from society's definition of what is right and wrong. This is, in fact, what we're seeing unfold before our very eyes.

In discussing these issues with me for this book, Josh McDowell recalled a proclamation a number of years ago from some professors who told him that they had a plan to "marginalize Christianity." He recalled asking how such a feat would be accomplished. Their response? "Through tolerance."[9]

The apologist also recapped his belief that a series of broader changes in human history helped to bring us to where we are today—to a place where a higher standard no longer matters in the minds of many men.

"When all truth becomes equal, Christianity will lose its sting. We went from where all truth was in a personal creator God...scientific truth, economic truth, historical truth, everything," McDowell said. "Then along came the Renaissance that said, 'Look how great man is.' That's when they started doing the sculptures of man, the painting of the human body, everything."[10]

The next movement—the Enlightenment—then said, "We don't need God. Look how great man can reason," McDowell explained. From there the Industrial Revolution kicked off, and yet another ideology took form, further alienating society from its need for God. "The Industrial Revolution came on the scene and said, 'We don't need God. We don't need a personal creator God, because see how great man can create,'" he said. "This is when all great machines of history, patents, everything, exploded."[11]

The next transformative ideology to emerge on the scene was Darwinism, a theory that involves the origination and evolution of species and life. It was this paradigm, McDowell said, that led human beings to conclude that "we don't even need the concept of a personal creator God." It was that idea that further helped to push the idea of God out of the minds and hearts of so many, he argued.[12]

McDowell dubbed this entire scenario the "God Is Dead Movement," using it to explain how culture ended up where it is today. "A concept of a personal, creator God [in] which all truth resides, that concept died," he said. "Out of this came the greatest virtue in culture today: tolerance. Every single university in America is based on tolerance, which is a false concept."[13]

In light of the definitions of relativism and tolerance, McDowell's theories seem to hold some merit. Universities have sometimes been critiqued for fostering the notion that one must be tolerant to the point of obliterating personal moral codes and ethical values.

"Tolerance came on because how could one person say to another person, 'Your values, your belief, your lifestyle, your claim to truth is lesser than mine. Where is your external reference point?'" McDowell said. "There is none, so all truth is personal."[14]

McDowell also spoke to the issue of multiculturalism, saying that it is "tolerance applied to culture" and that it can lead to a dynamic in which one concludes that "all cultural values, beliefs, lifestyles, and claims to truth are equal." That too, he argued, can come along with some dire consequences. "If you dare to say there's a value, belief, life-style, or claim to truth in your culture that's greater than the truth in another culture, then you are anti-multicultural," he said.[15]

Surely not everyone will agree with McDowell's take on the culture, and that's perfectly fine. We're all entitled to believe what we wish, though I'd argue that at least some of his core arguments hold merit. Many certainly see our current cultural trajectory as one that is taking us on a favorable or progressive move in the right direction; others, though—particularly people of faith and political conservatives—tend to see these tectonic shifts as problematic.

AMERICA IS CHANGING

What's perhaps most striking about the current cultural dynamic is that ten years ago—or even five—there was an entirely different societal vibe. Extend that back a few decades and the differences are even starker. What is it that has so fervently transformed American culture? What is it that has changed our fabric so intensely? I would argue there is what I call a *triangular dominance* at play surrounding how members of our society receive their information—a systematic control over educational content that has permeated our minds, our hearts, and perhaps most tragically, our souls. And the situation is only intensifying.

Through the media, entertainment, and university system—the three main information sources that shape the American conscience—people are bombarded with moral codes and messages that are anything but modest, restrained, or in line with biblical tenets. These educational spheres have become overridden with progressive ideals and biases that work against traditional moral understandings. Each sector incubates one worldview while filtering the other out or, more routinely, simply ignoring it all together.

Think about it. It's no surprise that millennials—the individuals who will pave the way toward the nation's future—are the adult generation that is most profoundly impacted by this dynamic since they grew up just as media and technology began to explode. And as a guy on the upper end of the millennial scale, I can speak from experience.

But the disproportionate informational focus isn't the only problem; there's also ignorance and complicity unfolding that, unless it is checked, will only incubate, empower, and metastasize this educational conundrum, and tragically many people today are likely too indoctrinated at this point to believe—or even recognize—that there's anything wrong with the paradigm shift in moral values undoubtedly slated to transform a wide array of institutions, including marriage, the economy, and the circumstances surrounding children's upbringing.

Big changes are already afoot—movements that most certainly carry with them consequences for faith and family structures. And don't just take my word for it; Gallup made this sentiment clear in its 2015 report on morality in America:

> This liberalization of attitudes toward moral issues is part of a complex set of factors affecting the social and cultural fabric of the US. Regardless of the factors causing the shifts, the trend toward a more liberal view on moral behaviors will certainly have implications for such fundamental social institutions as marriage, the environment in which children are raised and the economy.[16]

This dynamic was more pointedly captured by the Barna Group in a 2016 report titled "The End of Absolutes: America's New Moral Code." The study opens with this ominous line about where our culture currently stands: "Christian morality is being ushered out of American social structures and off the cultural main stage, leaving a vacuum in its place—and the broader culture is attempting to fill the void."[17] The natural resulting question is what are they filling the vacuum with? The answer: unrestrained chaos and confusion, or at the least, the impetus for such constructs.

I've heard some people scoff at the notion that something doesn't feel quite right in our culture; those who favor the move away from biblical or Christian sentiments see it as a societal benefit that we're abandoning what they see as a more limiting or conservative worldview—an abandonment that allows for a progressive and open society. And while it's true that many Americans do feel that way, the Barna study yielded perhaps one of the most bizarre statistics of all. While many people are expressing changing views on what they're willing to tolerate, the vast majority of the public also think that something doesn't feel quite right.

In fact, 80 percent of Americans expressed concern over the current "moral condition," with even 74 percent of millennials and 67 percent of people with no religion expressing concern. Not surprisingly, 90 percent of practicing Christians share these worries and concerns.[18] Of course, I should caution that the question itself about moral condition is a relatively benign measure, considering that, at this point, morals have become oddly subjective; a high proportion among various cohorts, in this case, could simply be rooted in a dissatisfaction over the failure to see one's personal values reflected in the broader culture. Still the numbers at least tell us that there's a sense that something isn't quite right, societally speaking.

Even more shocking is what Barna found when respondents were asked for their level of agreement with the following statement: "Whatever is right for your life or works best for you is the only truth you can know." A majority of Americans—57 percent—agreed, with 74 percent of millennials concurring either strongly or somewhat with this notion. Meanwhile 41 percent of practicing Christians agreed with this sentiment. What's perhaps most disturbing about these measures, though, is that the statement appears to link one's personal moral compass to whatever "works" for that individual person; it's quite a daunting measure when one truly pauses to consider the ramifications. But it doesn't end there. Sixty-five percent of Americans also agreed somewhat or strongly with the idea that "every culture must determine what is acceptable morality for its people."[19]

These statistics cause one to wonder if we have become so intellectually lazy and desensitized that we can no longer separate personal standards that are shaped by thought and reason from the broader societal narratives that are imprinted and reinforced through universities, media, and entertainment.

Have we become so inept and lazy that we can no longer learn to love and respect people while still being willing to say that their personal beliefs and practices cross our own moral barriers? It seems the moral barriers have come tumbling down as our society continues to push out biblical truths—the only collective benchmarks and standards capable of helping human beings fully make sense of the world around them.

In the end, despite the doom and gloom and the obvious moral bewilderment, 59 percent of Americans somehow still agreed that "the Bible provides us with absolute moral truths which are the same for all people in all situations, without exception."[20] So there's clearly at least a ray of hope for those concerned about the current state of morality.

WHERE AMERICA IS HEADED

Let's go back to that question that was asked earlier on in this chapter: If Christian influence over the culture is dissipating, what's replacing it? David Kinnaman, a researcher and the president of the Barna Group, offered up the idea that there is a "new moral code" that he calls the "morality of self-fulfillment"—and he believes it "has all but replaced Christianity as the culture's moral norm." Rather than being predicated upon biblical values or, at the least, the idea that a higher power has set standards and that those standards are good and enriching for everyone, the principles that comprise the "morality of self-fulfillment" are quite individualized.[21]

Kinnaman narrowed down six attributes that apparently form the basis for this newfound moral center. To begin, 91 percent of adults believe that the best way to find one's self is to look within, 89 percent believe that people shouldn't criticize others' life choices, 86 percent say that one should pursue the things he or she most desires in order to be fulfilled, 84 percent say that "the highest goal of life is to enjoy it as much as possible," 79 percent say that people can believe whatever they wish so long as it doesn't impact society, and 69 percent say that "any kind of sexual expression between two consenting adults is acceptable."[22]

I'll let Kinnaman summarize in his own words, as he did in his book *Good Faith: Being a Christian When Society Thinks You're Irrelevant and Extreme*: "The highest good, according to our society, is 'finding yourself' and then living by 'what's right for you.'" So rather than appealing to the Creator for guidance, we're apparently looking to the self these days—a troubling idea, to say the least, with some complex causal factors.[23]

It might not be possible to definitively prove all of the ways through which we got here culturally speaking, though the influences that have helped to create and reinforce the problem, as we'll discuss throughout this book, aren't too difficult to pinpoint.

The overarching reality is that America is changing, as the country continues to separate from the Christian roots that the majority of the population have historically embraced. In fact, PRRI (a nonprofit that conducts public opinion research) conducted a study in 2016 that found that only 41 percent of Americans believed that the United

States is and has always been a Christian nation. This is compared to 42 percent who said that America was once a Christian nation, but isn't one today, while an additional 15 percent said that the United States never was a Christian nation.[24]

Perhaps what's most notable is the difference that was observed among white evangelical Protestants when comparing the proportions in 2012 and 2016. "White evangelical Protestants are most apt to believe that the US has lost its Christian identity, and this belief has increased significantly over the last four years," the report read. "In 2012, 45 percent of white evangelical Protestants believed that the US is and has always been a Christian nation, while a similar number (48 percent) believed that the US was a Christian nation in the past but is not today." Those numbers changed profoundly in just four years, with the 45 percent who believe the United States always has been and still is a Christian nation dropping to 37 percent and with a stunning 59 percent suddenly believing that the United States is no longer a Christian nation.[25]

People are free to debate whether they believe America is or ever was a biblically in-tune nation, but what we can at least see from the numbers is that the culture has changed. Now, let's dig a little deeper into what's causing the moral uncertainty.

CHAPTER 2

WHAT'S REALLY GOING ON
WITH OUR CULTURE

WITHOUT A DOUBT there is a troubling triangular dominance influencing society as the nation's three main educational veins—the mainstream media, entertainment, and the university system—lean to the political Left and, on a theological front, typically misrepresent or underrepresent Christian values and biblical sentiment.

These important societal spheres all too often serve up deceptive content that biases citizens against faith while selectively offering up stories, programs, lectures, and content tailored to tout, embrace, or at least act as a sympathizer for secular ideals. As a result perspectives have been shaped over time and desensitization has run rampant, specifically among younger generations. And we now have increasingly graphic, bizarre, and morally defunct content that wouldn't have seen the light of day even a decade ago.

This wouldn't all be so terrible or concerning if there was an equal ideological playing field, but rather than welcoming or even seeking out all perspectives, the media, entertainment industry, and the educational system tend to eschew Christian values—many times doing so without recognizing the intensity or even the existence of the biases held, embraced, and echoed within.

Other sectors of society only add fuel to the fire. The government's anti-discrimination policies are in some cases further alienating Christian business owners. Additionally, atheist and secularist groups are organizing like never before in an effort to fervently spread their message of nonbelief on a massive scale—all while stripping faith out of the mix. Between government policies, activists' antics, and the progressive and secular dominance of media, entertainment, and education, the state of morality hangs in the balance.

Millennials have already been profoundly impacted by the

restriction of diverse ideals, with the next generation poised to grow up with an even more skewed perspective of the world around them.

ANTI-FAITH BIAS IN AMERICAN CULTURE

Over the years Christians and conservatives have continued to sound the alarm about their concerns surrounding a dearth of representation in society's three key educational sectors, yet when they voice those grievances, they are sometimes painted as paranoid or incorrect—and are dismissed altogether. But let's pause to think about this for a minute: shouldn't concerns over free speech and the constraints on reasonable self-expression at least be entertained or investigated, especially when there's evidence that a pervasive problem has taken root?

One of critics' favorite rebuttals to faithful individuals who claim there is an inherent anti-faith bias in the current culture is to cite the fact that—at least nominally speaking—the vast majority of Americans are Christians. It is an explanation that is, at its best, lazy and slightly dishonest and, at its worst, a data manipulation that is uttered with the intent of maintaining the status quo. While it's certainly true that 70 percent of the nation embraces a "Christian" label, using that statistic to act as though secular ideological dominance is a figment of Christians' imaginations is an exercise in intellectual malpractice.[1]

Atheist comedian Bill Maher, a man known for sometimes poking fun at faith and religion, is among those who have most blatantly articulated this faulty progressive argument. During the June 5, 2015, broadcast of his HBO Show *Real Time With Bill Maher*, he railed against the notion that Christianity is being marginalized in America, quipping, "Conservatives who constantly whine that Christianity is under attack from liberals have to explain why there are over 300,000 churches in the US, but only 400 Whole Foods. Clearly your side is winning."[2]

From there, Maher said that "Christians love to feel persecuted," because "it's part of their origin story," and went on to cite the 70 percent figure as the centerpiece of his pushback against claims that liberals are denigrating Christianity.[3]

Maher said he believes though liberal politicians, the media, and entertainers are often accused of being against faith, that accusation simply doesn't add up. "This idea that everybody on the Left is plotting against Christianity and wants to wipe out religion is offensive—to me," Maher continued. "I really want to know: Where is religion belittled in the liberal world? The *New York Times* editorial page? No. The *Times* op-ed page? No. Any newspaper's any page? No."[4]

There are so many things wrong with his claims that it's hard to decide where to begin. Perhaps we can start with the demographics, since people seem to enjoy bringing them up in this debate. Let's first focus on the fact that there was a substantial decrease in the proportion of Americans calling themselves Christians between 2007 and 2014, with the percentage moving from 78.4 percent to 70.6 percent, which Maher, of course, didn't give much attention to during his rant. At the same time, the proportion of unaffiliated Americans—those unaffiliated with a specific faith—rose from 16.1 percent to 22.8 percent. On that basis alone, one could argue that there is a troubling tick downward when it comes to the influence of Christianity on the masses.[5]

DECLINE OF CHRISTIANITY

This leads to a question, of course: What's causing the decline in the number of Americans calling themselves Christians?

No doubt, these changes have emerged, in part, because of the ceaseless messages that are being distributed through the triangular dominance of media, entertainment, and universities—messages that mesh more fervently with a secular worldview. Anyone who is looking objectively at the situation can see that faith is hardly a valued or prevalent sentiment in society's main educational spheres. And that has had a major impact.

Maher and others like him rail against those who caution that Christian values are under assault, using their elevated platforms to lecture the masses about how such warnings about the demise of these principles are essentially paranoid and silly.

But what these critics gloss over is the fact that secularists and some on the American Left have created and incubated a climate that is hostile to the very values that were once revered and protected in society—biblical sentiments that give individuals meaning and fulfillment and that connect them to the very Creator who they believe set the world in motion. And with Christians retreating from Hollywood, media, and education—yet another dynamic that's adding to this problem—the effects are unfortunate.

Before we continue, it's important to note that bias isn't always overt, which is yet another point that Maher seems to miss. It might not be a politician, entertainer, or professor vocally lambasting the Bible or dismissing the Christian faith; bias can emerge in many forms, including through a complete and consistent dearth of biblical or traditional values in media, education, and entertainment, or the cultivation of an environment in which those who embrace such sentiments either feel entirely unwelcome to express them or are chided when they do decide to do so publicly.

I teach speech courses at a New York City college, and one of the main points I always drive home to my students is that many times what is missing from a speech or address matters just as much as what is being said. This same ideal can be applied to media, entertainment, and universities when exploring bias; sure, there are many examples of overt bias, but there is also a general reality that something is missing from what's being taught at universities, aired in our entertainment, and reported in media. With the content worsening and with biblical and traditional values increasingly missing from these arenas, it's understandable why so many conclude there is a silent assault on those ideals.

While Maher appears to laugh off critiques from Christians who feel as if their worldview and perspective are increasingly absent from media, entertainment, and college classrooms, these concerns and claims are corroborated and validated by the cold, hard facts.

With 70 percent of the nation still embracing a Christian label, does it not appear odd to Maher that there aren't too many TV shows (outside of programs that air on Fox News, which, by the way, has had the highest cable ratings for eons, showing just how much this programming is craved) that espouse faith and traditional values? Sure, there's been *Duck Dynasty* among other outliers, but it's impossible for an objective observer to look at the TV lineup—especially prime time and what's airing on the most-watched networks—and conclude there is even a remote semblance of fairness when it comes to a representation of every worldview, particularly the Christian majority worldview.

Biblical sentiment is virtually nonexistent in entertainment, media, and the university classroom, yet many liberals—who tend to dominate these spheres—continue to dismiss complaints over the impact these education portals have on the American conscience, particularly among young people and millennials. (The responsibility isn't only on the Left, though. I'll note later on in this book that conservatives and Christians also bear plenty of responsibility for their role in avoiding these fields.)

While Maher tells us he finds offensive the "idea that everybody on the left is plotting against Christianity and wants to wipe out religion," the numbers don't lie. The cultural winds have swayed, whether intentionally or unintentionally, in liberals' direction, with a secular viewpoint being touted above all else. Christians and conservatives are all too often left out of the discussion.

Without a doubt, there has been a slow-paced indoctrination that isn't merely transforming individuals' minds; it is profoundly expediting our nation's trajectory toward moral and culture chaos. Why else do nearly 70 percent of Americans now have no moral qualms with premarital sex, with other moral parameters following suit?

Because the "free sex and multiple partners" message is really the only one that most Americans have been seeing in mainstream entertainment and media for eons now and because, as a result, it has been a force of normalization in the lives of millennials for quite some time, though, as we'll explore later on in the book, changing ideas on sex doesn't necessarily mean young people are engaging in it more. Either way, the triangular ideological dominance of media, universities, and entertainment has held quite a bit of sway over the masses.

Dr. George Yancey, a sociology professor at the University of North Texas who specializes in research on anti-Christian bias in academia and other societal constructs, told me in an interview for this book that he believes "cultural institutions" tend to hold a bias against faith—an assessment that I fully embrace.[6]

He told me he's found evidence of bias in media as well as the educational sphere, explaining his assessment: "It sort of confirms what I thought—that cultural institutions [are] where this is happening. Not just academia, but also in the media." The problem, of course, is that these "cultural institutions" are, again, the channels through which so many in our society consume information and learn, making such a paradigm more than concerning, as I will explore throughout the book.[7]

Chapter 3

MILLENNIALS: A COMPLEX GENERATION

W E'VE ALREADY COVERED the fact that around four out of ten Americans believe the United States has been—and still remains—a Christian nation, but when we dive deeper into the data, it becomes painfully clear that the youngest subset of US adults (those aged eighteen through twenty-nine) are much less likely to recognize the nation's Christian roots. When you consider the content this generation has been consuming for years now—an informational exchange that largely edits out those values—I suppose it's not too surprising. Either way, it's concerning.

"Only one-third (32 percent) of young adults…say America is and always has been a Christian nation, while nearly half (49 percent) of seniors (age 65 and older) say the same," reads a PRRI study from 2016. "Conversely, young adults are nearly three times more likely than seniors to say America has never been a Christian nation (24 percent vs. 9 percent, respectively)."[1]

Millennials, after all, are an interesting breed. Considered the youngest adult cohort, they generally fall between the ages of eighteen and thirty-five, though polling firms use different date ranges for classifying the cohort. The Pew Research Center said in a 2016 report that "the oldest 'Millennial' was born in 1981," while the Barna Group calls anyone born between 1984 and 2002 a millennial.[2]

Either way, this is clearly a group that was raised during an entertainment and media explosion. Even still the floodgates continue to open to new modes of content and a never-ending array of channels that are available on our phones, tablets, and computers. The millennials are a generation that has persistently been on information overload—so much so that one can't help but wonder how much more of an impact this dynamic will have on the next generation that's coming up behind them (a group that some now refer to as Generation Z), considering the continued influx of infotainment.

MILLENNIALS AND MORALITY

While we covered some of the statistics surrounding morality in previous chapters, it's essential to dive a bit deeper on the millennial front, especially considering that it appears a substantial proportion of the generation has become increasingly complacent when it comes to adherence to moral truths, falling prey to an ethical relativism of sorts. Don't believe me? Just consider that millennials are the most likely of any age cohort to believe that "moral truth is relative," with 51 percent embracing this sentiment compared to just "44 percent of Gen Xers, 41 percent of Boomers and 39 percent of Elders," according to Barna. (Those in Generation X were born between 1965 and 1983, Boomers between 1946–1964, and Elders before 1945.)[3]

But, again, what can we expect from them (or "us," I should say, considering that I personally fall on the upper end of the millennial spectrum)? Millennials grew up in a culture that was increasingly saturated with sexual themes, drugs, profanity, and the like. I believe this has led to amended standards of moral acceptability. But as I noted in previous chapters, it isn't only the millennials who have lost their way; Americans of a variety of ages have also ceded moral ground. With ethics in flux across the board, it's no surprise to see how "mixed up" young adults are when it comes to more specific indicators, such as their beliefs about sex, marriage, and relationships, among other issues.[4]

Let's start with a look at premarital sex, as studies have found that millennials differ quite a bit from past generations. Dr. Jean M. Twenge, a psychology professor at San Diego State University, found in her research, which was based on the 2012 General Social Survey, that 62 percent of millennials found nothing wrong with premarital sex.[5] Some critics might posit that young people are typically more progressive on issues like sexuality—and that's generally true.

But Twenge made another discovery when she dove a bit deeper into the research: millennials are more likely to see nothing wrong with premarital sex than members of past generations were at the same point in their lives. For instance, when baby boomers were between the ages of eighteen and twenty-nine, 47 percent of them took no issue with premarital sex, with just 50 percent of members of Generation X—those born between 1965 and 1981—saying the same.

When you compare that to the 62 percent of millennials who had no qualms about premarital sex, there's clearly a stunning difference.[6]

Twenge also found that there was a massive increase in the US population's overall acceptance of premarital sex from 29 percent in the 1970s to 42 percent in 2000 and then 58 percent in 2012—statistics that aren't all that surprising, considering the increasingly rampant sexual content in our music, shows, and films.[7] Meanwhile, Gallup pegged that proportion as increasing within the overall population from 53 percent in 2001 to 68 percent in 2015.[8]

One theory for the increase in the acceptance of premarital sex is that it increased as the median age at which individuals got married began to increase—a fair point, considering that the median age for women increased from 21 to 27 between 1970 and 2010 and from 23 to 29 for men during that same time frame.[9]

Despite millennials' loosened views on premarital sex, they were actually found to be somewhat more conservative on one measure: their number of sexual partners, which decreased from an average of 11.68 for those born in the 1950s (baby boomers) to 8.26 for individuals born in the 1980s and 1990s.

It's an odd dynamic: while the stigma surrounding premarital sex continued to dissipate, the number of partners, generationally speaking, didn't necessarily increase. Consider that in Twenge's study, millennials were more likely to admit to having casual sex, with 45 percent saying that they had sex with someone they weren't in a relationship with during their teens or twenties—a higher proportion than the 35 percent of Gen Xers who said the same when they were the same age.[10]

The researchers posit that casual sex could simply be unfolding with a more limited number of people, which could, in turn, potentially bring down the overall number of partners, according to the *Los Angeles Times*.[11]

And some curious findings about millennials continued to emerge not long after the aforementioned research was published, as Twenge attracted attention for a separate study released in August 2016 that found that Americans born in the 1980s or 1990s reportedly had a higher likelihood of saying they had no sex partners as adults when compared to Gen Xers born decades earlier. While 6 percent of Gen Xers born in the 1960s said they had no sexual partners since turning eighteen, this proportion was at 15 percent for millennials born in the 1990s, according to the study's abstract.[12]

If true, this raises a variety of questions about what could be driving such a dynamic. And while there isn't time in this book to embark on an exhaustive analysis of what could be unfolding, a number of theories have been floated. On the surface, some might applaud the data as evidence that more young Americans are "standing on the sidelines" when it comes to sex, as the *Washington Post* noted. But the outlet also reported that there is concern among some experts that this drop-off is reflecting "the difficulty some young people are having in forming deep romantic connections."[13]

What are the potential causal factors at the root of the issue? More on-screen relationships and social activities, pressure to succeed, and expectations surrounding "physical perfection" that aren't realistic, among other possible causal factors. Just pause and consider the "on-screen" element for a moment. Electronics and technology could surely be playing a role, with Twenge telling the *Post* that millennials are "the group that really started to communicate by screens more and by talking to their friends in person less."[14]

There are plenty of other theories out there as well, including the idea that millennials are more cautious as a generation and that they have increasingly turned to pornography, which they use to satisfy their pleasures virtually rather than through intimate relations with another real-life human being.

"I've seen a lot of patients—I have to say, young men who are not sexual at all, and it's partially because they satisfy themselves via the internet and porn," Dr. Ildiko Kovacs, a professor and psychiatrist at UC San Diego, told Vice. "We see early on, even from high school, that they turn to porn [and] get immediate gratification. They don't have to bother another person. They're not going to be rejected."[15]

Interestingly there has been quite a bit emerging of late about the negative impact of pornography as well. A landmark study released in 2016 by Josh McDowell Ministry found that the consumption of pornography has changed quite a bit among the nation's teens and youths. In fact, twice as many young adults between the ages of 25 and 30 (27 percent) first saw porn before they hit puberty compared to just 13 percent of Gen Xers. The study also found that teens and young adults "have a cavalier attitude toward porn," with only one in twenty young adults and one in ten teens saying that their friends see porn as a "bad thing."[16]

And it doesn't end there, as usage rates are also concerning. Eight percent of teens aged thirteen to seventeen watch porn daily, 18 percent weekly, and 17 percent once or twice per month, with 12 percent of young adults aged eighteen to twenty-four watching it daily, 26 percent weekly, and 19 percent once or twice per month. For twenty-five to thirty-year-olds, those proportions are 8 percent, 17 percent, and 20 percent, respectively.[17]

Researchers' findings about the impact of porn are, in themselves, worthy of an entire book. To summarize, studies have found that porn consumption can potentially lead to cheating, that it reduces individuals' commitment to their relationships, and that relationships are stronger without it.[18] But is porn impacting statistics surrounding sexual activity? That remains to be seen, though it's clear that young people have increasingly turned to it.

Either way, there is clearly a need to continue studying all of these issues, as some of the proportions might be confounding to observers. Consider that the Centers for Disease Control and Prevention has also found a decrease in sexual activity among high school students, with the percentage of those saying they have had sex in a 2015 survey standing at 41 percent versus 47 percent in 2013 and 54 percent in 1991.[19] Again, though, actions and beliefs are two different measures. While it's great that fewer young people might be having premarital relations, perceptions on sex—even if the acts aren't lining up with those looser ideals—continue to liberalize.

ENTERTAINMENT, MEDIA, AND SEX

There has clearly been a societal narrative at play telling young people, both overtly and covertly, that sex with multiple partners isn't only permissible, but that it's normative and encouraged. From TV shows to movies, a plethora of characters are shown shacking up and having sex at will, outside of the confines of marriage, and with little regard for emotional connections, consequences, or commitment. With entertainment and media continuously hitting society over the head with oversexualized plots, characters, and themes, it's hard to imagine that those elements haven't transformed perspectives.

Sex is quite obviously a primary driver of a great deal of our entertainment content, and it only seems to be worsening.

MILLENNIAL RELATIVISM

Over time, the once-helpful barriers, limits, and standards that came along with good morals have started to crumble, with relativism creeping in and taking root.

As I mentioned previously, a 2016 study from the Barna Group found that millennials—identified as individuals born between 1984 and 2002—were most likely of all generations (25 percent) to strongly agree that "every culture must determine what is acceptable morality for its people." And while that might not be an explosive red flag or an overt indicator of moral chaos, millennials are also the most likely—51 percent—to say that "moral truth is relative," with just 44 percent of Generation X, 41 percent of baby boomers, and 39 percent of Elders saying the same.[20]

Let this sink in for a moment and consider: just 39 percent of millennials said moral truth is absolute. That's pretty eye-opening.

LIVING ARRANGEMENTS

Not to be gloom and doom, but the shocking statistics don't end there. Young people today aren't just waiting longer to get married—they're also living at home longer than ever, with Pew analyzing 2014 data to proclaim that "for the first time in more than 130 years, adults ages 18 to 34 were slightly more likely to be living in their parents' home than they were to be living with a spouse or partner in their own household."[21]

That's right. For the first time since 1880 more young Americans are living with mom and dad than are residing with a significant other—a development that is troubling on a variety of levels. Experts believe the dynamic was sparked due to changes in educational attainment, employment, and marital status. And it appears as though romance is the key driver.[22]

"This turn of events is fueled primarily by the dramatic drop in the share of young Americans who are choosing to settle down romantically before age 35," Pew reported. "Dating back to 1880, the most common living arrangement among young adults has been living with a romantic partner, whether a spouse or a significant other." [23]

The research firm continued, "This type of arrangement peaked around 1960, when 62 percent of the nation's 18- to 34-year-olds were living with a spouse or partner in their own household, and only one-in-five were living with their parents." [24]

Those numbers transitioned quite a bit when 2014 came around, though, with just 31.6 percent of young people living with a partner or spouse and with 32.1 percent living with their parents. An additional 14 percent were heading up a single-person household, with 22 percent living with another family member, a nonrelative, or with a group of people. [25]

Much like Twenge, Pew cited the postponement of marriage as a key contributing factor, saying, though, that there is also some evidence that young Americans are potentially "eschewing marriage," with a separate analysis projecting that up to one in four youths might not ever get married. [26]

Considering the direction and stature of today's millennials and their morality, it's not entirely surprising that similar patterns of belief (and disbelief) are unfolding when one examines where the generation stands on God, the Bible, and other related indicators.

CHAPTER 4

MILLENNIALS: LOSING
THEIR FAITH AND RELIGION

IN **ADDITION TO** the state of millennials' views on moral issues, I'm also troubled by what's happening when it comes to their religious devotion. But before we dig deeper on that front, let's take a moment to explore the nation's self-described religious affiliation more generally, as there are clearly some important ties there worth exploring.

LOSING FAITH IN AMERICA

You may recall that a 2015 Pew Research Center study showed a stark decline in the proportion of overall Americans who call themselves "Christian." The study almost immediately ignited a firestorm of debate among academics, researchers, and the general public at large, with speculation abounding about what caused the proportion of Christian adherents in the United States to decline.[1]

There's no doubt that at 70.6 percent of the overall population, Christianity is still the largest and most prominent religious system— at least nominally speaking—but here's the more complex and concerning picture: that percentage is down substantially from the 78.4 percent who said the same back in 2007. So in just seven years, the proportion plunged around eight percentage points—a pretty notable decline that warrants much deeper exploration.[2]

THE REASONS BEHIND THE LACK OF FAITH

Naturally everyone has been debating about the cause of the drop, and if we're being honest, the true explanation is likely a complicated and multifaceted amalgam, though there is likely at least one cultural explanation that could be found among those potential factors.

Biblical values once held a prime spot in mainstream culture, leading many people to at least nominally associate with Christianity. But as the benefits of cultural Christianity—the natural societal and communal benefits that once came along with embracing biblical sentiment when it was deeply embedded in almost every facet of life— wore off, people without a deep devotion began to simply drop the label. But is that really all that's going on behind those numbers?

There's also the fact that America is a melting pot that continues to diversify on the faith front, though the gains among Jews and Muslims, among others, were pretty small between 2007 and 2014. There was one group, however, that experienced large-scale growth during that same time period: the so-called "nones."[3]

It's a cohort that is comprised of three groups: atheists, agnostics, and unaffiliated Americans. The latter group of "unaffiliateds" is comprised of people who are simply unattached to a religious construct, though that doesn't mean they reject God entirely. Some may, in fact, believe in God and have faith, though they simply aren't part of a broader construct or system.

The "nones"—this mix of atheist, agnostic, and unaffiliated citizens—grew from 16.1 percent of the American populace in 2007 to 22.8 percent in 2014—an increase that should shock Christians who, as a cohort, have made losses that mirror those gains. Of the 22.8 percent, 3.1 percent call themselves atheists, 4.0 say they're agnostics, and 15.8 percent report "nothing in particular."[4] And a separate study from PRRI and Religion News Service that was released in September 2016 found that the share of religiously unaffiliated Americans has grown even more since the Pew study, with 25 percent of the country—that's one out of every four Americans—now falling under that category.[5]

Clearly something is rapidly unfolding on the faith front. Sure, one can surely dismiss these changes as having everything to do with Christianity becoming more and more countercultural and thus less culturally beneficial to adherents, though that explanation still leaves a number of unanswered questions and issues on the table.

There is clearly a much larger cohort of unaffiliated people whom the faithful need to be engaging, and it's apparently an increasingly large segment of the population. We can debate the numbers all day and explain away the reasons behind the theological shifts, but there's something afoot that must be confronted, and it involves young Americans who are—more than any of their predecessors—being counted in ever-greater numbers among the "nones."[6]

It's also quite clear that many of these individuals have fallen under influences or messages that have somehow dissuaded them from their past religious beliefs. Just consider that Pew also found in a follow-up study that 78 percent of "nones" were once raised as a member of religion before later disassociating. And when they were asked why they left their faith labels behind, responses seemed to indicate that either secular messages drowned out their faith or that religious messages were no longer fervent enough or relatable enough to keep their devotion and attention.[7]

For 49 percent of the religiously unaffiliated who were raised in a religious home, it was a "lack of belief" that took them away from religion. Consider how one respondent answered when he was asked by the polling firm why he left his religious label behind: "I'm a scientist now, and I don't believe in miracles," with other respondents heralding the need for "evidence." Others said they simply had a distrust for organized religion.[8]

Perhaps many of these people faced a slow chipping away of their faith in a culture that values and routinely heralds countless viewpoints and positions that contradict traditional religious teachings. Just consider the fact that many agnostics—and the vast majority of those who selected "nothing in particular"—aren't willing to reject belief entirely, though they've clearly been dissuaded for some reason. It's as though something is distracting them and clouding their perspective.

"An overwhelming majority of atheists who were raised in a religion (82 percent) say they simply do not believe, but this is true of a smaller share of agnostics (63 percent) and only 37 percent of those in the 'nothing in particular' category," the Pew report reads.[9]

THE WANING FAITH OF MILLENNIALS

Now, here's where the millennials come into play. After releasing the 2014 religious landscape data, Dr. Jessica Martinez, a research associate at the Pew Research Center, told *TheBlaze* that Pew believes that "generational replacement" is one of the underlying factors behind the changing paradigms on the faith front. Basically younger generations are less religious than previous generations, and, as a result, they are impacting the overarching demographics.[10]

According to Martinez, millennials who are between the ages of eighteen and thirty-three are much less likely to embrace faith than are other generations. These younger, less religiously affiliated individuals are essentially replacing older, more faithful generations—and it's a pattern researchers believe is likely to continue.[11]

"This generation is much more religiously unaffiliated than older generations," she explained. "As the younger are replacing older, it's shifting the landscape in this way."[12]

In an interview for this book, Christian thought leader Dr. Ed Stetzer—who formerly served as executive director of LifeWay Research—further explained the generational cohort replacement dynamic, noting that people, over time, tend to progress in their personal religiosity, but that there's a generational problem embedded in the data that cannot be ignored.

"Each generational cohort that replaces the one before it has become a little less religious," he said.[13]

To put it into a statistical context, while 22.8 percent of the general American population falls under the "nones" category, 35 percent of millennials consider themselves atheist, agnostic, or unaffiliated—a pretty jarring prospect considering that these individuals will collectively be responsible for ensuring and progressing America's future. The "nones" are getting younger too, with the median age dropping from 38 in 2007 to 36 in 2014.[14] Some will dismiss all of this and claim that young generations are always less religious and not as likely to be affiliated as older generations. But there are some other elements at play that Martinez said could lead to continued demographic changes—mainly the notion that millennials appear to be less religious than past generations were *at the same time period in their lives.* "When we look by generation at people over time—older cohorts and what their levels of affiliation were, it's not necessarily the case that people have been more likely to be religiously affiliated over time," she said.[15]

Predicting the future trajectory of faith and religion is difficult to do with any certainty, but Martinez said it is likely that generational replacement will continue, with millennials leading the charge. In fact, Pew projected in early 2015 that Christians in America will decline from over three-fourths of the population in 2010 to two-thirds of the population in 2050.[16]

PRRI and Religion News Service bolstered all of these claims, finding in their survey that, as of August 2016, 39 percent of US adults between ages eighteen and twenty-nine are religiously unaffiliated. This is shocking because it is three times what was observed among Americans aged sixty-five and older. But that's not the only factor worth paying attention to, as the study also found that younger generations are less religious than previous generations were at the same time in their lives.[17]

"While previous generations were also more likely to be religiously unaffiliated in their twenties, young adults today are nearly four times as likely as young adults a generation ago to identify as religiously unaffiliated," the study reads. "In 1986, for example, only 10 percent of young adults claimed no religious affiliation."[18]

Speaking more broadly, the study found a massive gap when comparing Americans age fifty and below to those above the age of fifty, with 33 percent of those below that benchmark counting themselves among the unaffiliated compared to just 15 percent of those over age fifty.[19]

Again, there's debate over whether Christianity is actually in an authentic decline, or whether those abandoning the faith are merely nominal, unpracticing individuals who are simply shedding the label due to the fact that the once-robust social benefits of Christianity are eroding.

Regardless, the millennial factor is troubling and should be of grave concern to Christians. Stetzer pointed to generational research in further discussing millennials' moral standings, noting that there is actually "a robust Evangelical minority" that "are actually more devout than their predecessor cohorts, because I think they have to be." He proceeded, citing the American Religious Identification Study, to estimate that there are about a third of college students and millennials who are religious, a third who are spiritual but not religious, and then a third who are "secular."[20]

"What I would say, in recent history, millennials are starting off at a lower level of religiosity than any prior generation," Stetzer said, noting that he finds the situation "concerning."[21]

While he has his worries about that fact, Stetzer doesn't get himself too concerned with "self-identified Christianity" and is instead interested in "devout Christianity," stating that the population comprising the latter isn't much different from what we saw in prior generations. In the end Stetzer said we simply don't know what will happen when it comes to generational replacement.[22]

THE CAUSES OF MILLENNIAL DISCONNECT

Regardless of where the current and future generations are headed on the faith front, there is a key question that must be asked: What's causing the overarching millennial disconnect? Stetzer said it is certainly a "complex" dynamic and offered up a variety of potential causal factors he said are worth considering. Among them: "downward cultural pressure"—a dynamic in which changes in culture that conflict with faith values create a situation in which there are fewer believers over time.[23]

"Of course, it's complex. There's not one reason," Stetzer said. "I do think the downward cultural pressure is going to—it is already, and it'll have an increased impact—probably...produce a culture where you have [fewer] believers." He continued, "I think we would expect that. I think the downward cultural pressure is a big part of it." [24]

Additionally Stetzer pointed to factors such as immigration and the growing negative perceptions of Christian evangelicals, among other elements, that could be having an impact on the demographics and perceptions at play.[25]

While practicing Christian millennials who attend church at least once a month and who see faith as important to their lives have a high regard for the Bible, non-Christian millennials hold some beliefs that show hostility and skepticism toward the Scriptures. Not surprisingly, 45 percent of non-Christian millennials see the Bible as "just another book of teachings written by men that contains stories and advice." And just 27 percent say the Bible is either inspired by God or is actually God's Word, according to a 2014 Barna Group poll.[26]

Some of their other views, though, are a bit harsher. Barna explains: "About one in five say the Bible is 'an outdated book with no relevance for today' (19 percent) and more than one-quarter go so far as to say the Bible is 'a dangerous book of religious dogma used for centuries to oppress people' (27 percent)." And 62 percent of non-Christian millennials haven't ever read the Bible.[27]

Clearly there's quite a bit of work to be done to reach these individuals, but there's little doubt in my mind that much of the cultural perceptions these individuals have are the result of indoctrination perpetuated through the nation's main educational veins. After all, how can you expect people to be aware of a worldview—and a theological understanding, for that matter—that they've been shielded from? Now, let's dive deeper into the discussion by taking a look at how Hollywood has shaped our perspectives.

PART 2

CHAPTER 5

TV THEN AND NOW:
HOW THE TIDES HAVE CHANGED

HOLLYWOOD IS JUST one influential industry that often draws the ire of conservatives, evangelicals, and Christians more broadly. Sure, there's the tendency of celebrities to disproportionately support liberal causes and candidates: just consider a report in October 2015 that found that 90 percent of all political donations had, at that point, gone to Democratic candidate Hillary Clinton.[1]

But it seems the broader issue of concern is rooted not as much in political whims as in the increasingly raunchy content coming from Hollywood. Every year it seems TV shows and films get a little bit edgier, with many Americans wondering when the sex, violence, and other unpalatable themes will cease, or at least temper. With adult content that continues to worsen in some sectors—particularly television—it's not surprising that some people see Hollywood as hostile or unfriendly to Christian values. And, in fact, that's a common claim made by Bible-believers and conservatives alike.

It is a proclamation that Pure Flix Entertainment, the production house behind *God's Not Dead* and *God's Not Dead 2*, decided to investigate in 2016, with the company commissioning the Barna Group to ask Americans about this very subject. The survey question was worded as follows: "What is your opinion of Hollywood's treatment of Christianity?" Respondents were presented with a number of options: "They generally portray it positively." "They generally portray it negatively." "Neutral: they portray it neither positively nor negatively." "Mixed: sometimes negatively, sometimes positively." "They rely heavily on stereotypes." "They are faithful to Christian beliefs."[2]

Not surprisingly less than 1 percent of Americans agreed that Hollywood is faithful to Christian beliefs, with 15.6 percent saying that there is generally a negative portrayal, 7 percent saying that

Hollywood relies on stereotypes, and 29.3 percent saying there's a mix of some positive and some negative. Collectively this means that 51.9 percent saw negativity at least sometimes, with just 10.4 percent saying that Hollywood portrays Christianity in a positive light.[3]

Some of the more intriguing differences were among Democrats and Republicans. While 17.8 percent of Democrats said they believe Hollywood portrays Christianity positively, just 4.4 percent of Republicans and 9.3 percent of Independents agreed. Furthermore, while just 4.7 percent of Democrats felt that Christians are given a negative portrayal in Hollywood, 32.1 percent of Republicans and 14.8 percent of Independents felt the same.[4]

So how is all of this playing out in practice, and does it prove a bias? Well, that's a bit complicated, as public perception can only take us so far. What the results do show is that Democrats are less likely to see Hollywood as offering up a negative portrayal of Christianity than are Republicans and Independents. A larger proportion of Democrats also said there have been positive portrayals, while practicing Christians in the survey tended to align more with Republicans on the negativity front.

Either way, what's clear is that something has profoundly changed when it comes to the nature of our entertainment. Even if one argues that Christianity isn't being intentionally attacked and sidelined, there's surely a feeling among many that the values embraced by the faithful are either under assault in pop culture or are simply excluded from the majority of Hollywood content.

HOW TV HAS CHANGED

In recent years TV programming—particularly prime-time shows that air between 8:00 p.m. and 11:00 p.m.—has undoubtedly taken a stunning moral dive, with sexual themes becoming increasingly more prevalent. Gone are the days of *I Love Lucy*, when executives carefully navigated how actors Lucille Ball and Desi Arnaz—a husband and wife both on- and off-screen—were portrayed in the bedroom, typically showing the two lying side by side in separate twin beds.

If you're wondering just how shocking the disparity is when you juxtapose today's oversexualized content with what once graced the small screen, look no further than the controversy over how Ball's real-life pregnancy would be worked into the show's script. At the time the use of the word *pregnant* was reportedly banned by CBS, and instead they opted for the term *expecting*, as the former was considered too contentious for the airwaves.[5]

Don't believe me? Just consider what George Mason University history professor Michael O'Malley once wrote about how married couples were portrayed in the 1950s: "In the 1950s, for example, TV programmers would not show a married couple sharing a bed. Married couples, in 1950s TV-land, slept in separate beds." It was a restriction that O'Malley said Hollywood "voluntarily imposed...on itself." Imagine that? A standard based on moral platitudes.[6]

Some reports even claim that faith leaders were brought in to approve the scripts before they went to air—a prospect that would send most Hollywood producers into an uncontrollable laughing fit in the modern era.[7] Compare these to the fiery contemporary controversies over the graphic gay sex scenes in shows such as *Scandal* and *How to Get Away With Murder*—two programs that are executive produced by Shonda Rhimes—and the differences are astounding.

Rhimes has taken some of the scenes into such uncharted territory that one *Daily Beast* writer credited her with having "revolutionized gay characters on TV."[8] She doesn't appear shy about these controversies, either, as she took to social media to hit back at a critic who decried some graphic gay sex scenes as over the top and unnecessary.

What was Rhimes's response? "There are no GAY scenes. There are scenes with people in them."[9] Clearly she wasn't backing down from the challenge, though she's not alone. Hollywood has continued to push boundaries, no doubt in an effort to draw attention, ratings, and ultimately cash flow.

1950S TV STANDARDS

Today's TV world is a far cry from the small screen scene that unfolded between the 1950s and 1970s. After mass production of TV sets ramped up following World War II (the one million TV sets in use in 1949 reportedly skyrocketed to more than 50 million by the end of the 1950s[10]), it didn't take long for people to voice concern over the potential impact the technology could have on young people. Before the government could step in to temper those fears through regulation, the National Association of Broadcasters, which included the three networks around at the time, came up with a code to help self-govern the content it was churning out. Here's how the History Matters website explains the situation:

> With this relatively swift introduction of television into domestic American life, concern was voiced over the harmful influence that watching television might have on the nation's children. Although Congress held its first hearing on the subject in 1952, they chose not to take any action to interfere with the industry, in part because that year the National Association of Radio and Television Broadcasters adopted a code to regulate broadcast content.[11]

Stations could voluntarily follow the rules, which granted them the right to show the National Association of Broadcasters' "Seal of Good Practice" at the end of their shows. The code included a variety of points of guidance—parameters that must seem shocking to anyone consuming any considerable amount of television today. To begin, programs were encouraged to avoid selfishness, greed, and cruelty as motivations that were presented as worthwhile. Additionally the code called for an avoidance of explaining technical details of crimes, with brutality being avoided as well. And it didn't end there. The code also called for police officers to be shown respect, according to History Matters.[12]

One of the more intriguing points was that the code also specifically mentioned television's responsibility toward children, according to an edition of the text that was published in 1959. It read, in part, "The education of children involves giving them a sense of the world at large. However, such subjects as violence and sex shall be presented without undue emphasis and only as required by plot development or character delineation."[13]

Eventually the code was dissolved, but the details show a very different—and much more contained—entertainment universe when compared to what we're faced with today. I'm not advocating censorship per se, but I am noting that there was a time in which the moral and ethical impact of entertainment was given far more weight than it is today. Or perhaps more plainly stated, there was a time when society sought cleaner entertainment and when the industry took steps toward that goal.

THE LACK OF MORALS IN TELEVISION

Yes, the media world that we live in has dramatically changed over the decades. Hollywood has stretched, redefined, and torn to shreds decency standards in an effort to attract audiences by appealing to the most basic and human of desires—a tactic that has possibly paid off on the financial front, but likely not without its social costs.

It's been more than six decades since Lucy and Ricky graced the small screen. The world has changed; culture has transformed, with technological advances yielding a scenario in which audiences are inundated now more than ever with edgy messages. Meanwhile the individuals and companies behind many modern-day TV shows and films appear to be thinking little about the impact of the content beyond their own checkbooks.

In recent years youths and adults alike have been indoctrinated into accepting the bizarre level of sexual content that is disseminated through the entertainment industry, and the depraved nature of the content only seems poised to worsen. When conservatives and Christians bellow about what's on TV, opponents scoff right back, quibbling that these individuals should quit yammering and abandon their seemingly prudish protests. "Times have changed," these individuals say, while professing to be "open-minded" and "progressive" individuals who see nothing wrong with what's being disseminated.

But is it really that simple? Should everyone really just accept the increased nudity, overt sex, and loose ethical standards that society is foisting upon them? And do people really assume that these sentiments haven't—and won't—have a profound impact on the populace? The problem certainly isn't new, but with mass cultural confusion on the rise it is one we must address.

It was back in 2003 that the *New York Times* openly admitted that the "family hour [had] grown more permissive over the past few years." At the time the outlet noted that a study conducted by the Henry J. Kaiser Family Foundation found that one out of seven shows featured sex, or at least implied the act. The organization told the

New York Times that just four years before, that number was only one out of every fourteen shows, exposing quite the uptick at the time.[14]

It didn't end there, though. The 2003 report was followed up with a 2005 report about teens and sex—research that pointedly addressed the impact that TV has on individuals' perspectives and actions. A telling introduction to the Kaiser Family Foundation research details the slow trickle effect that entertainment can have on both hearts and minds. It reads as follows:

> In general, television's influence on social beliefs, attitudes, and behaviors tends to occur by a gradual, cumulative process that is most likely to develop with repeated exposure over time to common patterns of portrayals.[15]

This is precisely what our society has witnessed: a normalization of rampant sexual activity that has slowly infiltrated our TVs, smartphones, iPads, and every other device that we use to consume entertainment. These themes have been leaking into the tele-sphere for years, slowly gaining acceptance and culminating in a climax of moral chaos that we continue to experience today; this becomes painstakingly evident when we turn our TVs on and engage in a desperate search for acceptable content.

Or as Tim Winter, president of the Parents Television Council, aptly told me in a 2014 interview: "We look at this as a very classic case of the frog and the kettle where the boiling water heats up and you don't even notice, because [the] whole environment is becoming more explicit."[16]

Just consider what Kaiser found back in 2005 when analyzing more than 1,100 shows to uncover just how much audiences were being exposed to sexual themes. From talk about sex to passionate kissing and actual scenes featuring intercourse, the group found that 77 percent of the prime-time shows that they assessed included "sexual content," as did 70 percent of shows overall. If that's not stunning enough, consider that these proportions back in 1998 were 67 percent and 56 percent, respectively. The frequency of sex scenes was also up for each show that included sexual activity or discussions about sex—yet another troubling metric. Of course, these statistics are from more than a decade ago and—in media years—that's an eternity, especially when it comes to changing cultural trends and technologies.[17]

Unfortunately 2005 was the last time that Kaiser explored sex on TV, with widespread analysis by other groups remaining quite sparse over the past decade.[18] That said, it doesn't take a rocket scientist to see that sexual content is running more rampant than ever. I'd place a safe bet that more than 77 percent of prime-time shows contain sexual content today, with that proportion probably poised to grow.

Despite a lack of large-scale studies of late, organizations such as Tim Winter's Parents Television Council, a nonpartisan group that works to educate the public about TV content, continue to sound the alarm about our crumbling moral infrastructure. "What we're seeing, especially on prime time, is content that never, ever would have made it to air on prime-time broadcast TV as recently as five or ten years ago," explains Winter.[19]

Part of the problem, he said, is that broadcast networks, which are heavily monitored by the US government's Federal Communications Commission, are trying to compete with cable networks that have far less regulation and are prone to carrying more salacious and violent content.[20]

In turn, Winter said that the cable networks are competing "against the Internet," which is even less regulated than cable. It's a situation with a competitive trickle-down effect that he said is extremely concerning.[21] It's the industry's own "Amazing Race" toward total and utter moral depravity. And what is the prize? Fattened wallets with a side of cultural denigration.

Sadly many of us aren't blinking twice when these explicit scenes ofttimes awkwardly appear in the middle of our favorite shows. We're simply willing to look past it, accepting it all as the "new normal"—or we're so desensitized that we've become permissive, simply unaware that what we're seeing is problematic.

THE PROBLEM

Either way, it isn't a pretty picture. Ignorance, after all, isn't always bliss, with TV shows profoundly changing the ways in which young people and adults alike think, feel, and act. Consider that just two 2004 studies by RAND found that teens' consumption of shows with a plethora of sexual content "hastens the initiation of teen sexual activity" and that talk about sex on TV can actually have the same impact.[22]

Researchers surveyed 1,762 young people aged twelve to seventeen by asking about their TV viewing and sexual experience, following up a year later to ask again about these indicators. In the end, it was found that young people who watched the greatest amount of sexual content were two times more likely to have sex the next year.[23]

A separate study in 2008 yielded similar results, with RAND finding that young people are twice as likely to impregnate someone or get pregnant if they've been highly exposed to shows with sexual content over a three-year period when compared to young people who have not consumed the same sexualized programming.[24]

Here's how a brief explains the implications of the 2004 study:

> Taken together, the two studies suggest the need to reduce teens' exposure to sexual content on television and to explore greater use of entertainment shows to inform teens about risk. Reducing the amount of sexual talk and behavior on television, or the amount of time that adolescents are exposed to them, could appreciably delay the onset of sexual activity.[25]

More than a decade after this research was conducted, we've done little to heed this advice, with sex and violence running rampant in entertainment at an increasingly troubling rate.

It's not only about the negative impact it's having on children, though, as parents too seemingly run the risk of becoming so numb to these themes that they become subconsciously desensitized to the negative messages their kids are consuming. Consider a 2014 study by the Annenberg Public Policy Center that found that adults can actually become less aware of the dangers of these themes the more that they themselves are exposed to them.

For the purpose of the study, parents were confronted with three sets of movie scenes that had either violent or sexual content. As they watched those scenes, they provided a minimum age that they felt was appropriate for young people to consume the content. As it turns out, the more the parents were exposed to the themes, the less stringent their age requirements became.[26]

The average age for the first set was 16.9 years old for violent content and 17.2 for sexual content, but by the time the parents watched the final set, they had dropped the minimum age to 13.9 for violence and 14 for sex.[27]

Annenberg Public Policy Center associate director Dan Romer explained that parents became increasingly accepting of the sexual and violent content as they watched more of it, indicating a level of desensitization that could have a very real impact on the types of content that parents permit their children to consume.[28]

Tim Winter told me in an interview for this book that there are a few "broad strokes" that have him concerned about TV today. "One is the continued path of...so-called reality television, which continues to seek the lowest common denominator in humanity rather than entertaining and uplifting and inspiring, which reality programming, I think, is uniquely capable of doing," he said. "It tends to be following the most despicable human behavior."[29]

He did note that there have been some well-received programs in recent years such as *The Voice*, *American Idol*, and other similar performance-based shows, as well as live renditions of *The Wiz* and *The Sound of Music*, that have allowed audiences to enjoy content with little fear or worry surrounding what's being consumed.[30]

"These are shows...they're live television at its best," he said. "It's unscripted mostly, and...you're rooting for somebody or you're just enjoying the beauty of live entertainment."

Other unscripted shows, he said, rely on negative tactics to gain attention by breaking the mold and standing out—a dynamic that concerns him. "[They] try to figure out some really screwed up, pathetic family somewhere in America that's doing wretched things... [They] try to focus on it," he said. "It's shown, I guess, some sort of light that looks down on it, but at the same time you're almost validating...and normalizing the behavior." He continued, "Whether it's a Kardashian or...*Jersey Shore* or a Dance Mom or you name [it]...you're normalizing behavior that sometimes is very abnormal and something to be avoided."[31]

It all constitutes a slippery slope, but one that society continues to gleefully stumble down.

CHAPTER 6

SCRIPTING CULTURE: DRIVING HOME AN AGENDA

BIAS CAN BE found both in movies and in reaction to movies, and it isn't always intentionally fostered; it sometimes takes root in an honest misunderstanding, or even a lack of familiarity. Regardless of how purposeful or innocent its catalyst might be, systematic bias—particularly when we're talking about influential venues such as Hollywood, the media, and the university system—can have troubling ramifications.

In the case of Hollywood, anti-Christian sentiment is generally created as the result of a mix of intentional and unintentional paradigms, as overtly liberal members of the entertainment industry often overlook or steer clear of Christian and conservative themes; or, in some cases, perhaps they pointedly take aim at these worldviews.

FROZEN AND GOD

Perhaps one of the most intriguing utterances I've heard from people inside Hollywood about this paradigm unfolded during a 2014 NPR interview with Robert Lopez and Kristen Anderson-Lopez, the husband and wife duo who wrote the music for the Disney hit *Frozen*.

Lopez told host Terry Gross that working on edgy projects doesn't necessarily preclude someone from eventually working for Disney. "Disney is not this sanitized place that you might imagine it to be," he said. "I mean, they hired Ashman and Menken after they did 'Little Shop of Horrors' which was sort of the 'Avenue Q' of its day. It was very campy and very kind of…a little off color and racy."[1]

Lopez continued, "And I don't think Disney has any problem with employing people who have, you know, done off color stuff in the past." But it's what his wife said next that ended up capturing quite a bit of attention. Below, read just a portion of the conversation that followed:[2]

ANDERSON-LOPEZ: It's funny. One of the only places you have to draw the line at Disney is with religious things, the word God.

LOPEZ: Yeah. You just can't…

GROSS: You can't say the word God?

LOPEZ: There was even a—well, you can say it in Disney but you can't put it in the movie.

ANDERSON-LOPEZ: You can't put it in the movies.

GROSS: Well, OK. I'll point out, Robert Lopez you co-wrote "The Book of Mormon" which is a satire about the Mormon faith.

LOPEZ: And it's as equally a satire of Disney as it is of the Mormon faith.

GROSS: Yes. Right. Yes, strike two. Yeah.

LOPEZ: I mean, it really is.

The God comments quite naturally ignited controversy, with many wondering whether Disney had truly banned God from its films. But just a few weeks later, Lopez and Anderson-Lopez said their words were taken out of context.

"That is completely misconstrued," Anderson-Lopez told *Business Insider*, saying they were actually discussing one specific instance. The issue, according to her husband, was rooted in "using the Lord's name in vain," as there was a line they were considering in a song that read, "Couldn't keep it in, God knows I tried." [3]

In the end Anderson-Lopez said there were fears that the line would be taken to seem as though they were trying to use God's name in vain, so the team ended up not including it. She added, "Disney does not have a policy of not using the word 'God' at all." [4] Regardless of whether their clarification—which some saw as backtracking—was truly the original intent, the entire debacle is comical. But there's a reason so many people reacted to their initial claim, regardless of whether it was misinterpreted: there's a sense that Hollywood doesn't care much about the values Christians hold dear.

BIAS CHANGES CULTURE

Ideologies aside, money is what drives Tinseltown—a fact that must be confronted when addressing how entertainment content has drifted so fluidly into a land of total and utter moral depravity. In a world where sex sells, one can see why—from a profit perspective—Hollywood companies have increased the use of shock factors, including violence and explicit themes. After all, the intended goal is to capture and retain audience attention, with executives constantly looking for the latest and greatest methods to make that happen.

The unintentional consequence of using these tactics, though, is that many of the faithful are marginalized, cut out of the discussion, misrepresented, told that their values are antiquated and unworthy, or—at the least—are simply not served by what the industry is offering. What results is a cornered market that, over time, shapes hearts and minds. The forces that have the most power and prevalence over the masses will have the greatest ability to impact public thought and perception; that's just the reality.

While TV consumption has been on a slow decline in recent years as the public increases its consumption of Internet and on-demand video, consider that in quarter three of 2014, the average American spent 141 hours watching live TV a month.[5] That's a lot of TV, and it doesn't even include the mass consumption of movies and digital content via theater attendance, satellite or cable subscription, and online viewing platforms. Various forms of entertainment surround us at every turn, and no doubt collectively shape how we see the world.

And since Hollywood tends to alienate conservative and Christian values, it's no surprise that people—and particularly millennials— over time are becoming less interested in espousing these ideals. Much of the bias in Hollywood is unintentional, but that doesn't mean there aren't powerful movers and shakers in these spheres who have a vested interest in using their art to alter the public's perceptions, for better or worse.

Actor Eric Stonestreet, who plays Cam, a gay character on the popular ABC sitcom *Modern Family*, was careful not to overstate the show's social impact when he told HuffPo Live in a 2014 interview that he and fellow actor Jesse Tyler Ferguson, who plays Mitch, his husband on the show, "are normalizing what it is to be a same-sex couple."[6]

And despite the fact that *Modern Family* executive producer and creator Steve Levitan told *Gay Star News* in 2012 that the show doesn't have "an agenda," others don't quite see it that way.[7]

Just consider what Ryan Murphy, who cocreated *Glee*, had to say about *Modern Family* and the way it has shaped views: "I'm personally just so appreciative to 'Modern Family' and to 'Will & Grace' because they are huge successes. I think so many people watched those shows and are educated, and those shows changed views."[8]

SOME BIAS IS UNINTENTIONAL, SOME IS INTENTIONAL

Again, there's nothing wrong with exercising one's First Amendment rights to launch shows that have progressive (or conservative) agendas, but when Hollywood collectively chooses to present only one narrow lens, giving viewers little room to learn about or even consider alternative worldviews, the dynamic becomes troubling. That in mind, my broader point in mentioning gay characters and the like is really more for those who reject the idea that Hollywood has the ability to impact thoughts and perceptions; clearly some in the industry believe that shows and movies absolutely do hold that power—and they're using entertainment platforms to try and shape perspectives. So, why is it such a stretch then to fear for young people, among others, when it comes to sex, drugs, and other themes that are incessantly embedded in our entertainment? Can't those elements also have a transforming impact on minds and hearts, both young and old?

It's no secret that the entertainment world is overrun by progressive social and political agendas that run counter to the Christian worldview (and part of that, as I'll cover later on, is the fault of Christians themselves). Hollywood and the media are unfortunately helping to raise our children, and tragically the values that are streaming to TVs, smartphones, and other devices paint the picture that Christian values are no longer worth embracing. Perhaps Winter said it best when he told me that his work with the Parents Television Council and in entertainment has taught him a key lesson: "Hollywood is an echo chamber."[9]

Free from a diversity of perspective, he said it's an ideologically homogeneous sphere in which biased ideas are constructed, distributed, amplified, and—unfortunately—solidified in the minds of impressionable audiences.[10]

"It is not different from other echo chambers that are out there. If you're a conservative in Washington, you hang out with other conservatives in Washington," he said. "But Hollywood is the biggest echo chamber and the most powerful."[11]

It all starts with industry insiders who tend to hire others who share their worldview. This creates a cumulative scenario in which people who share the same worldview come together and create plotlines, characters, and projects that reflect those ideals. "People tend to hire other people who share their values," Winter said. "If you are of a certain opinion in Hollywood that goes against traditional family values, chances are you have people under you who share that belief."[12]

While some might claim there is a vast liberal and anti-faith conspiracy in entertainment, the truth might be a bit more complicated. Some in the industry might certainly have a bias against Christians and conservatives, but much of the cumulative end product—one that results in collective entertainment that eschews faith and conservatism—is quite possibly a by-product of this echo chamber mentality.

Phil Cooke, a Christian who is a TV producer and consultant in Hollywood and who was an executive producer of the documentary *Hillsong: Let Hope Rise*, said that his experience hasn't necessarily corroborated claims of a vast "anti-faith" conspiracy in the industry. "Obviously there are people in Hollywood who don't like religion, just like there are attorneys, school teachers, plumbers, and store clerks across the country who don't like religion," he told me. "But in my experience the vast majority of producers, actors, filmmakers, and studio executives in Hollywood are very open."[13]

Cooke said that many of these individuals simply weren't raised in Christian homes and are "largely ignorant of any knowledge about the Christian faith." This in itself, though, doesn't make them "anti-faith," he said. "Creative people create based on what they know, and frankly, as I mentioned before, most Hollywood professionals simply didn't grow up in Christian families, so to produce faith-based programming simply isn't on their radar," Cooke added.[14]

The consultant said he has spent time trying to help studios and executives realize, though, that they're often willing to bend over backwards when it comes to reaching special interest groups, including the military, the gay community, feminists, and others, yet they tend to ignore the largest special interest group there is—Christians.[15]

Some in Hollywood, though, are aware of these biases, or are—at the least—comfortable with quite possibly Hollywood's ideological bubble. Conservative author Ben Shapiro tackled this very subject in his 2011 book titled *Primetime Propaganda*, when he sat down for video-taped interviews with famous Hollywood TV producers and exposed what he said was overarching liberal biases. Many of the famed producers and heavyweights he spoke with seemingly had no problem openly proclaiming their progressive political alliances, giving the book a fair amount of publicity at the time, particularly among conservatives who felt it vindicated their long-held suspicion that Hollywood was intent on assaulting their deeply held convictions.

Friends creator Marta Kauffman was reportedly candid with Shapiro when he mentioned that some "cultural conservatives" took issue with the sitcom's handling of issues like gay marriage and with the show's consistently liberal take. Rather than retreat or avoid giving a definitive answer, she purportedly offered up her assessment:

> How could it now? You have a bunch of liberals running the show, which truly, we all come from a certain place, we're going to put out there what we believe. These characters mirror who we are. Um, and it has to. You write from what you know and what you research....And we put together a staff of mostly liberal people.[16]

Kauffman reportedly went on to admit that *Friends* was sending a powerful message to the "right wing" with a 1996 episode of the show that guest-starred Candace Gingrich, the half-sister of Republican politician Newt Gingrich, who was featured presiding over a commitment ceremony for two lesbians.

"I have to say, when we cast Candace Gingrich as the minister of that wedding, there was a bit of '[expletive]' in it to the right wing directly," she continued. "That was a choice and it was an exciting choice, and she made a statement during the wedding where she says something about, 'Nothing makes God happier than to see two people, any two people, together in love.'...And we felt that was honest."[17]

Countless others in Hollywood were quoted as making similar proclamations, adding fuel to the long-standing belief that the entertainment industry holds biases against Christians and conservatives alike.

All this in mind, I keep coming back to the fact that I'm not arguing to see progressive or even counter-Christian perspectives banned or removed from the airwaves—and I want to reiterate that. I'm simply wondering why Hollywood doesn't facilitate a more equal playing field, especially considering the demand for other types of content. It should also be noted that some, like Winter, point to an apparently mistaken belief in Hollywood that "people want dark, edgy, troubling, disturbing, especially violent, sexually violent material." As stated, this content has had a presence on some premium subscription networks, with Winter decrying the fact that it's also starting to emerge on broadcast TV and basic cable.[18]

"The violence is so grotesque, and it's more and more becoming sexually violent," he said. "You have more graphic gore, and it's computer enhanced. The computerized imagery is beyond realistic."[19]

CRITICAL BACKLASH INSIDE THE ECHO CHAMBER

It's not just about the content, itself, though, as movie critics are also part of the Hollywood echo chamber, as they are often unable or unwilling to look outside of their own worldview to offer fair assessments of the films they're reviewing. In fact, it's not uncommon for movie websites such as Rotten Tomatoes to show a wide disparity between audiences and top critics.

In recent years, two anecdotal examples stand out that show just how disconnected some of these professional reviewers are from mainstream America.

Moms' Night Out

Let's start with *Moms' Night Out*, a 2014 family-friendly film about a group of mothers—a pastor's wife, a stay-at-home mom, and a Sunday school teacher—who find themselves in a series of unfortunate yet comedic scenarios when they attempt to go out on the town for a night of relaxation. It's a light-hearted, fun-filled family movie that elicits some laughs while exploring some of the struggles that mothers and fathers face.

In the wake of its release, thousands of audience members flocked to Rotten Tomatoes to give the film an overall 85 percent favorability score. But while the masses loved it, professional critics found themselves in an absolute tizzy.[20]

Let me explain it this way: If an alien were to land on Earth with no knowledge of the *Moms' Night Out* plotline and only critics' rebukes to go by, they'd assume it was a diabolical film that was being used to denigrate and subjugate women. Glaring out from the sheltered insides of their echo chamber, some critics absolutely blasted the movie, shockingly giving it a collective 16 percent favorability score.

Christy Lemire of RogerEbert.com lambasted the film as "depressingly regressive and borderline dangerous," saying that it "peddles archaic notions of gender roles in the name of wacky laughs." She continued: "The ultimate message here is unmistakable, regardless of your religious beliefs: A woman's place is in the home, not out on the town."[21]

Yes, Lemire actually used the word *dangerous* to describe a benign film about moms having a night out on the town. She also went on to claim that the movie is "just as afraid to let loose as its characters are" and that the antics displayed "are all dismally tame."[22]

In case you're wondering, though, Lemire gave Lars von Trier's 2013 film *Nymphomaniac: Volume I* three out of four stars, describing the sex-infused movie as "unexpected and so refreshing."[23] Von Trier, who reportedly admitted in 2014 that he once made his films while under the influence of a bottle of vodka as he has tried to enter a "parallel world" of creativity, has purportedly been accused of misogyny for how female characters have been portrayed in his movies.[24]

But Lemire takes a starkly different view:

> Von Trier gets a bad rap for being a misogynist. I'd argue that he's the exact opposite—that he's fascinated by women in all their flaws and complexities, and he makes movies that are difficult to watch in hopes of understanding them better. His actresses are willing to put themselves through the wringer for him and he gets devastating, powerful work in return.[25]

One can't help but walk away from this review feeling a mixture of surprise, confusion, and frustration. *Moms' Night Out*—a movie about mothers who learn valuable life lessons without the use of sex or profanity—is "dangerous" and peddles "archaic notions of gender roles," but a movie chock full of sex is oh so "refreshing." This is the truly bizarre world we're living in.

I'm not dismissing the notion that *Nymphomaniac* might have a good storyline beneath all of the muck (personally I don't plan to find out), and Lemire is certainly free to dislike *Moms' Night Out*. I'm simply wondering how we've gotten to a place in society in which reviewers are actually calling wholesome movies dangerous, while praising others that are, well, filled with what many people would consider needless garbage.

Apparently "dismally tame" is echo chamber code for "a film with standards." Lemire wasn't alone in her opinions, though, as others unleashed similar sentiment against *Moms' Night Out*. The headline of Inkoo Kang's review for The Wrap summarized her opinion of the movie in three simple words: "Unfunny and Anti-Feminist."[26]

Jon Erwin, who wrote and directed *Moms' Night Out* alongside his brother Andy Erwin, held little back in responding to these critics, noting at the time that he believed that media bias and a failure to properly understand Christian audiences were at the root of the overtly harsh film rebukes.

Rather than a sexist movie with a "dangerous" agenda, Erwin told me he had repeatedly screened the film and that mothers loved it, proclaiming that it was, in fact, "their story," with a plotline many could relate to.[27] It's a disconnect that Erwin believes shows the true disparity that exists between the Christian world and Hollywood.

"What you see is a group of underserved people who have not felt appreciated who now have an outlet and a voice and an ability to celebrate themselves," he said of the film. "Hollywood and the mainstream press [don't] understand these people."[28]

Little Boy

And Erwin wasn't alone in his frustrations, as other films have experienced similar disparities between audience and critical reaction.

Little Boy, a heartwarming movie about an eight-year-old child who desperately wants to bring his father home from battle during World War II, also received excoriating reviews from critics. Audiences raved about the film following its April 2015 release, with 88 percent of the more than 3,500 people who reviewed it giving it positive marks on Rotten Tomatoes. At the same time, just 10 percent of reviewers found the motion picture favorable.[29]

Critics called it "phony-baloney," "shameless," "manipulative," and "horrifically misguided."[30]

Here's what the Village Voice's Alan Scherstuhl had to say:

> This marks a new low in movie miracles. Faith here isn't something private that might nurture us through this world's cruel caprices—it's a promise that everything will work out, that a Superman-God will spin the world backwards for you.
>
> Imagine a real child, of today, who has lost a parent in America's desert campaigns. Imagine that child puffed up on *Little Boy* and its ilk, praying, hurting, maybe shouting *arggggh!* Imagine that child taking to heart the lesson of this cynical, poisonous, deeply stupid film: If the miracle fails to come, you must not have believed enough.[31]

Producer Eduardo Verastegui didn't stay silent about these reactions, putting out a statement immediately after the film's release letting entertainment insiders—and the public at large—know that, though he values critics' views, his main concern was serving his audience.

"My first audience for my movies is always the people and I am thrilled that the people are responding so well to 'Little Boy,'" he said. "We made this movie because as first generation immigrants we love America. Even with her faults, America is the greatest country on earth."[32]

For whatever reason, movie critics simply failed to understand the overarching message embedded in *Little Boy*, but it's clear that many Americans who crave more profound and fulfilling content on the big screen found overwhelming favor with its deeply embedded themes of faith, love, and healing.

In the end, these are just a few examples of how some in Hollywood seemingly fail to comprehend certain facets of the Christian audience and the beliefs they hold dear. When it comes to entertainment, we're a far cry from where we once were, indeed.

Chapter 7

MOVIES THEN AND NOW: THE PARADIGM SHIFT

PEOPLE RIGHTLY COMPLAIN about the content seen in movies today, but it seems even the early days of Hollywood brought about controversies and debates over the content that was presented on the big screen. With that said, there has been a paradigm shift in the last few years.

THE CLERGY EFFECT

Societal discontent led Hollywood to self-censor, with the Motion Picture Producers and Distributors of America, an organization that later became the Motion Picture Association of America, creating a moral code that Hollywood studios subscribed to in making most films. It was after Hollywood was shaken up by a series of negative incidents—and press resulting from each—that industry insiders came together to form the organization, which was headed by former politician William H. Hays from 1922 to 1945, as an effort to stave off government censorship.[1]

What sort of incidents? In real-life scenes that mirror some of what has happened in Hollywood in recent decades, stars were overdosing on drugs, comic Fatty Arbuckle went on trial for alleged manslaughter over the case of a dead actress, actress Mary Pickford reportedly got divorced so she could marry fellow actor Douglas Fairbanks, projects presented morally questionable content, and plenty more, according to NPR.[2]

Such incidents made religious leaders nervous, leaving them looking for ways to try and stop the negative influence that was purportedly flowing out of Tinseltown. With the power and sway of the faithful influencing the national discussion—especially at a time when silent pictures suddenly morphed into talking films—state censorship boards began getting involved, with the government retaining the right, at that time, to censor movies. In fact, local governments essentially regulated film content from 1915 until 1952, Dr. Thomas Doherty, professor of American studies at Brandeis University, told me in an interview for this book.[3]

"Movies [had] no First Amendment rights, which means state censorship boards, city censorship boards, a sheriff who didn't like the film, could basically go in and shut down the movie," Doherty explained.

The *Mutual Film Corp. v. Industrial Commission of Ohio* Supreme Court case in 1915 essentially set this in motion, when the high court ruled that movies were not considered free speech and, as a result, could be regulated.[4] It wasn't until the *Joseph Burstyn, Inc. v. Wilson* case in 1952 that the court changed its mind, ruling that films were, indeed, a form of free speech—a result that set in motion an understanding that continues even today.[5]

But from 1915 through 1952, censorship boards in states and local areas alike reserved the right to either cut scenes in films before they aired or to ban movies entirely from being shown to the public. That regulation came after priests, among other faith leaders, demanded that Hollywood put a moral muzzle on itself.[6]

"Roman Catholics were upset about the moral and social content of Hollywood cinema in the 1920s, so in around 1930, a couple prominent Catholics—a guy named Martin Quigley, who edited *Motion Picture Herald*...and a devout Catholic, a big-time Catholic layman and a Jesuit priest, named Father Daniel A. Lord—got together and wrote a moral code for the movies," Doherty said. "It had a moral philosophy, and then a list of prescriptions, things you should do, things you couldn't do."[7]

The studios had already created the National Association of the Motion Picture Industry, a regulatory body aimed at tempering the public's call for censorship, and adopted a series of guidelines, but that apparently wasn't enough to halt critique. So the Motion Picture Producers and Distributors of America, under Hays's leadership, set up a series of control measures during his tenure that were aimed at trying to keep Hollywood in check.[8] Or as the *Encyclopedia Britannica* summarized Hays's efforts:

> As a respected national politician and dignified elder in the Presbyterian Church, Hays brought prestige to the

organization. He initiated a moral blacklist in Hollywood, inserted morals clauses in actors' contracts, and in 1930 was one of the authors of the Production Code, a detailed enumeration of what was morally acceptable on the screen, which was not supplanted until 1966.[9]

It was this production code that offered up strict guidance for what would absolutely not be tolerated in Hollywood productions. Sex, crime, offensive language, nudity, illegal drug use, the ridicule of religion, and certain other behaviors were cracked down on.[10] Interestingly these are the very underpinnings of a vast array of films that are coming out of Hollywood today, yet when society pushed back decades ago, the entertainment industry bowed down. Perhaps most noteworthy is just how fervent the Production Code is in noting the impact that Hollywood can have on society's moral underpinnings:

> Motion picture producers recognize the high trust and confidence which have been placed in them by the people of the world and which have made motion pictures a universal form of entertainment. They recognize their responsibility to the public because of this trust and because entertainment and art are important influences in the life of a nation.... They know that the motion picture within its own field of entertainment may be directly responsible for spiritual or moral progress, for higher types of social life, and for much correct thinking.[11]

Martin Quigley, a Catholic publisher who coauthored the Production Code and was heavily involved in urging for a cleaner Hollywood, expressed similar sentiment, writing:

> The motion picture has created problems which have not attended the development and extension of any other form of expression. This has been due to the circulation which the public's favor has given to it, to the vividness of the medium and to its facility in thought conveyance and in emotional stimulus.[12]

It should be noted, though, that the Production Code didn't have an immediate impact after its initial implementation, with many in Hollywood simply ignoring it. According to Doherty, the code was adopted by Hollywood in 1930 to "just get the Catholics off their back," with studios proceeding to essentially ignore it for the next four years; it's a period people now refer to as the "pre-code era"—a period of time during which the code was apparently active but wasn't yet fervently enforced.[13]

"The Catholics get very upset, and in 1933, '34, they form something called the Legion of Decency, which is a political action group," Doherty said. "Unlike today, when the Catholic Church could tell its parishioners to do something and [they'd] ignore it, back in the '30s they actually abided by it. So the Catholics could really keep people out of the seats of theaters if they condemned a movie, or if they said a movie would jeopardize your soul."[14]

This pushback created problems for movie moguls, which led to the creation of the Production Code Administration to ensure that the movie industry's moral code that had been ignored since 1930 would finally be upheld. Doherty said it was "basically a movement by American Roman Catholics to pressure Hollywood to abide by a set of largely Roman Catholic standards for the moral content of Hollywood cinema."[15]

Either way, it's clear that some with dealings in Hollywood knew they had a responsibility to ensure that what they put out didn't have a negative moral impact. At this point, you might be wondering if there were other reasons why Hollywood would abandon some of the edgy themes and ploys that hold the power to attract American viewers. According to PBS, much of the motivation boiled down to money. Hays was reportedly able to convince studios that abiding by the Production Code was the most prudent path forward. After all, if they didn't, they would end up doling out more money to change films once government censorship boards got a hold of them. And with the nation's financial woes ramping up in light of the stock market crash of 1929, cost-cutting simply made sense. That's why in 1930 the studios first signed on board to follow the strict code, ushering in an era of a more sanitized—and family friendly—Hollywood, though, again, it wasn't until a few years later that enforcement of the code truly took place.[16]

But Dr. Ted Baehr, a film critic and the founder of Movieguide, told me in an interview for this book that studio heads' hands weren't simply forced; they saw immense benefit associated with the Production Code. They believed that it "protected them against unfair competition, that the code protected them from a race to the bottom, that the code built the industry into being a more effective and successful tool." Many of these people, who he said were not Christians, wanted to create entertainment for "as broad an audience as possible"—a prospect that the code helped them achieve.[17]

It's the involvement of clergy in the process that might serve as the biggest surprise for some. In fact, faith leaders played a key role in the filmmaking process in the early days of Hollywood. As Baehr explained, "By 1910 to 1914, the majority of movies were screening in churches," with the content reflecting that sentiment.[18]

As Charisma News reported in 2014, "From 1933 to 1966, Christians were one of the predominant forces in Hollywood." There were two organizations in particular—the Roman Catholic Legion of Decency and the Protestant Film Commission—that were heavily embedded in Tinseltown, regularly reading and assessing scripts in an effort to be sure that they contained decent values and would put forward a healthy set of moral standards.[19] The National Legion of Decency, which was formed in 1934 by US Catholic bishops, routinely rated films on a scale. Any film that was deemed "unobjectionable" was given a Class A designation, with objectionable content being labeled Class B and condemned content being filed under "Class C."[20]

Doherty said the Catholics had more power than the Protestants, as the latter "are congregational in organization," with each Protestant church, in effect, serving as its own Vatican. Meanwhile Catholics have a broader structure and a more top-down ability to move adherents to action. "(They) are hierarchical, so they can really send the word down to twenty, thirty million Catholics, the way that the Protestants can't," he said. "That is what gave the Roman Catholics power over Hollywood cinema."[21]

Regardless of how it was accomplished, the faith effort helped turn Hollywood films and culture around from the debauchery of its early days to a more morally centered industry that took into account the impact that entertainment would have on the masses. These Christian organizations apparently made a pretty big difference, offering a buffer between Hollywood and the culture at large. Baehr has often spoken out about this history, telling Charisma News, "Prior to the involvement of these Christian men in 1933, American movies were morally bankrupt—full of nudity, perversity and violence." [22]

After all, in the years preceding the creation of the Production Code, Christians had tried to force Hollywood's hand to make the right decisions, resulting in the aforementioned ratings boards, though the involvement and hands-on inclusion of clergy in the movie-making process ended up changing all of that. Still, it should be noted that these faith-based organizations didn't necessarily hold any real or binding power. Baehr said that the late George Heimrich, who once ran the Protestant Film Office, once told him that the only real authority he had was to explain to the studios what was at stake if they kept in morally bankrupt content.

Baehr said George told him, "The only authority I had is I'd say to them, 'If you put this dialogue in here, you're losing part of your audience, so why do you want to lose part of your audience? Don't you want to make more money?' And they'd say, 'George, what can you do?' and he'd go off and rewrite the dialogue for the scene." Eventually, though, the influence of these religious bodies waned. The Protestant Film Office closed up its advocacy offices in 1966 after some denominational funding was pulled and the Christian groups connected to the effort reportedly didn't care to continue it—a scenario that Baehr believes had profound consequences on Hollywood and the culture at large. [23]

"It set the scenes for moral collapse and degradation, and you went from *The Sound of Music* to the first X-rated film," he told me. "The change that took place created a culture—because culture is downstream from the mass media of entertainment—created a culture which…got new scripts of behavior." Baehr continued, "The new scripts of behavior [were], 'Let's all go out and have sex out of wedlock, take drugs, and enjoy ourselves.'" [24]

Doherty said the Legion of Decency is still around, but has changed its name to the National Catholic Office for Motion Pictures. While the body still rates movies, he said the organization isn't as influential as it once was. [25]

Considering the cultural changes that have unfolded, that's not all that surprising. Once the Production Code was abolished, Hollywood switched to the current ratings system that we have today. Doherty explained the key difference between the old code system and what we now have today. "Under the code, Hollywood said to everyone, 'Be assured that nothing you see in this movie is going to be immoral, and it's all going to be good for your kids, and if there's a salacious line, your kids won't understand it,'" he explained. "Where rating says, 'Be warned'... 'This is PG-13, it's R, it's whatever, and fair warning if you're sending your kids to this.' That's... a very different model." [26]

While there is certainly an argument to be made against censorship, it's also quite notable that society was once so repulsed by negative content that Hollywood was forced to change its ways—and chose to do so accordingly.

If one compares Hollywood today to its standing decades ago, it is quite a stunning transformation. Decades ago the industry seemed to see itself as having a responsibility of sorts to protect—or at least consider its impact—on the nation's moral standing. Today, though, it's not uncommon to see many actors and actresses doing very little to ensure their work has a positive impact on society and, in particular, on youths. Many performers simply don't see themselves as role models, and there's much critique today of parents and how so many fail to protect their kids from the slew of negative content. But while parental responsibility certainly is a viable critique, it's also no easy feat to protect a kid from everything that is going on out there; after all, problematic and troubling content is around every bend.

Either way, one can't help but wonder why Hollywood has changed so dramatically. But perhaps that's the wrong area of focus. Maybe the real problem is the culture at large—a society that is increasingly alienating itself from the very moral fabric that once bound it together. Then again, maybe it's both, with the former impacting the latter and touching off a vicious cycle that has pushed the culture beyond the bounds of a rational perspective and worldview. After all, Baehr said "people buy their scripts of behavior from the culture." [27] And with the influence of media and entertainment only increasing, people are being bombarded with affiliated messages.

"Back in the early '90s...by the time a child was seventeen, they were consuming eight hundred hours at church, and two thousand hours with their parents, and eleven thousand hours at school, and they were doing about forty thousand hours in the mass media," Baehr said. "Two years ago...they were doing sixty thousand hours with the mass media." [28]

And it's apparently only increasing; the film critic says that many young people are multitasking and "amusing themselves to death" on iPads, TV, and other tools, and he believes that the consumption of so much information is having an impact, especially considering the state of much of the content that is streaming to youths. Baehr said it's absurd to assume that, at eleven thousand hours of consumption, a school could compete with the estimated sixty-four thousand hours that youths have spent with mass media by the time they turn seventeen. As a result, he said the media are, in many ways, dictating the "scripts of behavior."[29]

"You've got a culture that's been acculturated...we know what happens to the kids," Baehr said. "We know how it deals with their different propensities, how it shapes who they are, how it gives them new scripts of behavior."[30]

THE BIBLE INVADES HOLLYWOOD

With all that in mind, some light is boldly shining in the depths of the Hollywood abyss. Despite the fact that many of the movies produced today are not even remotely in line with Christian or conservative values, this dynamic is beginning to change; churches and Christian companies have emerged on the entertainment scene in recent years to create independent films and studio movies aimed at serving faithful audiences.

Christian movies, which are sometimes attacked for what some say is poor quality, started gaining increased steam back in 2003, when brothers Stephen and Alex Kendrick launched Sherwood Pictures, a media division of Sherwood Baptist Church in Albany, Georgia, where the two served as pastors. Their efforts yielded popular Christian films such as *Courageous*, *Fireproof*, and *Facing the Giants*. These movies came on the heels of the *Left Behind* movie, which starred actor Kirk Cameron and was based on a monumentally popular apocalyptic book series.

While these movies enjoyed success among Christian audiences who were elated to see their worldview represented on the big screen, it has taken some time for other films to emerge that don't necessarily seek to preach to the choir.

About a decade after the Kendricks took to filmmaking, critics and observers heralded 2014 as the "year of the Bible"—a twelve-month period during which numerous big and small faith-based studio projects emerged.[31] From *God's Not Dead* to *Son of God* and *Noah*, Hollywood was flooded (pun intended) with movies that were predicated, to some level, upon God, the Bible, or divine intervention.

Some of these films were well received among the faithful, though some of the bigger studio projects, such as *Noah*, created debate and consternation among Christians who felt the plots needlessly deviated from the biblical text.

"Noah's character is conflicted about whether or not human beings should survive," National Religious Broadcasters CEO Jerry Johnson said during a panel discussion I attended back in 2014. "I think he borders on looking crazy and it's hard to match that to the Genesis text...I just think it's overdone."[32]

Despite this fact, Johnson joined other faith leaders in encouraging Christians to use the movie as an opportunity to evangelize. Their mantra: beggars can't be choosers, so Bible-believers should take what they can get from Hollywood.[33] On some level, it's not a deficient viewpoint, considering that the Bible story was being given prime attention in Hollywood, though critics still took issue with that sentiment.

After seeing the film, conservative commentator Glenn Beck said, "If you are looking for a biblical movie, this is definitely not it...It's not the story of Noah that I was hoping for. If you are going for that, you will be horribly disappointed."[34]

Beck said the movie would more aptly be titled "Babylonian Chainsaw Massacre," explaining how Noah was "running around... trying to kill his whole family" throughout the 138-minute film.[35] And Beck wasn't alone. The debate was apparently so fierce that Paramount Pictures added the following explanatory message to its marketing materials to try and buffer the storm:

> The film is inspired by the story of Noah. While artistic license has been taken, we believe that this film is true to the essence, values, and integrity of a story that is a cornerstone of faith for millions of people worldwide. The biblical story of Noah can be found in the book of Genesis.[36]

As for *Exodus: Gods and Kings*, which topped off the "year of the Bible" when it was released in December 2014, there was also some controversy, particularly after lead actor Christian Bale uttered some tough words about the biblical figure in an interview he did ahead of the film's release: "I think the man was likely schizophrenic and was one of the most barbaric individuals that I ever read about in my life." [37]

The film, similar to *Noah*, also drew criticisms for deviating from the Bible, with Beck saying he found it even more disconcerting than *Noah*. "They slapped Moses in the face," Beck said. "They slapped religion and people of faith in the face. If you're going to say, 'I'm going make a movie that appeals to everybody,' you at least make the main character sympathetic. He's not sympathetic, nor was Noah. They were both killers. They were both psychotic.... It's insane. It's hostile. It's really hostile." [38]

The lesson? Even when Hollywood attempts to serve audiences by invoking biblical themes, the messaging sometimes misses the mark, delivering plots and projects that may not be true to the original text. Again, on one side, some might say they're happy to at least see the Bible getting some attention, though others, like Beck, were still frustrated by the depictions. If anything, the conundrum speaks to the profound disconnect between Hollywood and the faithful—one that hasn't yet been bridged, despite ongoing efforts to try and do so.

Still some believe Christians also need to be patient when assessing Hollywood. Producer Phil Cooke candidly told me "most filmmakers don't believe the Bible," but added that he doesn't think that this precludes them from seeing the book as containing worthwhile stories. Considering filmmakers' worldview, though, it's not surprising there are sometimes notable differences in how Hollywood handles the content when compared to how professing believers would. [39]

"Since they're not believers, they don't feel the loyalty that we do, so as creative artists, they don't see the problem [with] deviating from the storyline," Cooke said. "But it's not about 'mockery' or being 'anti-faith.'" [40]

There is no doubt a legitimate debate over whether Christians should simply take what they can get from Hollywood or squawk. Either way, one must at least consider an important point raised by critics: *Noah* and *Exodus: Gods and Kings* might be the only education that some people get on these biblical stories. Editing the story too much means that individuals won't be walking away with accurate depictions of some of the most important biblical stories out there.

But again that's probably not something Hollywood is concerned about, and filmmakers are, of course, free to creatively make changes to these stories. That said, if they intend to market their films to Christians, it makes sense that the content meshes well with what's actually in the text.

While battles over movie and TV themes and content persist, there is yet another entertainment area where bias can sometimes rage: music.

CHAPTER 8

LYRICAL CONUNDRUM: MUSIC'S DEVOLVING STATE

THE **MUSIC INDUSTRY** is without a doubt in a steep competition for the "most troubled entertainment realm award" due to its dark and morally defunct nature. Over the years lyrics have increasingly invoked sexual themes, with industry award shows proving themselves to be on a similar trajectory. Sure, music has always been edgy, but something has felt a bit different and more intense in recent years.

MILEY CYRUS

Perhaps an example of just how far down the rabbit hole the industry has gone unfolded in 2013 in a moment that, hands down, solidified just how troubling—and perplexing—the situation has become. That stunning wake-up call came in August of that year when singer Miley Cyrus—an ex-Disney star who has more than shed her once squeaky-clean image—took to the stage at MTV's Video Music Awards and delivered what *TheBlaze* called "an eye-popping, gasp-inducing, slack-jaw-prompting, confounding performance."[1]

It was a bizarre spectacle that started out with giant teddy bears gracing the stage, as Cyrus gyrated, touched another woman's buttocks, and "twerked" while performing her hit song "We Can't Stop." And that was only the beginning; it was when fellow pop star Robin Thicke joined her on the stage that things took an even starker and more shocking turn.

Cyrus proceeded to strip down to what appeared to be a costumed version of a bra and underwear, as she continued twerking while standing in front of Thicke—all while making some pretty graphic gestures. It was a disturbing scene from the twenty-year-old, who had just a few years prior been entertaining the masses in a very different forum through Disney's kid-friendly TV phenomenon *Hannah Montana*.

This wasn't the first time the MTV Video Music Awards had included some graphic or edgy content (let's not forget about the infamous, headline-grabbing on-stage kissing that unfolded between Britney Spears, Madonna, and Christina Aguilera during the 2003 ceremony), but there was something different about this performance—something that, I believe, pierced the American conscience.

Reactions to the performance were volcanic. A multitude of commentators sounded off, with Bill O'Reilly blaming Cyrus's actions on bad parenting and proclaiming that she "embarrassed herself and her family on worldwide TV."[2] But he also hit on an important point—one that it appears MTV executives either ignored or simply didn't care about: the fact that many youths were tuned in to the troubling scene.

"With millions of young people watching, the scene was as degrading as it was unnecessary," O'Reilly said, adding, "Generally speaking, there is an epidemic of bad parenting going on in America."[3]

And others agreed. One mother named Kim Keller penned a blog post titled, "Dear daughter, Let Miley Cyrus Be a Lesson to You," urging her child to respect herself and not to follow in the pop star's footsteps. The strongly worded open letter reads, in part:

> This is what happens when no responsible adult has ever said the word "no," made you change your clothes before leaving the house, or never spanked your butt for deliberate defiance.[4]

Keller concluded, "I am going to fight or die trying to keep you from becoming like the Miley Cyruses of the world."[5]

What was perhaps most interesting about the sweeping response to Cyrus's over-the-top performance is that some of her fellow entertainers even expressed worries over her antics. The late comedian Joan Rivers was candid in saying that she believed Cyrus simply went too far.

"This is such a bad message to send out to young girls," Rivers told *Entertainment Tonight* after Cyrus's MTV performance. "We get it: You're no longer Hannah Montana...but you can do it with a little more grace....This has gone too far."[6]

Rivers touched on an important point—the same one that O'Reilly was trying to hammer home: the TV audience that night was likely comprised of at least some of the children who had watched Cyrus on Disney and who were fans of her before she profoundly changed her image. That fact wasn't lost on some psychologists who weighed in on the issue in the wake of the debate, warning that the performance's potential impact was worth discussing.

Dr. Pamela LiVecchi said in an op-ed at the time that children and adults alike are impacted by what's on TV more than some might think, as perspectives are often shaped in very small ways. "What we see affects our ideas, beliefs, emotions, and behaviors, regardless of whether or not we agree with them," she wrote. "As we are confronted with images, statements, and attitudes, they seep into our minds." [7]

LiVecchi said this happens even if people disagree with the images they are seeing or hearing, because they embed into individuals' memories and have an impact. She argued Cyrus's performance left kids and teenagers with a view about what is acceptable in society, even if they disagreed with her antics. [8]

This, she said, should spark some concern, especially surrounding programs that are geared toward youths, as she encouraged parents to teach their kids to critically analyze what they consume and to openly decry negative messages. [9]

Dr. Azadeh Aalai, an assistant professor of psychology at Queensborough Community College in New York, said that she could barely call Cyrus's performance "provocative," because she felt "pornographic" was a better descriptor. She, similar to LiVecchi, worried about the impact that Cyrus was having on the masses. "Unfortunately, popular culture does not exist in a vacuum," she wrote. "There are real effects—subtle, implicit, and then more direct or explicit—that come from living in an era of ubiquitous media where women's bodies and personas continue to be objectified at every turn." [10]

When it comes to music performances, though, Aalai wondered where the chaos ends, decrying the fact that performers keep becoming more and more graphic in how they express themselves on stage. She said the ever-increasing dynamic is "a direct byproduct of the process of desensitization," adding a troubling, yet thought-provoking question: "At some point, simulating sex on stage or even taking off virtually all of one's clothes may not be enough—and then where will pop culture lead us?" [11]

BEYONCÉ

It would, of course, be wholly unfair to focus only on Cyrus, though it's important to note that her performance was, for many, a wake-up call to just how devolved entertainment culture has become. But again, she's not alone. A few months later, pop star Beyoncé strutted around the Grammy Awards stage in a performance that sparked similar discussion and debate. As the *Daily Mail* reported at the time, concerned parents felt the "risqué routine [was] too explicit for children to watch."[12]

Proceeding to explain the performance, the outlet continued, "She opened the show straddling a chair then proceeded to writhe around on it before twerking her way up to a standing position." When Beyoncé's husband, Jay Z, came on the stage to perform with her, she began touching him and delivered "moves Miley Cyrus would have been proud of," the outlet added.[13]

The *Daily Mail* proceeded to offer up some Twitter reactions that unfolded during the performance, including people who said the singer had "no class," wasn't giving kids anything to look up to—and that they would no longer allow their children to watch the Grammys. Some, in their disgust, noted that Beyoncé is herself a mother.[14]

Let's also remember that the evening concluded with a mass wedding comprised of both gay and straight couples. Officiated by Queen Latifah—and complete with Madonna and Macklemore & Ryan Lewis—the tying of the knots was certainly a bizarre display for an event that's intended to celebrate music.[15]

During his performance Macklemore railed against conservatives who believe people can be cured of same-sex attraction and those who contend that being gay is a choice; he also charged that people abandon the notion that God loves everyone while quoting from biblical texts.

EVEN THE CONTENT OF MUSIC IS CHANGING

I could go on and on with the examples, but perhaps the more pressing issue is the actual content of songs. While some music that is essentially played on loop on America's Top 40 stations relies on double entendres or more veiled sexual or explicit references, there are plenty of examples of performers who produce songs with no intent of hiding the dirty messages within.

One of the more interesting efforts to examine how music has changed over time was undertaken in 2014 by Nickolay Lamm, a researcher and artist. Titled "Money, Love and Sex," the effort involved Lamm looking into popular Billboard hits over time to trace the presence of some key words. He reportedly organized song lyrics and then made a program to analyze the database. Lamm was then able to type in a lyric and see when and where it would show up in songs; he subsequently created graphs to help visualize the changes, according to the *Huffington Post*.[16]

"I had a feeling...that songs these days are a lot about sex," Lamm said. "I also had a feeling that songs back in the day were more about love." So, what did he find, exactly?[17]

In the end, the outlet concluded that "pop lyrics have taken a turn for the dirtier." Topics such as sex, weed, and expletives appeared to ramp up after the 1990s. Lamm selected a variety of words for inclusion in his study, finding that terms like "baby" have remained consistent in music throughout the decades, while "I love you" has been on the decline; it wasn't until the 1990s that the presence of expletives started ramping up in music, according to the *Huffington Post*.[18]

Others have taken on similar tasks. Journalist Shane Snow penned an analysis piece for Contently in 2015 after wondering whether "society—and music—[is] really going downhill, or...[whether] our generational complaints [are] just about nostalgia." So he decided to find the top ten Billboard songs from the third week of April every ten years beginning in 1965 and analyze their content. While Snow admitted that the research was just a sliver of what was out there, he said he came up with some intriguing findings.[19]

"It looks like top artists of the '60s and '70s used a lot of typical poetry vocab...in the '80s we were obsessed with songs about 'the night,'" he said. "In the '90s...we get more diversity of vocabulary and topics, and in the next two decades there's more focus on self."[20]

While Snow found that people were essentially singing about the same feelings throughout the decades, the intensity changed. In fact, he wrote that the once more benign and sappy subject matter moved to dark topics predicated upon lust, partying, losing, loving, and other related subjects. The specificity of the subject matter, Snow said, has changed, but some of the values have seemingly evolved as well.[21]

It appears as if music is more about profanity and drugs, but "sex and violence haven't really increased—at least in top radio hits," he said, noting, though, that there might be more questionable content on the Internet these days that is more intense yet isn't really all that popular and wouldn't make the Billboard analysis.[22]

MUSIC'S EFFECT ON YOUNG PEOPLE

The oversaturation of negative themes at this point is concerning. It doesn't take a scientific study to tell us that bombarding young people—and adults—with messages about sex, drugs, partying, and promiscuity is probably not really all that culturally healthy. But don't just take my word for it; there are studies that have found problematic effects of music on young people, in particular.

A study published by the American Psychological Association in 2003 found that "songs with violent lyrics increase aggression related thoughts and emotions and this effect is directly related to the violence in the lyrics."[23] Citing a 2008 report from *The Archives of Pediatrics and Adolescent Medicine*, the *New York Times* noted that one out of three popular songs included references to alcohol or drugs at the time, meaning that teens—who were estimated at that point to be listening to two and a half hours of music per day on average—were hearing about thirty-five references to drugs or substances for each hour of music they consumed.[24]

As the *Times* reported, "Studies have long shown that media messages have a pronounced impact on childhood risk behaviors."[25] All of this was concerning at the time and continues to spark worries due to the fact that iPods, MP3 players, and other technologies are making it harder for parents to know exactly what their kids are listening to. The fact that content is seemingly worsening teamed with experts' claims that negative messages can impact behavior means there is much to consider.

But, again, don't just take my word for it. A 2009 policy statement published by the American Academy of Pediatrics and titled "Impact of Music, Music Lyrics, and Music Videos on Children and Youth" summarizes the issue quite well. In it the organization expressed concern over the impact of popular music on youths' behaviors and emotions, saying that the topic is of "paramount concern." Citing the obvious, the American Academy of Pediatrics noted that the contents of lyrics have come to include an increasing number of references to violence, sex, and drugs, among other subjects. "A teenager's preference for certain types of music could be correlated or associated with certain behaviors," the statement read.[26]

A number of studies were referenced in the text to highlight that music has a potentially negative impact on youths. Some songs, some of the studies found, can instill negative emotions in young listeners—feelings that can have a profound impact. For instance, some research reportedly found that heavy metal and certain forms of rock music have association with increased risks of suicide; heavy metal has also been linked to problems with listening, issues in school, increased depression, smoking, and other issues.[27]

While the American Academy of Pediatrics said it's difficult to determine cause and effect relationships, as correlation studies have limitations, there are many elements that emerged from research that should cause parents—and society—pause. We could certainly dive into each study mentioned in the 2009 document, though one reference in particular perfectly illustrates the concern: "A survey performed among 2,760 American adolescents demonstrated that listening to music and watching television and music videos more frequently was associated with increased risky behaviors."[28]

In an updated policy statement in 2013 titled "Children, Adolescents and the Media," the American Academy of Pediatrics noted that the rise of new media technologies such as more advanced phones and iPads is opening up more access to youths. The statement reads, in part: "The overwhelming penetration of media into children's and teenagers' lives necessitates a renewed commitment to changing the way pediatricians, parents, teachers, and society address the use of media to mitigate potential health risks and foster appropriate media use."[29]

Again, I could go on and on. The statements and studies on the matter are in no short supply, yet many in Hollywood and the music industry simply don't seem to care. Whether they like it or not, Beyoncé and Miley Cyrus—among many others—are role models.

Young people are watching their every move, looking to them as individuals to quite possibly emulate. Parents face quite a challenge.

The American Academy of Pediatrics spouted off some statistics that should certainly raise additional red flags, saying in a 2010 document that "more than 75 percent of prime-time programs contain sexual content, yet only 14 percent of sexual incidents mention any risks or responsibilities of sexual activity."[30] And, again, that was 2010; six years have passed, and anyone unaware of how much worse it has become is living in a dream world. The question to ask now is: Will we change course?

Now that we've explored Hollywood, let's dive into the second sector that I believe is having a deep impact on Americans' views: the university system.

PART 3

CHAPTER 9

THE GREATEST IRONY OF OUR AGE

PERHAPS THE GREATEST irony of our age is that colleges and universities—the very institutions that are intended to educate and intellectually challenge the masses—ofttimes foster environments that are routinely accused of being patently one-sided and biased. After all, college is intended to be an intensive time of self-exploration—one in which young people are theoretically opened up to the world around them, with diverse perspectives and experiences helping to shape their contextual understandings. Yet, in contrast, higher education today is often a breeding ground for exclusively progressive ideals and values that are masqueraded, paraded, and marketed to young minds as definitive, unadulterated truth.

Unfortunately young people are all too often fed this information from left-of-center professors who are injecting their worldview into the classroom with little regard for the need for divergent beliefs in the educational marketplace. Their ideals, presented as truth and many times so filtered that opposing views are either denigrated into silence or ignored entirely, are often pervasive and treated as gospel when in fact they're nothing more than mere personal opinion.

Don't get me wrong. There is absolutely nothing wrong with liberal professors being employed by colleges and universities (just so we're clear here); what is improper, however, is an environment in which young people are given an imbalanced perspective on key social, political, and international issues or one in which conservative professors are too afraid to share their views with colleagues for fear of reprisal.

Such imbalances create unaccommodating and uncomfortable environments for those who do not share left-of-center perspectives, though the more pervasive and concerning issue is the notion that young, impressionable minds are potentially robbed of the ability to make decisions for themselves, especially when they aren't presented with a fair assessment of all the available and pertinent information.

ANECDOTAL EVIDENCE OF
BIAS IN HIGHER EDUCATION

The problem with measuring bias in the classroom, of course, is the fact that so much of what is claimed to have happened is based on anecdotal examples and he-said, she-said claims, though such incidents certainly warrant attention and analysis.

I've heard many personal stories of bias in higher education, so I'll just share one with you—a classroom lecture about the power of words. It unfolded at an American university as a group of students listened to a professor describe images on a paper he had just passed out to the class. When one of the students looked down at the paper, she noticed a series of black squares with static white inside of them. It took her a moment to realize that the images were sonogram pictures taken from women who were very early on in their pregnancies. As the student examined the paper and internally wondered what in the world the lesson would be about, the professor told the class something along the lines of, "What do you see in these pictures?" Some students attempted to answer before the professor interjected: "Some people will say that this is a baby. Does it look like a baby to you?"

Of course the images didn't resemble fully-formed, gurgling babies, as the pregnancies were in the earliest of stages; naturally, most of the class responded in the way one could only assume the professor wanted them to: with a resounding "No."

The professor then went on to invoke the debate over abortion and discussed the power of words in eliciting emotion—but the female student was so bothered by the explanation and the activity that she raised her hand and proceeded to explain that, though the images didn't resemble fully formed babies, people of faith believe that all life is precious and that these unborn children—complete with beating hearts—should still be counted among the living. Her point was that the class was still looking at images of human life, albeit undeveloped at the time. The professor was gracious but clearly unmoved.

Though fleeting, that lesson was a moment that stuck with the student, as she realized just how simple—and pervasive—bias can be in the educational process, and how difficult it is for so many young people to hold on to their values in environments that tend to see so many aspects of life through a liberal and/or secular lens.

She remembers thinking at the time that the lesson about the power of words works both ways. For instance, labeling an unborn baby a "fetus" takes the humanity away from it, making it easier to accept or even ignore what happens in abortion clinics across the country. There's a reason some don't call it a baby, no? Saying such a thing is not passing judgment on anyone; it's merely making a point about the importance of truth and reality.

This classroom example is simply anecdotal, though I know many young people have faced similar—and far more pervasive—issues of bias at the college and university level. Another example includes a mock debate between conservatives and liberals leading up to the 2004 presidential election. The goal was to have one professor and a few students come together on both sides of the aisle to face off, though the Republicans—who couldn't find a conservative professor bold enough to participate—ended up having a liberal dean reluctantly stand in and pretend to be a Republican, reading responses from the GOP platform verbatim when the debate moderator called on her. Hey, at least she was willing to participate.

BIAS AGAINST CHRISTIANS IN ACADEMIA

These examples only scratch the surface. In fact, University of North Texas professor George Yancey has been more than vocal about the overt bias that he sees inherent in university environments, diving deep into that paradigm in an interview for this book.

On a broader level, Yancey, who authored *Hostile Environment: Understanding and Responding to Anti-Christian Bias*, rejected the claims of some in society who argue that, as a nominal majority, Christians can't possibly be the victims of discrimination, saying that he has conducted research that proves these individuals are flat wrong in advancing such claims.

"I always preface this by saying, 'I'm not saying that Christians are black. We're not talking about Jim Crow,'" he told me. "There's something to the fact that, at least in the past, Christians have been the majority—and maybe they still are in many ways today—but my research shows that if you are a conservative Protestant, you have a distinctive disadvantage going for a job in academia."[1]

Yancey's research involved a survey based on a national sample in which he presented professors with twenty-six potential characteristics and asked how they would react if they found out that a job candidate possessed each descriptor or characteristic. His question essentially asked, "If you found this out about a person, would it make you more or less likely to hire them?"[2]

In the end, the professor said it became more than clear that the academics surveyed were "definitely less likely" to hire Christian fundamentalists and evangelicals—characteristics that garnered the most negative reactions, even outpacing conservative political persuasions.[3]

"They were less willing to hire Republicans, for example, but that measure was at a much lower rate," Yancey explained. "That's why I say conservative Protestants are the ones that academics themselves will tell you, 'Yes, I'm less likely to hire you if I find out that you're a conservative Protestant.'" Half of them share this sentiment, as Yancey said. "About half. Obviously not all of them, but about half of them."[4]

It is those findings that lead Yancey to see roadblocks in academia for those who embrace conservatism and Protestantism, with the professor saying that other research conducted on the matter backs his theories. While some might scoff, Yancey offered up a powerful comparison to showcase the dire nature of the situation.

"If we had that sort of data on any other group—if we had that sort of data on Jews, that almost half of all academics are less likely to hire you if you're Jewish, no one would argue that anti-Semitism is not costing Jews in the academic world," he continued. "Really, there's no real argument that anti-Christian bias is not costing at least conservative Protestants in the academia world."[5]

In the end, Yancey said he was surprised by the results. He went into the survey assuming he would uncover bias, though he initially predicted it would be more prevalent on political indicators rather than religious parameters. Clearly he was wrong.[6]

With the aforementioned information in mind, it's easy to see how Christianity, God, and conservative values have been marginalized—and hold the potential to continue to be marginalized—in today's university system, but let's dive a bit deeper into corroboratory research.

POLITICAL BELIEFS OF
PROFESSORS IN AMERICA

As I said, measuring overarching bias can be a difficult feat, especially considering that there are thousands of colleges across the nation, but there is some data out there that can give us a clearer sense of what might be going on—at least when it comes to demographics.

So let's briefly explore what full-time undergraduate faculty members believe, politically speaking. How do we do that, you ask? It's a relatively easy task, considering that the Higher Education Research Institute at UCLA releases a study every two years offering a lens into the views of faculty members from across the country.

In the latest wave of the study, which was conducted using data collected in 2013 and 2014, professors were asked, "How would you characterize your political views?" The response? Eleven percent of educators described themselves as "far left," with an additional 48.8 percent saying that they are "liberal." Meanwhile, just 12.1 percent described themselves as "conservative," with .7 percent selecting "far right" as a descriptor; an additional 27.4 percent said they are "middle of the road."[7]

Collectively that means that nearly 60 percent of professors at four-year institutions are liberal, with only around 13 percent describing themselves as right-of-center. Flashing back to 1990, those proportions were around 45 percent and 16 percent among faculty at four-year universities, respectively.[8]

Clearly there has been some change afoot over the years, with progressives becoming more prevalent at the university level. The latest data also showed that professors at public universities are actually more liberal than those at private colleges—another odd dynamic considering that taxpayer dollars fund public institutions.

More specifically, in the most recent study, 63.6 percent of faculty at public universities considered themselves liberal (53.2 percent) or far left (10.4 percent), compared to 56.8 percent of professors at private institutions who selected either liberal (42.2 percent) or far left (14.6 percent). More than 16 percent of professors at private institutions are conservative versus just under 8 percent at public colleges.[9]

THE NEED FOR ALL
OPTIONS TO BE PRESENTED

I could go on and on…and on. I'm certainly not attempting to rant or cry victim by sharing these relatively benign examples, but rather I am concerned that they point to a troubling state of education in America. Can I definitively prove that every campus in America is filled with rampant bias? No, and I'd argue that there are certainly conservative and faith-based colleges out there as well; but there is surely a pattern that shows, on the whole, that some colleges can pose some challenges for Christians and conservatives—both academics and students alike.

At the core of the discussion is an important question everyone must honestly explore: If we truly want to raise freethinking citizens who are able to discern and make important life decisions, isn't it essential that they have all of the available options before them so that they can make the most appropriate and reasonable choices?

This shouldn't be a radical idea; in fact, it is one that many individuals—both liberal and conservative—have cited. Consider what progressive *New York Times* columnist Nicholas Kristof wrote about this very issue in a May 2016 op-ed. To summarize, Kristof concluded that universities disregard "ideological and religious" diversity. Speaking of the ramifications for such a dynamic, he wrote, "The stakes involve not just fairness to conservatives or evangelical Christians…but also the quality of education itself." [10]

Kristof pointed to a number of other important values, including the need for liberals to remain open and, thus, "true to their own values." Additionally, he said a dearth in representation of conservatives and evangelicals negatively impacts the quality of education. With some perspectives not being present at the table, he warned classrooms can become echo chambers and that, in the end, everyone loses as a result. [11]

The columnist went on to cite studies that he said showed clear disparities in professors' ideological viewpoints, saying that some inquiries have found that just 6 to 11 percent of humanities professors self-identify as Republican, with just between 7 to 9 percent saying the same in the social sciences. In that latter group, around 18 percent have called themselves Marxists—a fact that led Kristof to conclude that "it's easier to find a Marxist in some disciplines than a Republican."[12]

He also offered up a challenge to his fellow liberals: "Maybe we progressives could take a brief break from attacking the other side and more broadly incorporate values that we supposedly cherish—like diversity—in our own dominions."[13]

STUDENTS' VIEWS ARE SKEWED LEFT BEFORE THEY BEGIN COLLEGE

Again, the situation is disturbingly lopsided, with a majority of professors selecting "liberal" or "far left" to describe themselves and with conservatives constituting a very tiny sliver of the educational class. With that in mind, there are certainly some other key questions worth asking.

Can classroom discussions truly be fair and representative of the general populace if only one in ten professors consider themselves conservative? Are young people being underserved by a collective college experience that fails to consider diverse views? Is there really a respect for diversity if ideological views are so unevenly represented?

These questions are tough to answer, though what we can be certain of is that there is a dearth of educators in university classrooms who understand—or at least sympathize with—the Christian and/or conservative worldview.

In the end these biases matter. But as I've stated, it isn't only college where certain values are left out of the discussion, as the overarching university system is only one piece of the trifecta that appears to be impacting the views of young people in the modern era. Sure, professors and university environments might be skewing the views of kids and young adults, but as I've discussed in this book, the roles of entertainment and media have also been paramount, swaying the moral and ethical inklings of kids and adults alike. Many young people these days are entering college with values that have already been shaped and molded, in part, by the content coming out of those spheres.

The culture is changing, and those changes are being imprinted on the hearts and minds of both children and adults. Consider that a report from the Higher Education Research Institute titled "The

American Freshman" took into account the experiences of 141,189 first-time, full-time college students at 199 colleges and universities across America. The survey found that a higher number of students than ever before—27.5 percent—chose "none" as a descriptor of their personal religious beliefs in 2014. This is 2.9 percentage points more than the number of students who answered "none" in 2013 and 12 percent more than the same from 1971.[14]

When researchers decided to change the survey in the 2015 wave to include "atheist" and "agnostic," the overarching proportion jumped to 29.5 percent (a combination of 5.9 percent who called themselves atheist, 8.3 percent who called themselves agnostic, and 15.4 percent who selected "none").[15]

It's not just on the faith front, though, that the belief systems embraced by incoming freshman are seemingly evolving. Similar to the question posed to professors, incoming first-time students were also asked to select their political persuasion, with those metrics seemingly evolving.

"For the past several years, greater proportions of students have identified as either 'liberal' or 'far left,'" the report reads. "Roughly one-third of the students (33.5 percent) who entered a four-year institution in the fall of 2015 identify as 'liberal' or 'far left,' 1.8 percentage points higher than in 2014 and 3.9 points higher than in 2012."[16]

The text continues, "About one in five students (21.6 percent) identify as 'conservative' or 'far right,' which was similar to 2014 when 21 percent of students did the same."[17]

Similar findings unfolded when incoming students were asked about other more specific indicators, including majority agreement—52.3 percent—with the idea that students from disadvantaged backgrounds should be given preferred treatment, 56.4 percent supporting marijuana legalization, and 63.5 percent saying abortion should be legal.[18]

There's clearly a societal change afoot, and it's impacting people across the generations, though changes among millennials and younger generations are perhaps most concerning due to their implications for free speech and America's future.

CHAPTER 10

CAMPUS CHAOS RAGES

THE DEARTH OF conservative ideals among professors is certainly an area of concern, but a variety of other factors are also worth exploring, including the massive battle over campus buzzwords such as "trigger warning," "microaggression," and "safe spaces." If you're unfamiliar with these concepts, I'll briefly take you through the debate over each.

TRIGGER WARNINGS

Let's start first with trigger warnings, which are typically used "to alert or warn students that something they're about to read, watch or discuss could cause them distress," according to the *Lafayette Journal & Courier*.[1] These warnings might be uttered as a cautionary note just before showing material with themes surrounding sexual abuse or violence, among other potentially troubling ideals.

The idea, according to some, is that certain students might respond better to course content or messages that deal with controversial subject matter if they are warned and prepared for it beforehand. This subject matter might include disturbing elements such as rape or violence—themes that might be embedded in poems and books. But it seems there's some debate about the concept, as a 2015 nonscientific study from the National Coalition Against Censorship found that 45 percent of the eight hundred professors surveyed believe trigger warnings are or will negatively impact the classroom setting, with 62 percent saying it will negatively impact academic freedom. But, despite those views, only 15 percent said trigger warnings had been requested, causing some to wonder just how widespread they are.[2]

Many critics have cautioned that trigger warnings, while seemingly beneficial, could also have some unintended consequences. Alan Levinovitz, an assistant professor of religion at James Madison University in Harrisonburg, Virginia, wrote a piece for the *Atlantic* saying that students' free speech could, in fact, be endangered. "I know firsthand how debates about trigger warnings and safe spaces can have a chilling effect on classroom discussions," Levinovitz wrote.[3]

While he said he isn't concerned about his own speech, as professors are generally fine to present contentious material, he said students might be particularly vulnerable, adding his belief that trigger warnings and safe spaces can sometimes stifle free speech.[4]

"Students should be free to argue their beliefs without fear of being labeled intolerant or disrespectful, whether they think certain sexual orientations are forbidden by God, life occurs at the moment of conception, or Islam is the exclusive path to salvation," he wrote. "And conversely, the same freedom should apply to those who believe God doesn't care about who we have sex with, abortion is a fundamental right, or Islam is based on nothing more than superstitious nonsense."[5]

Levinovitz said these freedoms simply are not in place in many academic settings, adding that this is particularly troublesome in a religious studies class. Considering how deep some religious views run, it's possible that questioning those ideals could be seen as an attack on one's identity. And considering the definition of respect that is being embraced by many—the idea that no one can ever say anything offensive or question one's identity—the professor warned "the only respectful discussion of religion is one in which everyone affirms everyone else's beliefs, describes those beliefs without passing judgment, or simply remains silent." Clearly that poses a problem for both free expression and learning.[6]

SAFE SPACES

Now, let's move on to discuss safe spaces. Safe spaces, to dig a little deeper, are contentious in that one side sees them as designated areas that allow for respectful discussion and debate, while the other believes they are locations at which free speech is curtailed.[7]

Pushing back against some conservatives who he said tend to mischaracterize safe spaces, Vox's German Lopez wrote that "allowing safe spaces doesn't mean that whole campuses are cordoned off as places devoid of any controversial or challenging ideas." Rather, he added, "Safe spaces are, instead, a specific place where people of certain groups—racial, religious, and so on—can go temporarily to talk to and hang out with peers in a similar place without having to do the kind of cultural translation that a more diverse crowd might require."[8]

Grand View University professor Kevin Gannon also added his perspective to the debate, saying that dismissing safe spaces as "an uncritical, everyone-gets-a-trophy type place" is "inaccurate." He continued:

> They *are* a place where students can find mutual support and "their people" when they need. Not all the time, but when they want...Examples are useful here. Hillel, the campus Jewish fellowship, is a safe space. The Catholic Student Union or Wesley House are too.[9]

But while some see no problem with safe spaces, others have voiced their concerns. *Newsweek*'s Nina Burleigh pointed out that young people who might seek protection from certain troubling ideas likely won't be greeted with the same reality in the real world. Additionally, she charged that more than half of the colleges and universities in the United States have "restrictive speech codes." All of this, she argued, could lead to some negative fallout.[10]

"Graduates of the Class of 2016 are leaving behind campuses that have become petri dishes of extreme political correctness and heading out into a world without trigger warnings, safe spaces and free speech zones, with no rules forbidding offensive verbal conduct or microaggressions, and where the names of cruel, rapacious capitalists are embossed in brass and granite on buildings across the land," Burleigh wrote. "Baby seals during the Canadian hunting season may have a better chance of survival."[11]

MICROAGGRESSIONS

And the debate doesn't end there. Microaggressions—which have been given increased attention of late—"are the everyday verbal, nonverbal, and environmental slights, snubs, or insults, whether intentional or unintentional, which communicate hostile, derogatory, or negative messages to target persons based solely upon their marginalized group membership," according to Dr. Derald Wing Sue.[12] These cultural statements have, in fact, been dominating headlines more frequently of late.

There was a controversy in 2015 over a list that the University of California reportedly published outlining race and sex-based microaggressions. Though these statements weren't banned, UCLA law professor Eugene Volokh said at the time that they sent a "powerful message" to professors and students about what wouldn't be accepted. Volokh said that it collectively constituted "a serious blow to academic freedom and to freedom of discourse more generally."[13] In a previous piece, he warned that it was really all about "suppressing particular viewpoints."[14] Here were some of the examples of statements that he cited from the UC document:

- "Affirmative action is racist."
- To a person of color: "Are you sure you were being followed in the store? I can't believe it."
- "I believe the most qualified person should get the job."
- "Of course he'll get tenure, even though he hasn't published much—he's Black!"
- "Men and women have equal opportunities for achievement."
- "Everyone can succeed in this society, if they work hard enough."

The University of North Carolina also reportedly published its own list of microaggressions, which included lines such as, "When I look at you, I don't see color" and "You don't look Jewish/Native/Muslim." The document also said that any "unit celebrations, academic calendars and encouraged vacations" being "organized around major religious observances" also constitutes a microaggression, as it "further centers the Christian faith and minimizes non-Christian spiritual rituals and observances," according to *TheBlaze*.[15] Uh, Christmas vacation, anyone?

BACKLASH AGAINST SUCH BUZZWORDS

Again, not everyone is on board with heralding trigger warnings, microaggressions, and safe spaces as good and viable academic tools. Consider the letter that John Ellison, dean of students at the University of Chicago, sent to incoming freshman back in 2016. In it Ellison did anything but mince words on these issues, warning incoming students that free speech reigns on campus.

While the dean wrote in the letter to the class of 2020 that "civility and mutual respect are vital to all of us, and freedom of expression does not mean the freedom to harass or threaten others," he said discussion and debate will both challenge students and quite possibly give them discomfort—but that the school is devoted to enriching educational experiences.[16]

"Our commitment to academic freedom means that we do not support so-called 'trigger warnings,' we do not cancel invited speakers because their topics might prove controversial, and we do not condone the creation of intellectual 'safe spaces' where individuals can retreat from ideas and perspectives at odds with their own," he wrote.[17]

SPEAKERS ON CAMPUS

It should be noted that Ellison hit on a topic I haven't yet addressed: speakers on campus. Some estimates have claimed that liberal commencement speakers generally outpaced conservatives—by a four-to-one margin in 2016 alone[18]—but it appears there is a broader problem of conservative speakers claiming they've been banned from campuses. Consider just one example involving conservative author and speaker Ben Shapiro, who was reportedly nearly disinvited from speaking at California State University, Los Angeles, due to his "controversial" views.[19]

Rather than allow Shapiro to speak on his own as liberal speakers had allegedly been permitted to do, university president William Covino purportedly sent an e-mail to the head of the campus organization that invited Shapiro and said that Shapiro would be rescheduled along with others who could balance his message. Here's how the purported e-mail read:

> After careful consideration I have decided that it will be best for our campus community if we reschedule Ben Shapiro's appearance for a later date, so that we can arrange for him to appear as part of a group of speakers with differing viewpoints on diversity. Such an event will better represent our university's dedication to the free exchange of ideas and the value of considering multiple viewpoints.[20]

Shapiro ended up speaking anyway to the chagrin of angry pro-testers who some said actually blocked doorways to the venue.[21] Clearly this is the sort of issue that Ellison was possibly referring to when he said that the University of Chicago doesn't "cancel invited speakers."

When I spoke with Shapiro in an interview for this book, he told me he believes he's been banned from some campuses "because of the rioters' veto." He said, "Most of these students have no idea who I am or what I've said. They simply buy what their radical professors tell them about me, and they resonate to it," Shapiro said. "The same freedom of speech and expression that protect your ability to protest protects my ability to disagree with you. Undermining that freedom out of a myopic hatred for my point of view is dangerous for everyone, including you."[22]

And it seems some—even in academia—agree. As you can imagine, Ellison's letter gained quite a bit of attention, with many praising him for seemingly railing against political correctness; others, of course, were less enthusiastic.

UNIVERSITY REACTIONS TO THE ELECTION

The 2016 presidential campaign took the definition of "sensitive snowflake" to entirely new levels. Case-in-point: an event that was reportedly planned at the University of Michigan Law School to help students cope with the electoral results. The event titled, "Post-Election Self-Care With Food and Play," came along with the fol-lowing description: "Join us for delicious and comforting food with opportunity to experience some stress-busting, self-care activi-ties" and listed activities such as such as playing with Play-Doh and blowing bubbles. It was apparently cancelled after the Internet under-standably erupted with ridicule and quips.[23]

Another college reportedly reminded students that therapy dogs were available to those who needed them, and the list goes on.[24] The weeping and gnashing of teeth following the election apparently trig-gered some shocking responses on select college campuses, with emotions taking precedence over logic, calmness, and restraint. It's understandable why people might be sad and frustrated when their chosen candidate looses, but offering adults Play-Doh to cope is utterly bizarre.

THE LEFT-LEANING WORLD OF ACADEMICS

Summarizing what has been happening on America's college campuses, the *Washington Post*'s Catherine Rampell wrote, "Today's students are indeed both more left wing and more openly hostile to free speech than earlier generations of collegians," before going on to cite some troubling statistics from the Higher Education Research Institute.[25]

The organization, which surveys first-year students each year, found in 2015 that 71 percent of freshmen agree with colleges prohibiting "racist/sexist speech on campus," up from 60 percent in the early 1990s. Meanwhile, 43 percent support colleges having the "right to ban extreme speakers from campus." The problem with these statistics, according to Rampell? "What speech counts as 'racist' or 'sexist' is of course in the eye of the beholder."[26]

Perhaps the most telling portion of her piece, though, was the note the author made at the end of it. Citing the notion that these worsening statistics were collected from incoming freshmen and not students who yet had the chance to be liberalized by a college campus, Rampell suggested that "colleges themselves are not wholly responsible for rising liberal and illiberal tendencies on campus—even if they do sometimes aid and abet both trends."[27] Clearly something is happening in the culture that is creating and incubating these views before students ever set foot on campus.

CHAPTER 11

THE RISE OF COLLEGES' ALL-COMERS POLICIES

WITHOUT A DOUBT one of the most sinister developments (or at the least, problematic) on American college campuses has been the rise and impact of so-called "all-comers policies."

These anti-discrimination regulations, which appear to be beneficial and inclusive on the surface, bar officially recognized campus clubs from requiring their leaders to embrace specific viewpoints. Again it all sounds wonderfully intended. After all, no one wants another person or organization mandating what he or she believes; so, theoretically, an all-comers policy means every student has the chance to both participate in and to theoretically lead a club, even if his or her personal views run counter to that of the organization in question.

But here's the problem: all-comers policies—to some degree—defy logic, as some clubs actually depend on their leaders holding specific viewpoints. Take, for instance, a Bible study group that looks to its leaders to guide members through Scripture. It would seem pretty counterintuitive to allow that club to be led by an atheist or even a nominal Christian who lacks information or context about the faith.

VANDERBILT'S ALL-COMERS POLICY

Vanderbilt University in Nashville, Tennessee, is just one private college that found itself in the crosshairs of the all-comers debate in 2010 and 2011 after the school changed the language of its nondiscrimination provision to clarify that registered student groups—those that can apply for funding, use campus listservs and group mail, and benefit from recruitment activities—must allow *all members* in good standing to apply for leadership roles.[1]

So, while a club is welcome to require membership dues, auditions, regular meeting attendance, and other similar provisions, a Bible study group is barred from asking that the head of its club actually be a Bible-believing Christian.

A response under a FAQ question on the university's website addressing whether a registered student organization (RSO) can "impose faith-based or belief-based requirements for membership or leadership" reads:

> No. The policy provides that all Vanderbilt students are eligible for membership in all RSOs. The policy requires that any member in good standing of any RSO must be eligible to compete for any leadership post in that RSO. For example, Republicans and Independents are eligible to join the College Democrats, and any member may run for office, though it is up to the members to select their leaders. This is true for all RSOs at Vanderbilt.[2]

While the university chose a political example, one can take that same logic and apply it to a gay and lesbian student support group, concluding that, under the policy, the club would hypothetically be forced to consider an anti-same-sex marriage activist for a key leadership role—a nonsensical provision, regardless of how unlikely it is that such a person would win member support in a campus election. Still, doesn't going down this route potentially open up a can of worms?

Vanderbilt acknowledged fears that the policy could lead some clubs to be intentionally infiltrated by members who disagree with the message being espoused and "want to take it over," explaining that attendance and other "neutral requirements" could be created to help prevent this. But those parameters aren't clearly laid out.[3]

The Vanderbilt all-comers debate reportedly began after a gay student claimed he was kicked out of Beta Upsilon Chi, a Christian fraternity. He purportedly filed a complaint with the school, which launched a discussion about whether every campus group was abiding by Vanderbilt's nondiscrimination policy—the mandate requiring that clubs allow students to be both members and leaders.[4]

WHAT ALL-COMERS POLICIES ACTUALLY DO

But as I shared with the aforementioned example, religious clubs, unlike some other groups, generally hinge on having strong leaders who not only understand Scripture and theology, but who also embrace it in their own lives; these are people who hold the ability to teach, lead, and instruct members in a variety of faith matters. It absolutely makes sense for a Christian club to expect its leaders to believe in the Bible as the infallible Word of God; what doesn't make sense, though, is leaving the door open for someone who rejects Christian teaching to become a "Christian" club leader.

As Christian researcher Dr. Ed Stetzer proclaimed while addressing a similar campus issue, "Only in a modern American university would this make any sense."[5] In an interview for this book, Stetzer said that these policies might be "well intentioned," but that it "really fundamentally undermines the ability of people to create groups that actually live what they believe."[6]

He added, "Basically what [they're] saying is your association and your religion can't actually be held in the way that you think it should."[7]

HOW ALL-COMERS POLICIES
PLAY OUT IN PUBLIC SCHOOLS

The fight over all-comers policies, of course, becomes even more contentious when one considers how the regulations play out at public versus private universities. Considering that Vanderbilt is a private college, the school holds the right to govern its clubs in such a manner. But it appears that public schools too had their all-comers policies validated by the US Supreme Court in the 2010 *Christian Legal Society v. Martinez* case.

It is a decision that John Inazu, an associate professor of law at Washington University, said was "unwisely" made by the high court, which ruled in favor of a nondiscrimination policy at Hastings College of the Law in San Francisco.[8] Reportedly at the center of the dispute was the fact that members of the Christian Legal Society, a Christian campus group, believed that "homosexual conduct" was a sin and that leaders should also share in that view.[9]

The college, though, wasn't willing to treat the club as an officially recognized campus group, which led to a legal battle over whether Hastings College was discriminating against the Christian Legal Society. In the end, though, neutral all-comers policies were upheld in a 5-4 decision—one that Christian campus group InterVarsity Christian Fellowship said led to additional colleges across the nation challenging the rights of its affiliated clubs to be officially recognized due to the requirement that all leaders be Bible-believing Christians.[10]

Just a few years after that decision, the California State University system, California's twenty-three-school public college system, announced at the end of the 2011–2012 academic year that it too would be adopting Executive Order 1068, a similar requirement for all campus groups.[11] As a result InterVarsity—which has 985 chapters on 649 campuses around the county—ended up being derecognized in these universities.[12]

Gregory L. Jao, vice president and director of campus engagement at InterVarsity, said that the California State University system initially gave the organization a one-year exemption during the 2013–2014 school year to study the issue, but that the club was no longer recognized on its campuses the following year.

Being derecognized came with a steep set of challenges for InterVarsity, putting the group's chapters at a severe disadvantage. For instance, its chapters no longer had free access to rooms to hold meetings; this meant they had to pay to use space, while also doling out cash for insurance. Additionally they could only book rooms after other officially recognized organizations had the chance to do so.[13]

But it wasn't just meeting space that became a problem. Advertising the club via electronic channels and through bulletin boards was also restricted, with InterVarsity no longer being seen as part of university life—something that Jao said impacted how leaders interacted with faculty, administrators, and other student groups on campus. These restrictions significantly increased the cost of being on campus for InterVarsity chapters, including one group that reportedly had to pay $30,000 to reserve meeting rooms for a year.[14]

Despite all of the restrictions, though, Jao said he doesn't believe there was any intentional ill will behind Executive Order 1068. "I think it was administrators in good faith trying to do something that they thought was important," Jao said of the implementation of the policy. "And later, they thought it was legally required."[15]

It took the organization quite some time to dialogue with the university in an effort to find an official route back on campus. After a long dialogue and interactions with officials in the California State

University system, it was announced in June 2015 that InterVarsity could return to campuses as an official club.[16]

"We were trying to listen to their concerns and goals as well as to communicate our goals," Jao told me of the reconciliation process. "Out of those conversations came an opportunity to return to campus in a way that takes seriously the university's legitimate [quest] to create an inclusive environment as well as allow our groups to have processes that satisfies our need to have leaders who actually believe in the message of the group."[17]

He said InterVarsity leaders worked hard not to demonize the university and to listen and respond in the same way that the group trains students to interact in its evangelism efforts. In the end InterVarsity affirmed that all students are, indeed, welcome at its twenty-three chapters on nineteen of the California State University system's campuses, coming to an agreement that it believes will allow for genuinely Christian students to lead these groups.[18]

"[Cal State] said that their primary concern is to be sure every student has the right to participate," he said. Concerning leadership, Jao said "they wanted to make sure every student had the ability to apply so that there was a fair entry point for every student, which made sense. And we wanted to make sure we had a robust selection process that included an ability to ask about faith and belief that are necessary to help select leaders that can carry the message with integrity."[19]

In the end InterVarsity struck an agreement with California State in which the all-comers policy remained intact but officials clarified its intent. InterVarsity must allow everyone to become a member of its chapters—something that has always been permitted. While all students must be permitted to apply for leadership roles, the organization is allowed to have a strict and rigorous process.[20]

Despite feeling good about this decision, Jao said the quest for inclusive policies on campuses across America is far from over. In fact, InterVarsity is facing similar situations at other colleges across the United States.[21]

Jao differentiated the situation at California State from some of the other battles such as the stalemate at Vanderbilt University, among other campuses, as he felt leaders in the California university system were consistent in trying to work with InterVarsity to find a way to help the ministry—and other religious groups—get back on campus.[22]

As for the overarching level of hostility that is driving some of these all-comers policies, Jao said he believes it's been fifty-fifty when it comes to the motivations for pushing student groups like his off campus. "I think there [were] some campuses where it felt like certainly there was animus," he said. "[And then there are a] number of cases [where] they've implemented a rule and they didn't [consider] the disparate impact."[23]

Jao noted that these nondiscrimination policies will preclude a group such as InterVarsity from requiring Christian leadership for its clubs, while still permitting athletic programs that allow for able-bodied discrimination as well as performing arts groups that obviously discriminate based on talent—an intriguing comparison worth considering.[24]

As for the other battles that Jao and his fellow Christian leaders will be fighting on campuses across America, he said the primary attempt at remedying these policies is to "have a conversation." There are times in which it's essential to consider other options, including legal avenues, though he said that's never ideal. "The campus is our mission field . . . suing your mission field for access is always a bit awkward," he said. "You can win a fight and lose a war. We filed suit in other places before, but that's not our favorite tool."[25]

REACTIONS AGAINST ALL-COMERS POLICIES

Detailing his own views on the matter, University of North Texas Professor George Yancey agreed that these all-comers policies might appear very neutral on the surface, but that, in practice, they seem to unfairly target Christians.

"If a policy says, 'There are certain beliefs I don't like and if you have those beliefs and act on them we're going to punish you,'—well, who's going to have those beliefs?" he rhetorically asked. "Conservative Christians tend to have those beliefs. They believe that their leaders should be of their religion."[26]

In the end Yancey said Christian groups are essentially punished under these policies for acting based on their beliefs, citing the concept of "disparate impact," which is defined as "a test or other tool used for selection that, though appearing neutral, actually has an adverse effect on a particular protected class of individuals."[27]

"To me, this is a form of institutional Christianphobia," Yancey said.[28]

David French, an attorney who formerly worked for the American Center for Law and Justice, a conservative legal firm, has represented InterVarsity over the years and is an expert in campus religious freedom issues.

"You are talking to the lawyer who has sued more universities over constitutional and religious liberty issues than any other living lawyer," he quipped while speaking candidly about how he views the impact of these all-comers policies.[29]

As for the Vanderbilt battle, he said it was an "ideologically-driven effort from the very top of the university to exclude Christian groups that maintained their faith-based leadership standards." Vanderbilt, he said, had told many Christian students on campus that it was the college's goal to be seen as a leader in the academic community when it came to "mandating their particular brand of inclusiveness."[30]

But French said the blatant "malice" he observed in that situation wasn't unique, as he had seen it in other cases as well. Still, he said there were some elements that differentiated it from past cases.[31]

"What was unique was the backlash from the students and the community—for the first time, a broad-based student-led backlash," French said, adding that this was almost immediate and that it was fueled, in part, because there was more than one Christian group on campus that was impacted by the controversial policy.[32]

French said that in a situation like what unfolded at Vanderbilt, typically one group would be under fire by administration while others would sit on their hands "not wanting to raise a stink." But in that particular all-comers case, all of the Christian groups came together to voice their opposition, which created a critical mass of individuals pushing back against the provision.[33]

"The administration was so ham-handed and [disrespectful] in dealing with them that it only motivated them more," French said. "There was a moment...when a senior administrator compared them to segregationists. The room erupted in anger."[34]

Students with the Vanderbilt College Republicans produced a video slamming the nondiscrimination policy, with one individual claiming that it "threatens to destroy the integrity of each of our religious organizations." Another accused the school of "going somewhere where no other university has gone before," and yet another called it "nonsense." [35]

Students and club leaders clearly weren't backing down. But it wasn't just the campus groups who were up in arms. Considering that Vanderbilt is smack dab in the middle of the Bible Belt, religious conservatives in the area who hadn't previously been paying attention to the nondiscrimination policy issue were apparently suddenly in tune with what was going on.

French said the controversy likely cost Vanderbilt a fair amount in donations, as some alumni reportedly pushed back against the crackdown, with the state government also taking action to try to remedy the situation.

The Tennessee legislature responded to the furor by passing a 2013 bill that was signed into law prohibiting public colleges "from denying recognition, privileges or benefits to a student organization or group on the basis of religious content of the organization's or group's speech or the manner in which the organization or group determines its organizational affairs." [36] While Vanderbilt wasn't included in this due to its standing as a private institution, the move sent a powerful message.

This came after a broader bill that also targeted private schools, including Vanderbilt, was vetoed by Governor Bill Haslam, who said at the time that he disagreed with Vanderbilt's policy but did not believe it was appropriate for the government to intervene in a private school's policies. [37]

Vanderbilt officials continued to double down in the midst of the initial debate over its policy, with Beth Fortune, vice chancellor for public affairs, stating the following in 2012: "All registered student groups at Vanderbilt must be open to all students, and members in good standing must have the opportunity to seek leadership positions. This debate is about nondiscrimination, not religious freedom, and we stand behind our policy." [38]

Despite a refusal to publicly back down, French said the battle at Vanderbilt has ended up in an intriguing place. "Because the university was taking such a black eye publicly [over] their policy…while they never backed away from the policy, they never fully implemented it either," he said. "The result, at the end of the day, was essentially that there's a cease-fire." [39]

French said some groups still meet on campus, resulting in an "uneasy truce."[40]

But the attorney also warned that the all-comers battle is only one issue that he believes will negatively impact people of faith on college campuses around the country, predicting that the "ideological cleansing of the helping professions"—social work, psychology, and other medical fields—is also percolating.[41]

When asked why college campuses have become more abrasive when it comes to conservative Protestants and why we've seen an increase in all-comers policies, among other elements perceived as hostility toward the Christian faith, Yancey said that he could only speculate, as he has not researched the historical trends and details. He proposed, however, the idea that the secularization of culture has, in turn, led some to take more overtly oppositional stances against Christianity.

"I think at one point there was a lot more social pressure to accept Christianity, and so people, they may like it, they may not like it, but it's irrelevant," he said. "You really couldn't go out and do something that Christians did not like. That has obviously changed."[42]

The lack of religiosity in academia, he said, isn't a new development, though the ramping up of these issues could, in fact, be directly tied to cultural shifts. "It may be now, in our changing culture, that it's seen as OK to be a little more aggressive toward Christians and that may be what's occurring here," Yancey said.[43]

Despite being both Christian and African American, Yancey said he has experienced more bias due to his faith than his race. While this hasn't necessarily been true of his life more generally, it certainly has been in his university experience, with Yancey explaining that in some ways in academia, "being black has been an advantage." In fact, he said overall "there's a dearth of anti-black bias in academia."[44]

"Systematically I've seen more bias against me as a Christian. Now is it a lot? I don't think it's that way," he said. "Maybe because I don't complain a lot...but I know others have had a harsher time, so I don't want to dismiss it."[45]

Yancey's point about cultural changes impacting just how fervently some might push back against faith is intriguing. As it turns out, some of these cultural changes are creating notable difficulties for Christians in academia, as critics are becoming increasingly concerned and are closely watching the landscape to see what's next.

CHAPTER 12

THE TRUE IMPACT ON ACADEMIA

SO, WHAT'S REALLY happening in the academic world—and how sweeping are the ramifications? It seems there is a clash unfolding between people of faith who wish to sincerely live out their religious convictions and the rules and regulations that govern certain disciplines. While all-comers policies can prevent campus groups from fully exercising their mission, some say there's another battle being fought that could have a more personal impact on the lives and careers of various students.

David French told me he believes there is an "ideological cleansing of the 'helping professions,'" such as nursing, psychology, social work, etc. He said that the "LBGT issue is so deeply entrenched in these positions," and went on to warn that "they are beginning to affirmatively require agreement [and] validation of LBGT lifestyles as a condition of entering into professions." In recent years, French has had three cases involving counseling students, noting that the variety of conclusions to those cases has created concern about where the issue could go next.[1]

COUNSELING STUDENT JULEA WARD'S FIGHT FOR RELIGIOUS FREEDOM

Julea Ward, a former student at Eastern Michigan University who was studying to be a K–12 school counselor, was involved in one such case. She was assigned a case file during her practicum back in 2009 for a man whom she noticed had been counseled about a gay relationship in the past. Ward, a Christian, reportedly told her supervisor that she would not be able to work with the individual and requested a different case.[2]

According to reports, Ward wasn't refusing to work with gay clients, though. In fact, according to the United States Court of Appeals for the Sixth Circuit, which eventually ruled on a religious discrimination case on the matter, she asked her supervisor whether she should meet with the client "and refer him only if it became necessary—only if the counseling session required Ward to affirm the client's same-sex relationship" or whether he should simply be referred from the start.[3]

The client was referred, but disciplinary action commenced against Ward, who was subsequently told that she would need to comply with the American Counseling Association's Code of Ethics, which barred discrimination based on sexuality, among other protected classes. She was then reportedly permitted to make a choice between going through a formal hearing, entering into a remediation program, or leaving the school's counseling program altogether. After she chose a hearing, she was expelled from the program purportedly for violating the aforementioned Code of Ethics.[4]

Rather than back down, though, Ward approached the Alliance Defending Freedom (formerly the Alliance Defense Fund), a conservative legal firm, and sued. Her initial religious discrimination complaint was dismissed, though the Sixth Circuit ordered that the lower court rehear it. Ward later won a $75,000 settlement from Eastern Michigan University, and the expulsion was removed from her record.[5]

Eastern Michigan University framed the settlement as one in which the school's policies—the ones that punished Ward for standing by her faith—would be left intact, with Walter Kraft, vice president for university communications, proclaiming that "The faculty retains its right to establish, in its learned judgment, the curriculum and program requirements for the counseling program at Eastern Michigan University."[6]

The school said that the $75,000 was paid out to Ward in an effort to best serve students and taxpayers, as a trial would have been costly.[7]

But Jeremy Tedesco, an Alliance Defending Freedom attorney who also represented Ward, saw the settlement as a victory for religious freedom, calling the conclusion of the case "a big win for students everywhere."[8]

"The settlement…leaves the Sixth Circuit's opinion intact, which is a major win for religious liberty," Tedesco wrote in a 2013 op-ed. "The opinion held that 'the First Amendment does not permit educators to invoke curriculum as a pretext for punishing a student for her religion.' Regardless of what policies a public university puts into place, it cannot use them to target students' religious beliefs for punishment."[9]

Tedesco also clarified that the request for reassignment was not about the client being gay and that it was a more general "religious objection" about being mandated to counsel an individual about a sexual relationship outside the bounds of marriage, an objection that applies to gay and straight relationships alike.[10]

JENNIFER KEETON

Ward isn't alone, as others have faced similar battles. Consider Christian counseling student Jennifer Keeton, who was reportedly expelled from Augusta State University in Augusta, Georgia, after expressing her disagreement with same-sex relationships and reportedly saying in class that it would be difficult for her to counsel gay clients.[11]

Students at the college were purportedly told that they could not discriminate in their treatment of clients, with Keeton suing in 2010, alleging that the school demanded she alter her biblical worldview or be removed from the college. A central claim in her lawsuit was that school officials recommended that she complete a "remediation plan" that would have reportedly dealt with her organizational and writing abilities, while also helping her learn to work with "gay, lesbian, bisexual, transgender and queer/questioning populations," after she voiced her traditional views on sexuality in both the classroom and her assignments.[12]

Her legal representation, the Alliance Defending Freedom, claimed that part of the "re-education program" she was required to attend if she wanted to continue at the school involved "diversity and sensitivity" training, which reportedly included Keeton reading and writing about the issue. She was also allegedly told that she would need to be around gay individuals, which accompanied a suggestion that she attend a gay pride parade.[13]

Keeton had said she would counsel gays and lesbians, but she also expressed her view that homosexuality is immoral. She reportedly initially agreed to the remediation program but then retracted that agreement and took legal action. When the lawsuit was first filed, Augusta State University pushed back against the claim that it was attempting to change Keeton's views, but said there are very specific protocols for how counselors must handle their clients.[14]

"The professional counselor's job is to help clients clarify their current feelings and behaviors and to help them reach the goals that they have determined for themselves, not to dictate what those goals should be, what morals they should possess, or what values they should adopt," the college said in a statement.[15]

In the end, the courts sided with Augusta State, finding that Keeton's personal religious views were not impeded by the university's attempts to abide by the American Counseling Association's guidelines that would require students to counsel everyone in a supportive manner; she was expelled. Southern District of Georgia Judge J. Randal Hall said as follows:

> The remediation plan imposed on Keeton pursuant to those policies placed limits on her speech and burdened her religious beliefs, but, as the allegations show, the plan was motivated by a legitimate pedagogical interest in cultivating a professional demeanor and concern that she might prove unreceptive to certain issues and openly judge her clients...
>
> Keeton's speech and conduct were evidently impelled by the absolutist philosophical character of her beliefs, but that character does not entitle her to university accommodation and it is irrelevant to the court's analysis.[16]

WILL THOSE AT CHRISTIAN UNIVERSITIES FACE SUCH ISSUES?

These cases have naturally led some to wonder what's next on the religious liberty front, as the results weren't necessarily the most rousing of victories for those seeking exemptions for their Christian beliefs. Let's just assume for a moment that a faithful individual simply wants to be a Christian counselor who helps fellow believers journey through life. French said that such people might be in for a rude awakening.

"Let's say you're a Christian. You can go to a Christian school and say you're part of whatever Christian counseling group, but then what if you're needing state licensing," he said, citing the American Psychological Association and the National Association of Social

Workers. "That's where you're going to begin to have some...problems...you might have even limited ability to become a licensed counselor, even if you're only counseling the Christian community." [17]

In the Ward case, for example, the American Counseling Association filed an amicus brief—also known as a friend of the court—with the Sixth Circuit Court of Appeals, siding with Eastern Michigan University's decision to expel the student. It argued that Ward was in violation of its code of ethics.

"When she refused to counsel assigned clients based on her objection to homosexual relationships—and stated a further refusal to counsel any clients with views about premarital sex that differ from hers—she violated the ACA Code of Ethics and demonstrated an unwillingness and inability to perform competently as a counselor," the document read, in part. "Having refused to accept her supervisors' remedial assistance, dismissal was proper." [18]

Clearly tolerance isn't as rabid as one might hope in some spheres of higher education for individuals who wish to practice counseling while holding close to their religious views. While these policies—much like the all-comers policies—are likely well intentioned, the fallout could clearly end up hampering the beliefs and rights of the faithful. It also sends a powerful message to students, both young and old, who enter these programs: you are not free to pursue your dreams if you do not comply—even if that means violating your sincerely held ideals.

CHALLENGES TO GORDON COLLEGE'S HOMOSEXUALITY STANCE

Two additional issues that have emerged of late are fears surrounding accreditation and tax-exempt statuses for Christian schools across America—the latter of which has become a more pronounced fear in the wake of the Supreme Court's *Obergefell v. Hodges* decision that legalized same-sex marriage across America in June 2015.

Let's start by looking at how Gordon College, a Christian institution in Wenham, Massachusetts, ended up landing in the crosshairs of media and activists alike over the college's traditional stance on homosexuality. Here's how the school describes its long-standing view on same-sex relations:

> We affirm God's creation of marriage...as the intended life-long one-flesh union of one man and one woman....There are clear prohibitions in the Scriptures against sexual relations between persons of the same sex.[19]

Despite the fact that the college has asked students and faculty to sign a statement affirming these ideals for more than five decades, problems began for Gordon College in 2014. The situation quickly ignited after school president D. Michael Lindsay joined other Christians and faith leaders in signing a July 2014 letter to President Barack Obama that asked that faith-based groups that are federal contractors be exempt from mandates that they hire people who are in gay relationships.

While Lindsay signed the letter as an individual and not as a representative of the college, confusion set in and protests aimed at the college began to take form. Naturally media coverage followed, with the city of Salem, Massachusetts, responding to the controversy in July 2014 by taking a very public early opt-out of a long-held facilities agreement that the city had with Gordon.[20]

A representative of Gordon described the defunct deal at the time as "a reciprocal arrangement where we provided management of the facility in exchange for using it for educational programs connected to Gordon, and as well as 'curation' experiences for history majors at Gordon."[21]

The move seemed political, considering that Lindsay's signing of the letter was in the headlines at the time. Another oddity? The agreement between the college and Salem was reportedly already set to expire the following month anyway.

"The city does not contract with private parties that willfully discriminate on the basis of...sex or sexual orientation," Salem Mayor Kimberley Driscoll said at the time, citing the college's standards on "homosexual behavior" in her decision.[22]

But Gordon faced other more pronounced obstacles at the time. The New England Association of Schools and Colleges' Commission on Institutions of Higher Education—the board that oversees Gordon College's accreditation—had announced that it would be considering whether the college's ban on "homosexual practice" runs contrary to its Commissions Standards for Accreditation.[23]

Lindsay told me in an interview for *TheBlaze* in early 2015 that though he believed there was virtually no chance the board would revoke the school's accreditation and that the inquiry that was launched is common for any school that finds itself in the headlines, he had already assembled a twenty-person panel in late 2014 in an effort to accomplish a number of objectives.[24]

From exploring the theology that has driven preclusions of same-sex relations to assessing how the college handles scenarios in which students deal with same-sex attraction, the panel's scope was wide, according to Lindsay. Those taking part in the effort had in-depth conversations about the issue.[25]

"We recognize that there have been some changing attitudes…and so we wanted to look at the issues as thoughtfully as possible," he said. "We hosted twenty-four forums on our campus…we brought in theologians, social scientists, scholars, pastors, counselors—helping our trustees and campus leadership to look at this holistically." Lindsay said the decision to explore the issue was in place well before the controversy, as he had previously predicted that these issues would soon be on the docket for discussion at colleges across America.[26]

"My sense is that Gordon has been at the tip of the spear of a very significant cultural conversation," he said at the time. "And the kind of conversations and issues that we have faced over the past nine months are coming to every single Christian institution in this country in the days ahead."[27]

In the end, after nine months of deliberations that began in late 2014, he told me in March 2015 that the panel came to a number of conclusions, the most noteworthy of which was an affirmation of its policy upholding traditional unions and precluding sexual acts between individuals of the same sex.[28]

"In the end, the board concluded…we really do think the college's traditional position is exactly right for an evangelical institution, so the board of trustees unanimously reaffirmed the theological position," Lindsay said. "I feel really good about where we wound up."[29]

The behavioral policy that remains in place reads, in part:

> Those words and actions which are expressly forbidden in Scripture, including but not limited to blasphemy, profanity, dishonesty, theft, drunkenness, sexual relations outside

marriage, and homosexual practice, will not be tolerated in the lives of Gordon community members, either on or off campus.[30]

Lindsay also said that a number of other provisions were put in place as well, including a stronger anti-bullying policy, better training for residence life staff, and a "Life Together" task force. This task force is comprised of "students, staff and faculty who will work together to think through best practices and protocols on these issues in the context of our Christ-centered community."[31]

Despite sticking by the school's values, Lindsay said he's fully aware of the challenges young people face in today's culture—issues that make averting sex and upholding personal ethics quite daunting. "We are a sex-saturated culture. Pornography is rampant; it's all around us," he said, noting that Gordon plans to continue maintaining its high moral values. "It's really hard for a young man or young woman to keep their way pure."[32]

As for the accreditation issue, the New England Association of Schools and Colleges released a joint statement with Gordon College in April 2015, commending the college for providing a report that detailed a "careful and extensive process of engagement and reflection regarding Gordon's issues of sexual orientation and gender identity." In the end, the release noted that Gordon remains "accredited in good standing."[33]

ACCREDITATION ISSUES AT CHRISTIAN UNIVERSITIES

While the Gordon issue ended up concluding without much fanfare, David French believes that accreditation more generally will be a problem in the days and years ahead, saying that all it takes to ignite a firestorm is for a Christian school to become clumsy or to err in how it handles these sensitive issues.

"I worked with Gordon College, and they've made it through the initial crisis there, but that is going to be even more of an issue post [gay marriage legalization]," he predicted. "They're going to be facing questions about tax exemptions and accreditation."[34]

French said he doesn't think Congress will move forward with any overt bills to strip tax exemption from faith-based colleges; instead, he believes it will take just one institution to handle matters poorly before controversy leads to bigger problems for Christian colleges and universities. "There will be a school that handles a situation with an LGBT employee or student in a way that is particularly clumsy or particularly hurtful—and the Left will fixate around that case and the poster child of that case to begin whittling away at accreditation and tax exemption," French predicted. "I don't see an immediate, short-term issue where the IRS promulgates a rule where they say, 'We're pulling the exemption.' I don't think right now they have the political strength to do that on a political basis." [35]

Some might call forecasts that predict the targeting of religious schools a bit premature—or even needless fear mongering—but just weeks after gay marriage was legalized in June 2015, activists were already addressing the issue.

Barry W. Lynn, executive director of Americans United for Separation of Church and State, a First Amendment watchdog, reportedly told the *Christian Post* that he believes it is "on the edge of the indefensible" for Christian colleges that receive government money to refuse housing to married gay couples. He said:

> I think that the issue with [LGBT] rights is a little bit different [from race]. The evolution of the issue is moving at least as quickly as we have moved in the area of race and that this is a national dialogue that ought to begin about, should in fact benefits be given to educational institutions that do in fact discriminate...I would not want to be a person at a fundamentalist academy who is trying to defend the practice, that is taking a reasonable amount of government funds and refusing to allow a same-sex married couple to live in the married student housing. [36]

With some colleges' faith-based policies being called into question in the wake of gay marriage legalization, critics are looking back to *Bob Jones University v. the United States*, a 1983 Supreme Court ruling that found that a college can be denied tax-exempt status if it refuses to allow admission based on racial parameters.

"Petitioner Bob Jones University, while permitting unmarried Negroes to enroll as students, denies admission to applicants engaged in an interracial marriage or known to advocate interracial marriage or dating," read the case syllabus. "Because of this admissions policy, the IRS revoked the University's tax-exempt status."[37]

With gay marriage now legal, some wonder how this past court battle could be used against Christian colleges and universities who have qualms with sexuality rather than race. With many unknowns still on the horizon, Frank Ravitch, a professor at Michigan State University's College of Law, said that though the gay marriage ruling itself "doesn't actually have any impact at all outside of recognizing same-sex marriage as a fundamental right," tax-exempt status and federal benefits could hang in the balance. "At least for religiously affiliated entities, the risk isn't interfering with their beliefs or practices," he told the *Grand Rapids Press*. "It's going to be more a question of whether or not they're going to be subject to revocation of tax-exempt status down the road."[38]

Mat Staver, founder and chairman of Liberty Counsel, a conservative legal firm, used stronger language when he told me not long after the Supreme Court's legalization of gay marriage that he believes Christians are poised to encounter increased challenges in the public square. "The assault against Christians will increase, but the resistance will also increase," he said. "We are entering a cultural civil war."[39]

Now that we've covered claims of bias in both Hollywood and universities, let's move on to the final piece of the trifecta: the mainstream media.

PART 4

CHAPTER 13

THE MEDIA PARADOX:
IGNORANCE VERSUS INTENTIONALITY?

LIKE **HOLLYWOOD AND** universities, the media too are routinely accused of holding anti-Christian and anti-conservative biases, and when you dive deeper into the issue and examine reporters' personal views, demographics, and expert analysis, the roots of the bias conundrum start to become clearer.

It's no secret that many critics see the media as unfair and politically biased, but a topic that gets somewhat less attention is the "God gap" that has apparently taken root in many newsrooms. What do I mean by this? Well, on the whole it seems there is a disconnect between journalists and the public at large when it comes Christianity and, more specifically, evangelicalism—a fact that is quite ironic considering that the nation overwhelmingly embraces the Christian faith, with evangelicals forming a sizable portion of the population.

Some will dismiss critiques that the media—much like Hollywood elite and universities—are overwhelmingly biased against faith, though there appears to be plenty of evidence to at least show that religious representation in American newsrooms isn't necessarily reflective of nationwide demographics. And while that doesn't directly prove bias, it is a factor worthy of discussion.

CONSERVATIVE POLITICIANS ROUTINELY CLAIM THEY EXPERIENCE MEDIA BIAS

Perhaps the best evidence of at least an overarching feeling that there is bias at play (again, not definitive proof that there is, indeed, bias) is the fact that Republican politicians often successfully seize upon the theme in an effort to rally the conservative and Christian base.

There are plenty of examples of politicians doing just that, though 2008 vice presidential candidate and former Alaska governor Sarah Palin perhaps best exemplifies the efforts of public figures to vilify the media, with her repeated use over the years of the term "lamestream media" and overt claims that "the media has always been biased."[1]

Palin's relationship with the press, of course, has been less than warm—and people can judge for themselves whether they believe she's been treated unfairly or has received the treatment she deserved. Either way, her comments provide a useful lens into the views that many conservatives and Christians have about the media's treatment of right-of-center issues, causes, and candidates.

It was back in 2011 that Palin published a Facebook post taking direct aim at "the never-ending issue of media bias"—a rich example of the aforementioned rhetoric. She wrote, in part:

> The media has always been biased. Conservatives...have always been held to a different standard and attacked. This is nothing new. Lincoln was mocked and ridiculed. Reagan was called an amiable dunce, a dangerous warmonger, a rightwing fanatic, and the insult list goes on and on....
>
> Let's just acknowledge that commonsense conservatives must be stronger and work that much harder because of the obvious bias. And let's be encouraged with a sense of poetic justice by knowing that the "mainstream" media isn't mainstream anymore. That's why I call it "lamestream," and the LSM is becoming quite irrelevant.[2]

Again, Palin isn't the only politician to have made these claims, with other Republican leaders also accusing the press of slanted reporting when it comes to faith and politics. While the veracity of the former vice presidential candidate's claims might come under attack by some on the left and right alike, others have followed a similar script. Just consider a CNN.com headline from October 2015 that read, "2016 Republicans vs. the Media." Written well before Donald Trump officially became the GOP nominee, the piece highlighted the ways in which Republican candidates had railed against CNBC over questions the network asked during a GOP primary debate.[3]

"The questions that have been asked so far in this debate illustrate why the American people don't trust the media...This is not a cage match," Texas Senator Ted Cruz said at the time.[4] During that same debate, Marco Rubio took aim at a *Sun-Sentinel* editorial that criticized his absences during Senate votes, saying the piece was "evidence of the bias that exists in the American media today." [5]

And Carly Fiorina also jumped in on the anti-media bandwagon, lambasting apparent liberal bias. "News flash: The media is biased," Fiorina said in an interview with Fox News host Bill O'Reilly while discussing a double standard she felt she was observing on the campaign trail involving Democratic candidate Hillary Clinton. She added, "This isn't anything new. And we just have to deal with it, unfortunately." [6] Fiorina had also taken aim at the *Washington Post*, among others, throughout the campaign. [7]

But it was the 2016 general election that perhaps ushered in the most flagrant season of media bias in recent memory, with journalists seemingly setting their sights on taking down Republican presidential candidate Donald Trump. Sure, Trump said some objectionable things throughout the campaign—comments and claims he deserved intense scrutiny for—but the overarching media tone became so negative that reporters' hostility toward Trump as well as their true persuasions were routinely on full display. There should have been a balance between holding Trump accountable and remaining objective, but that line was crossed too many times in 2016, further putting the media's credibility at risk.

Watching many reporters deliver 2016 election night coverage as the returns came in was akin to observing mourners at a funeral. So many in the press simply couldn't understand why Trump had resonated with the masses, easily soaring to the 270 electoral college votes needed to secure the White House; they found themselves in total and utter shock as the reality set in. That in mind, there are a few troubling election-related statistics that should put the media on notice: 78 percent of voters said after the election that presidential coverage was biased, with 59 percent saying the media were for Democrat Hillary Clinton and 21 percent for Trump, according to a poll commissioned by the Media Research Center. Additionally 32 percent of Clinton voters admitted the press had a pro-Clinton bias, yet 97 percent of overall voters said they didn't let the media influence their vote. [8] And it doesn't end there.

Republicans have consistently alleged in the past that the media were taking aim at their candidacies. How intensely? Just consider an April 2012 *Washington Post* article that opened with the following line: "Charges of media bias have been flying like a bloody banner on the campaign trail."[9] Months later, Republican candidate Mitt Romney cited a "vast left wing conspiracy" that was setting out against him and said that "many in the media are inclined to do the president's bidding." He even said that he'd face an "uphill battle" with the media.[10]

Eight years before that, the Associated Press summarized this dynamic in the lede to a story titled "Evangelicals Say They're Not Represented in Newsrooms." The text read, "Here is a foolproof way for politicians to score points with evangelical voters: Attack the media, an institution widely seen as lacking conservative Christian voices."[11]

Again, none of this is new, and it only scratches the surface of the claims surrounding media bias that have come from political candidates. It's not just about the political candidates and parties, though. The main issue for many—particularly Christians and the faithful— is how individual issues are handled, mishandled, and poorly framed by the press. Since candidates and parties take stances on these issues, there is a clear tie between the political realm and the more general framing of moral views on a litany of perspectives. So with all that said, do these politicians' claims about liberal bias hold any merit? Let's dig even deeper.

LARGELY LIBERAL NEWSROOMS

Critics of the media sometimes assume there is truly a "vast left-wing conspiracy" (to borrow from Romney's words) at play in which values and political inclinations are strategically targeted and taken down, and that could, of course, be true in certain anecdotal scenarios. But there's a deeper form of bias that is equally concerning: a lack of perspective as a result of not having enough people who understand faith working in American media.

First, let's consider newsroom ideology. While there is not a ton of data revealing where journalists see themselves on the political spectrum, Pew Research Center's Journalism Project (formerly the Project for Excellence in Journalism) has, over the years, asked reporters to name their political inclinations.[12] In 2008 the survey found that a majority of national (53 percent) and local (58 percent) reporters called themselves moderates. That said, an additional 32 percent of national and 23 percent of local reporters classified themselves as liberals. Perhaps the most stunning line in the report, though, reads as follows: "Relatively small minorities of national and local journalists call themselves conservatives" (8 percent national, 14 percent local)." [13]

And with the growth of Internet news sites and blogs, the finding that online journalists tend to be even more liberal than national and local reporters was intriguing; 46 percent said they were moderate, 39 percent said liberal, and just 9 percent self-described as conservatives. Now, when you compare that to the country's political breakdown around the same time, there was clearly a divide. Around 2008, 36 percent of the country called itself conservative, 39 percent moderate, and just 19 percent liberal, according to Pew. [14] (Gallup found that the proportions were at 37 percent, 35 percent, and 24 percent a few years later in 2015. [15]) Unfortunately 2008 was the last time Pew asked reporters these political questions, so there aren't more updated figures to share.

That said, there are a few things worth mentioning at this point. First and foremost, the Internet has quickly changed and evolved, with conservative media outlets emerging and thriving in recent years—a dynamic that has potentially altered the situation on the ground. Still, it's unclear whether conservative outlets should or can truly be counted as having an equalizing effect on potential bias in mainstream media.

Another potential caveat is that many reporters believe themselves to be unbiased—or at least they pine to be—so some journalists opt out of voting in elections and work overtime to try to appear as though they're centrists. While this is wonderful and noble, one can't help but wonder if that quest can sometimes lead a reporter to inaccurately self-select "moderate" or "independent" in these surveys even if he or she, in reality, falls somewhere to the right or left of the middle. We can't be sure, of course, but it's worth considering since it would further impact the numbers found in the Pew poll.

Either way, Pew isn't the only research center to churn out data on reporters' political ideologies. As it turns out, journalism professors Lars Willnat and David H. Weaver published a study in 2014 titled "The American Journalist in the Digital Age"—a study that looks at, among other things, political affiliations of members of the media. Researchers at Indiana University started the effort in 1971, following up with additional waves of the study in 1982, 1992, and 2002; the 2014 report is the latest to emerge, offering a more contemporary lens into newsroom ideologies.

The study found that there was an 8 percent decrease in journalists who called themselves Democrats between 2002 and 2013, when the data was collected; there was an even starker decrease in Republican-aligned reporters during that same time, with the proportion decreasing from 18 percent to 7.1 percent. Meanwhile, 50.2 percent of respondents self-described as independents.[16]

And it doesn't end there. Democrats have always had a more sizable representation among journalists, with 35.5 percent of reporters embracing the label in 1971—a figure that ticked up to 44.1 percent in 1992. As for Republican affiliation, the survey showed 25.7 percent of reporters calling themselves GOP-affiliated in 1971. In subsequent decades, the proportion hovered between 16.4 percent and 18.8 percent from the early 1980s to the early 2000s before dropping in 2013 to 7.1 percent.[17]

The imbalance is more than clear, though some correctly say that a journalist's political affiliation does not necessarily prove a definitive bias in that person's media work. These people say that liberal and conservative journalists alike are perfectly capable of putting their personal views to the side while still remaining fair and impartial. Again, this is a perfectly valid argument and one that must be considered. That said, we also must confront the reality that liberals and conservatives tend to see the world through very different lenses—and those lenses impact us as individuals, professionals, citizens, and most certainly as reporters.

It's hard to imagine that an imbalance in ideology inside newsrooms doesn't impact, to some degree, everything from story selection to how coverage is carried out. Let's say these biases do somehow—even unintentionally—shape news, impacting the selection of experts as well as the types of stories that are ignored by the press. Would it be safe to say that, over time, this would create an unfair environment in which the masses would be given imbalanced information? The tougher question, of course, is how to remedy the problem if it does, indeed, exist (which I believe it does).

FAITH IN THE NEWSROOM

Imbalanced statistics among reporters when it comes to their political and faith views most certainly point to a dearth of cultural diversity in American newsrooms. In simple terms: there aren't enough journalists who are familiar with the deep impact that faith has on people's lives; it's is an odd dynamic considering that diversity is generally embraced and sought out in almost every other respect.

"Journalism has become more of a white-collar field that draws from elite colleges," columnist Terry Mattingly told the Associated Press back in 2008. "While there's been heavy gender and racial diversity...there's a lack of cultural diversity in journalism."[18]

The belief among many is that some worldviews—particularly an evangelical one—are lacking. But there are certainly some roadblocks when it comes to attempts to accurately assess the number or proportion of religious reporters working in American newsrooms. To begin, questions about religious observance are legally problematic, thus inquiring about a prospective candidate's beliefs or practices would be unacceptable. Just consider what the US Equal Employment Opportunity Commission had to say about the matter: "Questions about an applicant's religious affiliation or beliefs...are generally viewed as non job-related and problematic under federal law," although religious organizations are exempt from this federal instruction.[19] So unless the information is willingly provided once media outlets hire individuals, it's tough to assess the religious presence—or lack thereof—in newsrooms.

That said, the Pew Research Center for the People and the Press revealed survey results in 2007 that found that just 8 percent of journalists at national media outlets attended church or synagogue each week, with 29 percent saying they never attend services; an additional 39 percent said that they do go, but only a few times per year.[20]

At the time, the Associated Press noted that Pew's polling of the general public found a major disparity, with 39 percent of Americans going to church weekly—a major difference when compared to the fewer-than-one-in-ten reporters who said the same.[21] That difference is clearly worth noting, but as the revered Poynter Institute noted in a piece titled "There's No Good Data on How Many Christians Are in

Newsrooms," it's important to remember that "attendance and belief don't always correlate neatly." [22]

While that is surely true, it's difficult to ignore the fact that people who attend church weekly are much more likely to be devout believers; or, at the least, they are exposing themselves more regularly to the theological ideals that would, at a minimum, help foster and condition an understanding about Christianity in America. Such a lens would provide some clarity for reporters, especially when covering complex moral and ethical issues for which an understanding of biblical values would seem paramount. I'm a firm believer that, in the end, a lack of representation of Christians in media is ideologically dangerous. Fixing the problem, though, involves engaging an ignorance of sorts—an ignorance of the problem itself and a failure to understand why it really matters.

Religious adherence is unlike any other personal attribute; it plays a deeply intricate role in shaping the thoughts, feelings, and actions of the faithful. Few descriptors or personal ideals hold such fervent power. Here's why that matters: true faith isn't merely a nominal marker. Rather than serving as a mere system that someone subscribes to by slapping a label on himself and marching on his merry way, Christianity calls on its adherents to live out its values in every area of their lives.

There are often intricate reasons why believers hold various stands on social and political issues. What seems like bigotry to some critics is quite often a sincerely held religious belief that is rooted in a long-standing theological explanation that goes far deeper than critics comprehend. Understanding these intricacies is key because faith shapes how millions upon millions of Americans live their lives; it helps to mold and solidify beliefs, practices, and actions like no other force.

But if mainstream reporters truly have little exposure to what Christians believe and why they believe it, is it really possible for outlets to always get it right when it comes to covering topics such as abortion and gay marriage, among others? And what about locating the best, most articulate—and representative—individuals among the evangelical ranks to discuss those issues? Without base knowledge of something as important as religious motivation, coverage gets a bit complicated.

THE REASON CLAIMS OF BIAS CONTINUE

There is a reason claims of bias haven't ceased—and that has very little to do with some sort of unfounded paranoia on the part of Christians and conservatives, as some critics might assume. There is a legitimate feeling among many Americans that the media simply do not understand conservative values or, for that matter, faith. It's this very topic that columnist and commentator Matt K. Lewis tackled in a controversial 2013 op-ed for *The Week*, writing that "conservatives have long lamented our East Coast secular media, charging that its worldview bias…skews America's information supply" and that "too often, Christians feel like they're cast as the type of fringe characters one might associate with the bar scene from *Star Wars*." [23]

Lewis went on to say that he believes it's time for media outlets to make a concerted effort to include the Christian worldview in their newsroom culture, though he did add that some outlets do, indeed, already have some faithful on staff, citing the *Washington Post* as just one example. Still, Lewis argued that the situation across media outlets most certainly warrants improvement.[24]

"Media outlets who want to understand America should at least have a few journalists hanging around who share—or at least, aren't hostile to—the Christian faith," he wrote, later adding, "Why does this matter? This sort of diversity isn't just important because of the creeping worldview bias, but also in terms of selection bias." [25]

So, Lewis's argument is twofold: without a fair number of faithful reporters working in American newsrooms, there is a "worldview bias" that impacts coverage; but there is also a "selection bias" when it comes to the stories that are (and aren't) chosen by outlets to make air, print, or digital publication. When we consider the informational flow and the impact that the media have on the populace, these are certainly concerns worthy of consideration and, I would argue, exploration.[26]

A great many reporters and commentators have made similar claims about the imbalance seen in newsrooms, with David Shaw writing the following in the *Los Angeles Times* back in 2003:

> People of faith have long complained that the mainstream news media pay too little attention to religion—except, of course, when there's a controversy or a scandal, like the ongoing story on priests as sexual predators. Absent such

a scandal—or the death of a pope and the election of his successor—the news media often seem indifferent to, ignorant of and, at times, downright hostile toward religion.[27]

Interestingly Shaw, who wrote that he was "not a very religious person," quoted the late Robert Bellah, a sociology professor known for studying religion, as once telling him that most journalists are "simply blind to religion," saying that they see faith as something that "ignorant and backward people" believe. Rather than constituting an overt bias that is being consciously acted upon, Bellah said these beliefs are essentially part of reporters' worldviews. Shaw noted that universities, among others, were trying to bridge the religious divide—and that was back in 2003. But despite those efforts, the disconnect clearly continues.[28]

Evening the playing field is a difficult task, though, as we will cover, the responsibility isn't solely on mainstream media outlets; Christians too must make an effort to come into the fold, and—as Mattingly told the Associated Press—they must do so with the right intentions.

"They have to be journalists first. You don't need more Christian journalists," he said, noting that these reporters would be able to help shape coverage. "You need more journalists who happen to be Christians if they're going to contribute to any real diversity in newsrooms."[29]

CHAPTER 14

IS THERE PROOF THE MEDIA ARE BIASED?

I THINK THERE'S LIBERAL bias in the media." That's what veteran reporter and former *Meet the Press* moderator David Gregory told me when I asked him on *The Church Boys* podcast to respond to the long-held conservative claim that the media hold an anti-conservative—or pro-liberal—bias. But he did add some caveats.

"I say there is…I think there's liberal bias in the media, but I always add to that: I don't think it's that simple. It's not just about a liberal bias," Gregory said. "It is about a bias toward conflict, it is sometimes geographic bias, it's sometimes cultural bias, sometimes it's secular bias."[1]

Gregory went on to mention a particular incident that stuck out to him—debate surrounding a quote that President George W. Bush once uttered about how he appeals to a "higher father." The comment was made after journalist Bob Woodward asked Bush if he had ever consulted his father, former president George H. W. Bush, for advice before invading Iraq in 2003. The younger Bush's full response? "He is the wrong father to appeal to in terms of strength; there is a higher father that I appeal to."[2]

It was a statement that led to quite a bit of discussion and debate in media, as some seemingly didn't understand what Bush was saying, though Gregory told me that people of faith very clearly knew what the president meant. "People of faith get that. He's praying to God for strength and comfort," Gregory said.[3] The veteran reporter previously made similar comments in other interviews as well, delivering a particularly intriguing response when *New York Magazine* presented him with the critique that Bush "put faith above reason."[4]

"That's something that I don't think is accurate. I just have never put much stock in the idea that he had a messianic view of Christianity that led him to make certain decisions or that appealing to a higher Father rather than his own father was somehow code for *God tells me what to do,*" he told the outlet. "For me, I feel like his faith was something that helped him stop drinking and helped him deal with weakness in himself and get a little more self-mastery."[5]

SEVERAL WORKING IN MEDIA ADMIT TO BIAS

Gregory hasn't been the only person in the media to point to bias, though, as former NBC News reporter Luke Russert—a professed Catholic—answered candidly when CBN News's David Brody asked him about the issue. "Do you believe the media…has some sort of bias against whether it be a strong conservative evangelical or maybe a strong Catholic…people of faith?" Brody asked. "It just seems like if you wear it on your sleeve too much you can get bit to a degree."[6]

Russert responded to Brody's question by calling it "absolutely accurate," adding that, in the current world—and specifically in American media—"'snark' is valued." With that in mind, Russert said it's often easy to go after people of faith, and provided examples of what such treatment might look like. "You're sort of tagged with this label of being puritanical and not understanding of others or of different viewpoints, and I think that's kind of lazy, number one, and I think it's just something that sort of feeds the snickering masses," Russert said, adding that faith is a complex paradigm—and that reporters should be careful.[7]

Russert said reporters need to be careful not to put people of faith—individuals with complex viewpoints—into those boxes, which he believes many journalists often do.[8]

And who could forget CNN president Jeff Zucker's candid admission in response to critics of his network who have alleged a liberal bias; Zucker said they had "legitimate" concern—so much so that network executives took steps to try and even the playing field. Zucker told the *Wall Street Journal* that he felt the news network had made an effort during the 2016 presidential campaign to create an equal playing field by focusing on the unconventional campaigns of Republican candidate Donald Trump and Democratic contender Bernie Sanders.[9]

"I think it was a legitimate criticism of CNN that it was a little too liberal.… We have added many more middle-of-the-road conservative voices to an already strong stable of liberal voices," he said at the time. "And I think that we are a much more-balanced network and, as a result, a much more inviting network to a segment of the audience that might not have otherwise been willing to come here." [10]

How's that for not only seemingly admitting to bias, but also acknowledging the potential impact of skewed coverage?

JOURNOLIST AND CLAIMS OF MEDIA BIAS

Over the years there have been plenty of events that have fueled claims of media bias. There was the now-infamous JournoList listserv—a secretive, online gathering of left-of-center bloggers, reporters, policy wonks, and others who came together to discuss their views. The forum, which was founded in 2007, was shut down after garnering negative press. While critics decried alleged bias due to the individuals who were on the list, others likened it to a simple online discussion forum for like-minded individuals. [11]

Either way, controversy erupted and *Washington Post* blogger David Weigel, who was a JournoList member, resigned. The *Post* explains:

> Weigel, whose tenure lasted three months, apologized Thursday for writing on a private e-mail exchange that Matt Drudge should "handle his emotional problems more responsibly and set himself on fire." He also mocked Ron Paul, the Texas congressman, by referring to the "Paultard Tea Party"...
>
> [Weigel lamented] news organizations' "need to give equal/extra time to 'real American' views, no matter how [expletive] moronic." When Rush Limbaugh, who has called for President Obama to fail, was hospitalized with chest pains, Weigel wrote: "I hope he fails." [12]

Many conservatives believed that the listserv was a slam-dunk that proved bias was afoot. While it certainly raised some eyebrows, others countered that journalists have every right to communicate with one another, though the problem seemed to be the claim that these were liberal-minded professionals who were sharing ideas and perspectives. The main allegation was that reporters and activists were sharing notes about specific stories—or, as some saw it, colluding.

One example centered on questions that emerged in 2008 about then–presidential candidate Barack Obama's relationship with his pastor, the Reverend Jeremiah Wright. Some members of JournoList were reportedly worked up after ABC News's George Stephanopoulos asked Obama the following question about his controversial pastor: "Do you think Reverend Wright loves America as much as you do?" Here's how *The Daily Caller* framed the reaction some in the listserv had to that question:

> "George [Stephanopoulos]," fumed Richard Kim of the Nation, is "being a disgusting little rat snake."
>
> Others went further. According to records obtained by The Daily Caller, at several points during the 2008 presidential campaign a group of liberal journalists took radical steps to protect their favored candidate. [...]
>
> In one instance, Spencer Ackerman of the Washington Independent urged his colleagues to deflect attention from Obama's relationship with Wright by changing the subject. Pick one of Obama's conservative critics, Ackerman wrote, "Fred Barnes, Karl Rove, who cares—and call them racists."
>
> Michael Tomasky, a writer for the Guardian, also tried to rally his fellow members of JournoList: "Listen folks—in my opinion, we all have to do what we can to kill ABC and this idiocy in whatever venues we have. This isn't about defending Obama. This is about how the [mainstream media] kills any chance of discourse that actually serves the people."[13]

And this is only one example of an incident that made a splash, leaving some to conclude that the sweeping bias they had suspected for so long was absolutely provable. Some critics, including State University of New York political science professor Jim Campbell, called the JournoList fiasco "troubling."[14] "At one level it could be thought of as just colleagues throwing ideas out to one another, but from another standpoint it almost looks like collusion...where virtual talking points are shared and solidified in a group," he said at the time, according to the *Christian Science Monitor*. "That can't be healthy for the country—or for the media, for that matter."[15]

PUBLIC OPINION OF MEDIA BIAS

I could go on and on. But while anecdotal examples and internal inklings might convince some that bias is afoot, is there actually evidence to corroborate the claim?

Personally I've always felt that bias is most certainly at play, but it's making the concept provable that is quite complicated.

First, we can look at how the public assesses its own confidence in the press to explore that paradigm. In a June 2016 Gallup poll, only 8 percent of Americans expressed "a great deal" of confidence in newspapers, with an additional 12 percent saying they have "quite a lot" of confidence in periodicals.[16] That means that just two in ten Americans have a great deal of confidence in newspapers—and TV news doesn't fare much better, with 8 percent selecting "a great deal" and an additional 13 percent expressing "quite a lot" of confidence. Other institutions such as public schools (14 percent and 16 percent, respectively), the medical system (17 percent and 22 percent), small businesses (30 percent and 38 percent), and the military (41 percent and 32 percent), among other institutions, fared much better.[17]

The confidence proportions have changed in recent years when it comes to both newspapers and TV news. While just 20 percent of the public expressed a great deal or quite a lot of confidence in newspapers in 2016, that same measure was at 30 percent in 2006 and at 51 percent in 1979 (though it largely remained in the 30s over the years). Meanwhile, TV news has also experienced changes over the decades. While 21 percent expressed, at the least, "quite a lot" of confidence in the 2016 poll, that proportion was at 46 percent in 1993. Clearly an erosion of trust has unfolded over the years.[18]

The Newseum Institute also asked a question about bias in its "The 2016 State of the First Amendment" report, finding that only 23 percent of American respondents "believe that the news media attempts to report on news without bias." Meanwhile, 74 percent disagreed with this notion. The report found, more specifically, that 85 percent of conservatives disagreed with the idea that media outlets report without any bias, with 71 percent of moderates and 68 percent of liberals disagreeing.[19] And the deep trust issues don't end there.

Consider another Gallup poll that was conducted in September 2015; it found that the nation's trust in the media remained at a "historic low," offering additional data that backs up the idea that Americans are skeptical about what's being reported. Respondents were asked, "How much trust and confidence do you have in the mass media—such as newspapers, TV and radio—when it comes to reporting the news fully, accurately and fairly?" and were offered up a number of choices, which included "a great deal," "a fair amount," "not very much," and "none at all." While the public's trust was at 55 percent in 1998 and 1999, with people saying that they had at least "a fair amount" of trust at the time, the proportion was at just 40 percent in 2015.[20]

Again, there is more evidence of the erosion of trust: "Since 2007, the majority of Americans have had little or no trust in the mass media," Gallup reported. "Trust has typically dipped in election years, including 2004, 2008, 2012."[21] And guess what? When the question was again asked in 2016 amid the heated presidential campaign, the firm found "32 percent saying they have a great deal or fair amount of trust in the media"—the lowest proportion in Gallup history, topping even the shocking 2015 proportion.[22]

At this point you have to wonder: What's driving those dips, especially during politically charged election years? Something the media are doing is simply turning the public off. Perhaps a 2016 Pew Research Center poll further spoke to this dynamic, finding that 74 percent of Americans said they believe the media "tend to favor one side" when covering social and political issues, with just 24 percent saying outlets tend to "deal fairly with both sides."[23]

Now here's the piece of the Gallup puzzle that is, perhaps, most fascinating: for more than a decade Democrats have been significantly more likely than Republicans and Independents to express trust for the mass media. Let's just quickly recap the proportions of Democrats over the years that have said that they have a great deal or fair amount of trust for the media. In 1997, 64 percent of Democrats fell into this category, with that proportion reaching 70 percent in 2005. After that, it moved into the 50s before popping back up to 60 percent in 2013, 55 percent in 2015, and 51 percent in 2016. While there has been a general consistency among Democrats, the story is entirely different for Independents and Republicans.[24]

While 53 percent of Independents said that they had a great deal or fair amount of trust in media in 1997, only 30 percent said the same in 2016. It should be noted that the highest this proportion reached between those years was 55 percent back in 1999. There is a similar dynamic for Republicans, who saw their highest trust come in at 52 percent in 1998.[25]

But Republicans have consistently not had majority trust in the media, with the proportion found in 1998 standing as the only time between 1997 and 2015 that the combined percent of those who selected a "great deal" or "fair amount" of trust crossed the 50 percent threshold. Only 32 percent of Republicans said that they had trust in the media when asked this question in 2015, putting them on par at the time with Independents. But in 2016 that proportion dipped to just 14 percent.[26]

Forgive me for all the data and numbers, but it seemed prudent to delve into exactly where Americans stand when it comes to confidence and trust in media. The main takeaway is that Democrats have consistently had a higher regard for trust of the media. While that is not a smoking gun on the bias front, it's telling that more people who describe themselves as left-of-center would have fewer qualms with the mass media. Are they seeing more of their values being represented and are thus less perturbed by what they're observing on the news front? Perhaps.

And just when you thought we might be done with the data, let's look at yet another Gallup question that asked Americans a bit more directly what they believe about perceived bias in the news media. The polling firm said in a 2014 report that "historically, Americans are most likely to feel the news media are 'too liberal,'" finding that year that 44 percent of Americans felt the press were too left of center, compared to 19 percent who said too conservative and 34 percent who selected "just about right." [27]

As for those saying the press is "too liberal," the proportion has fluctuated from between 44 percent and 48 percent since 2002. Meanwhile, the "too conservative" cohort has been as low as 11 percent in 2002 and has never exceeded 19 percent. Republicans (71 percent) were the most likely to select "too liberal," with 42 percent of independents and only 20 percent of Democrats doing the same.[28]

With all of this in mind, Gallup concluded in its 2014 study that trust in media likely won't be improving anytime soon: "The overarching pattern of the past decade has shown few signs of slowing the decline of faith in mass media as a whole." [29]

ASSESSING MEDIA BIAS

Of course, public opinion polling is just a small sliver that gives us some ideas about the situation surrounding media bias, but is there a more scientific method for assessing actual bias in practice? That's a question that Professor Tim Groseclose has studied in-depth in recent years, working to quantitatively assess media bias.

When asked in an interview for this book what most convinces him that the mainstream media hold a bias, Groseclose was candid. "Just seeing the surveys of reporters saying who they voted for in the previous election," he answered. "If you're a national news network that deals with politics—say, your survey is of Washington DC reporters—then the number is like 92 to 8. It's not like 70/30 or 80/20."[30]

And let's just consider for a moment what Groseclose had to say about this dynamic in his 2011 book, *Left Turn: How Liberal Media Bias Distorts the American Mind*:

> According to surveys, in a typical presidential election Washington correspondents vote about 93–7 for the Democrat, while the rest of America votes about 50–50.
>
> What happens when our view of the world is filtered through the eyes, ears, and minds of such a liberal group?
>
> As I demonstrate, using objective, social-scientific methods, the filtering prevents us from seeing the world as it actually is. Instead, we see only a distorted version of it. It is as if we see the world through a glass—a glass that magnifies the facts that liberals want us to see and shrinks the facts that conservatives want us to see.[31]

In his interview for this book, Groseclose pointed to a groupthink mentality among reporters that he believes could be having a profound impact over how they cover the issues. If a newsroom lacks dissenting voices, he said the impact can lead to a problematic situation—one in which false assumptions are potentially made and then "magnified."[32]

"It's twelve liberals to one conservative, but the twelve liberals are just going to feel like, 'Oh no, everyone feels like this. What we're saying, these points about [how] taxes should be higher, abortion should be legal,'" he said. "To them that's going to sound like a fact that no one will dispute—a fact like 'Oh the sun rises in the east.' Everyone agrees with that." [33]

And Groseclose isn't merely speaking out of turn, as he and fellow professor Jeffrey Milyo crafted what they said was an academically rigorous method for studying media bias back in 2004. Their study, titled "A Measure of Media Bias," attempted to use a statistical technique to build an objective measure of conservative or liberal news bias in major US television and radio stations, newspapers, and magazines, and on the Internet.

Interestingly enough, Groseclose and Milyo's study started with exploring the voting records of members of Congress rather than the media itself. The researchers looked to see the pattern or tendency of Congressional members to cite two hundred prominent think tanks. The researchers then chose twenty prominent media outlets and measured the tendency of these outlets to favorably cite the same two hundred think tanks legislatures invoked in their speeches and presentations. Common sense implies that the outlets routinely referring favorably to conservative think tanks could reasonably be labeled conservative and vice versa. The study found that the mainstream media slanted to the left. Out of the twenty media outlets examined, only two emerged as conservative: *Fox News Special Report with Brit Hume* and the *Washington Times*. The other eighteen outlets came in either slightly or far left of center. [34]

This was, of course, years ago, and the media landscape has changed quite a bit, but Groseclose has kept up with his research, arguing through op-eds, his book, and academic discussions that bias has a real impact on the public at large.

"The bias makes us more liberal, which makes us less able to detect the bias, which allows the media to get away with more bias, which makes us even more liberal, and so on," he wrote in *Left Turn*. [35]

Relying on his "slant quotient" theory, Groseclose described in the book—much like in his 2004 study—how he believes it is entirely possible to measure bias quantitatively. Using his methodology, the professor claims he has been able to prove that every mainstream national outlet in America has a bias and that the "effects of media bias are real and significant." [36]

"My results suggest that media bias aids Democratic candidates by about 8 to 10 percentage points in a typical election," Groseclose wrote. "I find, for instance, that if media bias didn't exist, then John McCain would have defeated Barack Obama 56–42, instead of losing 53–46." [37]

Media bias, much like biases in Hollywood and universities, is prone to leave many people with complaints and frustrations, especially when considering the impact that these areas of society can have on the lives and perspectives of citizens.

And if all of what you've read in this book is true, you're likely wondering how, exactly, did we get here? That's what we'll explore next.

CHAPTER 15

HOW DID WE GET HERE

T'S ONE THING to pinpoint a bias, but it's an entirely different animal to dive deeper into what has caused such an unequal playing field. On one side there are those who believe wholeheartedly that a more secular and liberal class in the media have intentionally kept conservatives out of the loop and, to a larger degree, out of newsrooms. Then there's the more benign theory that with more liberals working in newsrooms, it's likely these people tend to gravitate toward others who are like-minded—especially when it comes to filling staff positions.

TWO IDEAS EXPLAINING HOW WE GOT HERE

This dynamic of differing viewpoints explaining how we got here was discussed in detail by Chris Field, former executive editor at *Townhall Magazine*, onetime executive editor of *TheBlaze Magazine* and a senior editor at *TheBlaze,* in an interview for this book. Field told me he believes "the media are generally negative toward conservative/Christian/biblical values." But that negativity, he argued, comes in two forms that, while different, end up having a similar impact.[1]

"There are those who are openly hostile to values held by conservatives and Christians," Field said. "This crowd stands in opposition not only to conservative economic principles on capitalism, free market, and low taxes but also to cultural principles people on the right tout (including many who might not consider themselves 'born again'): sanctity of life, traditional marriage, monogamy, etc."[2]   .

He continued, "This crowd shows utter disdain for anything that might impose on their progressive—and libertine—agenda."[3]

But rather than a flagrant disregard for right-of-center values, Field said the second form of anti-biblical and anti-conservative values is rooted entirely in an ignorance surrounding what Christians and conservatives actually believe. More importantly, he said there's confusion about "*why* conservatives and Christians believe what they do." [4]

"They are far less likely to display contempt for conservatism and biblical values but will reveal more of a naiveté regarding the 'what' and 'why' of those worldviews," he said. [5]

Field points to the same dynamic that I have hinted at throughout this book—the idea that those in the media aren't necessarily out to destroy conservatism and that many, in fact, simply don't "get" it. But that doesn't necessarily matter, as the end result—a potentially skewed populace—remains the same.

"Christian conservatives seem to get an extra level of scrutiny: both groups—regardless of why—treat Christianity and biblical principles as though they are just plain weird or old-fashioned," Field said. "And because living a life of conviction has become rare in much [of] the media, they tend to bristle at any attempt to offer some sort of standard for good living, and they offer to the faithful a collective 'lighten up, Francis.'" [6]

But there is an ideological price to pay when it comes to a lack of representation, or even misrepresentation, in the press, and considering what we've seen in terms of cultural shifts, it is certainly problematic to continue ignoring the issue.

HOW WE GOT HERE

It's clear that blame can be placed on both intentional acts of bias and, perhaps more rampantly, ignorance. However, there is another possible explanation as to how faith and conservatism have become so foreign in American newsrooms and beyond: conservatives and Christians have retreated and isolated themselves and, in doing so, have only furthered the ideological and theological gaps we see in many contemporary American newsrooms.

Scott Baker, a veteran journalist and the former editor in chief of TheBlaze.com, is not only a good friend of mine but also a mentor who hired me as the faith and culture editor at *TheBlaze*, helping to guide my coverage throughout my five years at the outlet. Baker has a deep sense of the roles—or the lack thereof—that conservatives and Christians have played in the American press, and he's worked in almost every facet of the industry, serving at various times as a journalism instructor, broadcast journalist, and digital media entrepreneur.

So when I asked Baker to share with me the first thought he typically has when he hears fellow conservatives complain about media bias, I wasn't surprised to receive his candid response: "My short answer—it's our fault." In short, he believes that conservatives have largely avoided working in the media, leading to the conundrum of unequal ideological representation in newsrooms.[7]

"Here's my logic. Even though we have seen more conservatives involved in journalism in the last ten to fifteen years, it has not been enough to undo decades of conservative avoidance of the field," Baker explained. "We love being commentators. Radio talk show hosts. Columnists. Prime-time analysts on cable TV. Pumping out our opinions on social media. But the day-to-day jobs of journalism? Not so much."[8]

Baker said this dynamic is particularly true at the local level, stressing that his concern stretches well beyond the realm of on-air talent. He argued that conservatives should be playing key roles in a variety of capacities inside American newsrooms—roles that some people might not even consider when they lash out about frustrations over media bias.[9] "Who are the people holding the cameras? Or assigning the stories? Or creating the graphics you see on the screen?" he said. "Conservatives should be doing all of those jobs. But I think young people growing up in conservative homes don't often hear a great deal of esteem being expressed for those kinds of careers."[10]

NO QUESTION, MEDIA BIAS EXISTS

It's not as though Baker ignores the many examples of skewed coverage that are there, as he said that none of his views on what has caused the dearth of conservatives in newsrooms excuse "a zillion examples of egregious liberal bias." Despite these incidents, though, the veteran reporter and editor said conservatives really don't have the right to complain if they aren't willing to do these jobs themselves. Overall, he said conservatives in media aren't where they need to be, though they are improving.[11]

Field shared similar views, saying he believes the ship has sailed on the debate over media bias, as "no one with integrity or a clue actually makes the argument that media bias doesn't exist." Despite the obvious, he encouraged conservatives to realize that endless complaining also isn't the answer; in the end, he said it makes them appear to simply be whining and complaining.[12]

"Though I agree with the sentiments, I get that 'Oh, not again' feeling. The Right has made that complaint—correctly—time and again," he said, noting, though, that he doesn't believe bias claims can always be conservatives' primary argument. "They have begun to sound like whiners looking for an excuse for our failed efforts."[13]

PROGRESS IS BEING MADE, BUT THERE IS STILL WORK TO BE DONE

Field, similar to Baker, also made another important point: the media landscape is changing. While the big and traditional mainstream outlets haven't become less liberal or biased, he said "the conservative counterbalance has become greater." Field maintains "the Internet— for all its faults (filth, hate, lies)—has begun to 'bring balance to the Force,'" referencing *Star Wars*.[14]

Still, there are clearly some challenges worth considering. Baker said the media are more attuned to conservatives' feelings on being marginalized, and that many of the liberals he worked with in newsrooms "really felt that they were trying to be fair." Unfortunately he said this sentiment can only take the industry so far, as "trust and understanding develop over time." And with barriers due to not understanding the impact that faith, among other attributes, can have on a person, tensions are sure to be felt.[15]

"We all come to our own presuppositions about the world. School. Family. Church. They shape us," he said. "If church was not a part of your socialization—you may have a harder time understanding the nuance of what faith means to a given community."[16]

Both Baker and Field believe that the media have had a major collective impact on society, with Field offering a short summary of his take on the matter, saying, "The media have remade society in their image—vacuous, conviction-less, impious."[17] Baker, though, sees the catalyst of societal change as extending far beyond the confines of the media landscape. When asked how he would frame the collective impact that media bias has had on society, he said it's "significant," but that he's more prone to looking at entertainment as a more powerful catalyst.[18]

"The entertainment culture is probably even more of an important shaper of our society," Baker said. "If there are few conservatives working in day-to-day journalism, there are even fewer working in the day-to-day entertainment fields."[19]

With that in mind, the journalist said he doesn't think people are doing enough to train, encourage, and support "thoughtful young people" to enter these fields, reiterating that he believes conservatives must look to themselves when it comes to the absence of the Christian and conservative perspectives in media, entertainment, and university cultures. "Plenty of people make [a] great argument blaming the people in those industries. I still feel it's our fault," Baker said. "If you are not willing to go and do those jobs, is it fair to sit around complaining about the people who do?"[20]

Field echoed this sentiment, pointing to some missteps and missed opportunities he believes have helped perpetuate the problem. "For a [long] time, Christians were told to stay out of the culture—don't go to movies, don't read books, don't pick up magazine[s], don't, don't, don't, don't," Field said. "The church in America wasted a lot of time telling Christians what not to do instead of telling them what they should do."[21]

As with Baker, Field blamed retreat and disengagement for much of the current situation that conservatives and Christians find themselves in. "The church chose not to engage, chose to pull back—and in doing so, the church gave up a lot [of] ground," he said. "Now we're trying to reinsert ourselves, and we're being mocked because we don't fit in. And we don't fit in because of bad teaching from the pulpits."[22]

While working to correct the dynamic mentioned in Field's latter point has its complications, a step in the right direction is most certainly increased engagement. How can media transform and become more representative of the public at large if conservatives and Christians fail to enter into the machine and become reporters, editors, camera operators, etc.?

"Set aside your reservations. Go tell good stories. Don't have a chip on your shoulder. Learn the craft. And be patient," Baker said to young people who might consider entering the field. "Malcolm

Gladwell has always said that it took him ten years as a newspaper reporter before he even really started to understand how to write." [23]

Now that we've talked through some of the causes, I think it's important we circle back at the impact that media, entertainment, and university bias has had on the masses. We've already covered changes in moral understanding, though there are some other broader issues—including religious liberty—that are at stake. The situation, as you'll see in the next chapter, has worsened in recent years, and unless Christians and conservatives become more engaged, that's only likely to continue.

PART 5

IS FREE SPEECH UNDER ATTACK?

IS FREE SPEECH under attack? That is a question that has dominated the sociopolitical landscape, with many decrying what they see as a dangerously potent level of political correctness that is curtailing the ability of people—many times conservative individuals—to share their sincerely held views in public forums.

And before we continue, I should note that these lamentations shouldn't be taken to mean that those who oppose a growing sense of political correctness are seeking the unadulterated right to totally and utterly obliterate and attack others, spout off offensive sentiment, or harass their ideological foes. Quite the contrary, most people are simply looking for the right to share their sincerely held views without fear of being maligned, shut down, and—in the case of public figures—shamed to the point of widespread embarrassment and retreat.

There's a "freedom for me and none for thee" mentality that has somehow come to dominate our discourse. Over time, it feels as though many people have become so consumed with their own views, opinions, and inclinations that they've come to reject the presence and worth of opposing positions. And with this environment persisting, it often seems as though people are willing to fight tooth and nail for their own causes while simultaneously denigrating or attempting to silence those who simply share divergent views. This becomes particularly problematic when a perspective doesn't align with the values espoused by and in the main educational veins—education, media, and entertainment.

This has led to a dynamic in which many are so fearful of offending others—or of becoming public enemy numero uno—that they hold back on sharing thoughtful commentary or sincerely held beliefs. Or in other cases they simply sanitize their true feelings in an effort to protect themselves from explosive and over-the-top fallout.

This has all been perpetuated by the fact that there has been a vicious turn of events in recent years—one that has given birth to concerted efforts to shame and destroy reputations, businesses, and the like. Rather than a more general call for respect, it sometimes feels as though critics want their opponents to not only tolerate behavior and belief systems, but also to fully embrace them; if they refuse, efforts are made to force their hands. These initiatives, unfortunately, often put free speech and expression at risk.

And free speech is directly tied to concerns over bias in that there is a danger when one side (in this case progressives) starts to dominate most of the educational channels in society. In such an instance, those with the firmest hold on media, entertainment, and universities unfortunately end up controlling, via messaging, a solid chunk of the news, entertainment, and university instruction we receive; one side loses its voice and influence while the other completely dominates the conversation. It's a dynamic that can quickly lead to some serious consequences for those who hold moral views not traditionally heralded in those venues, especially when the law suddenly starts to reflect opposing sentiments.

CONSULTING THE EXPERTS

With these dynamics in mind, I decided to consult revered legal mind Eugene Volokh, a professor at the UCLA School of Law who is known for his expertise on free speech and religious freedom. I started our interview by asking him an admittedly general—and loaded—question: "What would you say the state of free speech in America is right now? What's happening in your view?" Volokh said that it's essentially a mixed bag.

"By the standards of American history, by the standards of the world, it's very good, but I think it is more in peril than it was say five, ten years ago," Volokh said. "I think there are more attempts to censor speech that is seen as, say, religiously bigoted or racist or sexist or anti-gay, and increasingly all it takes to be called a racist is to express skepticism about immigration or to express plausible concerns about, for example, the spread of Islam throughout the world and the like." He continued by noting that "there are important issues that need to be discussed," but charged that one side is often trying to silence the other—a dynamic he called "dangerous for freedom."[1]

CARRIE PREJEAN: ONE OF THE FIRST TO BE CHALLENGED ON FREE SPEECH

With the media, entertainment, and university landscape reinforcing certain narratives—and with conservatives and Christians lacking a presence within those venues—the free-speech conundrum should come as no surprise. At some point these biases boiled over, with conservative or Christian people sometimes finding themselves in the crosshairs for simply stating their views on an issue. And while it's probably impossible to trace to the exact originating moment that the chaos began, in my mind the first notable event that left me with intense head-scratching and total and utter confusion unfolded on April 19, 2009, when an otherwise unsuspecting and routine beauty pageant somehow erupted into an endless media hoopla characterized by intense rage and consternation.

It all began when a beautiful young woman named Carrie Prejean gleefully walked across the Miss USA stage on live television that night to answer a hard-hitting question from one of the judges. As a smile stretched across her face, Prejean listened intently to judge Perez Hilton, a well-known entertainment blogger, who proceeded to ask her the now-infamous question that ignited the firestorm.

"Vermont recently became the fourth state to legalize same-sex marriage," Perez proclaimed. "Do you think every state should follow suit? Why or why not?" [2]

Prejean maintained somewhat of a smile as Perez delivered his question, though the internal strain and conflict that it brought about was evident from the slight and immediate change in her facial expression. As a large audience and millions of Americans watched in anxious anticipation, Prejean turned to the microphone and immediately responded.

"Well, I think it's great that Americans are able to choose one or the other. We live in a land that you can choose same-sex marriage or opposite marriage," she said, before offering her own personal view on the matter. "In my country and in my family...I believe that a marriage should be between a man and a woman." Prejean then added, "No offense to anybody out there, but that's how I was raised, and that's how I think that it should be—between a man and a woman." [3]

It was a simple response to an intensely complex and politically loaded question—an answer that, at the time, was reflective of the majority of Americans' views on same-sex nuptials. In fact, in May 2009, Gallup found that only 40 percent of Americans felt that same-sex marriage should be seen under the law as valid and legal, having the same benefits as traditional marriage, compared to 57 percent who disagreed with that sentiment.[4] Somehow, though, Prejean's response—one that was representative of the majority of Americans—exploded across the media landscape. She ended up losing the pageant with some, including Prejean herself, feeling as though the marriage response was the sole reason she ended up first runner-up.[5] But it was the aftermath that was perhaps the most disturbing. Prejean, now a married mother of two, reflected on the intense experience she faced in the midst of national controversy during an interview for this book.

Prejean started by discussing her pageant win that preceded the Miss USA controversy. "The day I won Miss California USA was the day my life had changed forever. I had competed against nearly ninety of some of the most beautiful, intelligent, driven, and articulate women from throughout the state of California—some say the toughest state to win," Prejean said. "Next up was to prepare for Miss USA. I was a twenty-one-year-old, attending a conservative, Christian college, and working two jobs. I was physically preparing myself with a daily rigorous training schedule, which took up most of my time, in preparation to compete at the Miss USA pageant."[6]

Prejean said she also dedicated her time to being mentally prepared, studying questions, surveying people around her on contemporary issues, and participating in "mock" pageants to practice answering difficult questions. Her ultimate hope? Not only to win the Miss USA title but also to go on to claim victory at the Miss Universe pageant as well.[7]

"I was ready for important issues that that could possibly be asked of a young woman vying for the title of Miss USA," she said. "[But] I never thought something as politically explosive as this would be asked at a beauty pageant. After all, 57 percent of the nation—and President Obama—had already confirmed that marriage was to be defined between one man and one woman."[8]

Prejean said she was always told in pageant training that if she knew what she believed in and always told the truth, she could handle any question—something she contemplated in her heart and mind as she stood on the Miss USA stage.[9]

"I just knew that God had prepared my way and this is what I was supposed to do, so when I got called into the top five, I stayed calm, and I felt prepared and ready for my final question." Prejean said. "I said a prayer, and felt God was with me before the question was asked. I had a sense of peace. I felt ready and prepared to win, move to New York, and be given a platform for causes and charities that would allow me to give back to my country, and serve as an ambassador…I was ready to represent America, the greatest country in the world."[10]

But Perez Hilton's question ended up being an unforeseen curve-ball. The entire scenario is one that she now looks back on as a "setup" aimed at drumming up controversy that would also attract media attention. "In promoting his own agenda, he decided to ask a political question that should have never been asked in the context of a beauty pageant, hoping 'Miss California' might agree with him just to snag the crown," Prejean said. Prejean continued, saying she believes the question was asked "to promote (Hilton's) own self-serving agenda at the expense of a young, intelligent, honest beauty queen exercising her First Amendment right."[11]

"He didn't just accept my answer as being different than his, and agree to disagree. He penalized me…and launched a vicious, abusive attack against me personally, calling me explicit names. He tried to exploit and abuse me for ratings and self-promotion," she said. "All of the things that he wanted—tolerance, love, acceptance, diversity, and peace—were the simple things that he couldn't even exercise himself."[12]

Prejean also explained the internal challenge she faced while standing on stage before the nation. After all, she could have simply taken the easy way out and answered in a vague or politically correct way, but in making a split-second decision, she felt compelled to stand by her truth. In that moment Prejean said her mind instantly went back to her pageant training and, while she was stunned the question was being asked, she said she knew she had to answer it one way or another. "I knew I had to speak from my heart and be truthful and not compromise my beliefs," Prejean said. "It taught me how important it is to always tell the truth, and speak from the heart…The crown didn't mean anything to me at that point. I would rather tell the truth and get first runner-up than sell my soul for the crown."[13]

It was an important lesson for Prejean, but one that didn't come without a plethora of public haggling and debate—a furor in the wake of the pageant that Prejean has described as total "chaos." The intense media scrutiny began right after the Miss USA competition concluded. Prejean recalled doing a few interviews immediately following the televised event during which she was asked by reporters if she stood by what she said; she affirmed that she did. Then, she headed back to her hotel not thinking too much about what had unfolded.[14]

But when she got back to her hotel room, she said she saw that Perez Hilton had uploaded a public video reaction to her on-stage answer to the gay marriage question—and it left her in shock. The blogger lambasted Prejean, reportedly calling her incredibly derogatory expletives both in that video and in the subsequent days.

"I was disillusioned that [a supposedly] unbiased judge at the Miss USA pageant would demonstrate his biased attack and try and bully a beauty contestant who didn't agree with him," Prejean continued. "I was disappointed that a man would attack a woman, and be so sadistic that he thought it was necessary to harass and intimidate and verbally abuse her—all the while, not a single women's rights group reached out to me in support of this unimaginably vicious attack."[15]

In one video uploaded after the pageant, Perez reportedly dubbed Prejean's response "the worst answer in pageant history" and said that it was "an awful, awful answer which alienated so many people." He also called Prejean a "dumb [expletive]," and suggested Prejean could have offered a more sanitized alternate answer.[16]

"I would have said, 'Hmm, Perez, that's a great question, that's a very hot topic in our country right now. And I think that's a question that each state should decide for themselves,'" Perez said, offering up his proposed alternative.[17]

It was a response that only added fuel to the media fire being kindled by Prejean's original pageant comments about gay marriage. But rather than back down and remain quiet amid the chaos, the beauty queen decided to defend herself, speaking out about her views on marriage and her belief in a freer and unadulterated state of free speech. In the process, others joined Perez in attacking her—and some of it was pretty ugly. Overnight, Prejean went from a hopeful and bubbly pageant contestant to a media sensation who had fallen under intense fire from her critics.

"At this young age, I got a quick understanding of political correctness and how biased and one sided the media can be if you are a conservative Christian blonde beauty queen who dared to stand up for what…she believes in," Prejean said. "My free speech wasn't accepted in this case, and the left-wing media would conspire to silence me." [18]

Prejean outlined some valid concerns that should give us all some pause, regardless of where we stand on gay marriage, or any other issue for that matter. First, to her point: she was asked a question and she proceeded to answer it. What was the problem? Her answer didn't align with what the person asking it and other critics wanted to hear. Rather than people having the maturity to respect a divergent view, Prejean was treated like a pariah. Looking back now, the entire scenario was a warning sign of the cultural chaos that would soon unleash.

"I didn't even quote Bible verses in my answer. I just said, 'This is the way I was raised and this is what I believe. Marriage should be between a man and a woman,'" she said. "My answer should have been accepted by the judge for what it was, without any penalty, persecution, or spiteful, vindictive attacks." [19]

While she was surely attacked by a great many critics, including liberal commentator Keith Olbermann, Miss California also had her supporters. Former Alaska Governor Sarah Palin came to her defense, as did commentator Roland Martin. In fact, Martin wrote an op-ed not long after the furor unfolded in 2009 that also offers some much-needed truth for the current culture. Martin offered direct advice to Perez—but also delivered a broader lesson that could benefit us all. [20]

"Hey, Hilton, from a real journalist to a wanna-be who traffics in gossip: Never ask a question if you're unprepared for the answer!" Martin wrote. "Isn't the whole point of asking a question to get someone's true feelings, rather than the plastic and superficial answers we are all used to receiving?" [21]

He added, "The day we condemn folks for speaking honestly is the day we become a bland society." [22]

Today, Prejean has moved on with her life, but the lessons she learned from the chaotic media furor have remained with her. "I really experienced firsthand how vicious the media can be, when your opinions don't align with their agenda...but, I am hopeful that I can pave the way for other young women to never back down from the bullies...[and those] who want to discredit conservative values," she said.[23]

More than seven years after her pageant debacle, Prejean has no regrets about what unfolded, and said she's now able to teach her own children about the importance of telling the truth and standing by their values, even when their beliefs aren't "popular."

Prejean has continued to speak out and defend her values, writing a book immediately after the controversy titled *Still Standing: The Untold Story of My Fight Against Gossip, Hate, and Political Attacks*. In addition to saying she has no regrets, she said her views on marriage still haven't changed. "I am still standing, all these years later, stronger than ever before. I will never back down. I stood up for my faith and what I believe in my heart," Prejean said. "Everyone is entitled to his or her opinions and freedom of speech, just as I'm entitled to mine."[24]

Prejean concluded by saying that she's "hopeful that political correctness will not ever replace our precious right of free speech."[25]

WHAT IS REALLY AT PLAY HERE

Some critics will surely dismiss Prejean and other conservatives who share her views as people who simply wish to stand in the way of freedom and equality, but those who stop there and fail to dig deeper into the broader issues at play, I believe, miss the point entirely. Part of the problem is that many of the contentious issues we're talking about here—gay marriage, abortion, and other highly debated subjects—tend to gin up emotion. And when emotion takes over, it's all too easy for us to stop in the midst of those feelings and decline to challenge ourselves to explore what's really going on.

When you peel back the layers, it becomes evident that Prejean's story and many others like it involve some complex issues, including the freedom of speech and expression. It's easy to dismiss those with whom we disagree, looking at them as backward, wrong-headed, or silly. But we live in a free society—or should, anyway—in which engagement and dialogue, and not cheap tactics of tearing down ideological opponents in an effort to silence them, should win out.

It requires a deep emotional capacity for each of us to consider how we would like to be treated if we were in Prejean's situation. While it's truly a juvenile lesson—the ability to have respect even in the midst of disagreement—it appears many of us either missed that message entirely or are intentionally deciding that certain opinions and perspectives are the only ones worthy of being heard.

As a result, what we're witnessing today is a sad state of affairs—one in which we have seemingly allowed society, or at least the loudest individuals in it, to go a bit too far in attempting to restrict rights and perspectives. Why is it that we can't simply have mutual respect? For too long many gays and lesbians were mistreated by opponents in mainstream culture (and yes, that included Christians). Now, with the cultural tides changing, some activists appear more than willing to use those same tactics against Christians. Finding a middle ground can't be that complicated; yet we've somehow sadly allowed the pendulum to swing from one extreme to the other.

Now, let's briefly get back to Prejean's case. While Volokh said private entities such as beauty pageants have the right to disassociate from people who have certain objectionable views, and that these private enterprises might be right to separate from those who spout extreme opinions, he sees a problem with the extent to which this paradigm is now playing out in society. Here's what he told me:

> The problem is this category of beyond the pale opinions has been extended so far that even mainstream opinions that are held by 50 percent or more of the population—or maybe a little less than 50 percent, but still part of very much continuing debates—lead to people being threatened essentially with loss of a job, loss of various other positions, and the like. I think...that's bad for democracy. How can we have a sensible discussion as to whether there should be, for example, anti-discrimination laws based on sexual orientation? Or whether the Obergefell same-sex marriage decision—which at the time was only in the future—whether that's wrong? How can you have such sensible debates if essentially the message to one side of it is if you speak up...you're going to lose your job? [26]

The problem with the reaction, Volokh said, is that it has a sweeping impact and can "carry over to everybody who says something that is then noticed by people who want to retaliate against this person." This, he argued, essentially breeds an environment that can become rabidly unhealthy. "Again, I think that's dangerous. I think that's intolerant," he continued. "I think that is disrespectful of what it takes to run an effective democracy." [27]

The public shaming of people into retreat has Volokh concerned, as he said using this tactic to shut down debate on an issue in which the public is deeply split is improper. Reiterating this point, Volokh said it is "wrong to try to stop or to have one side win the debate by basically threatening the other side into silence." [28]

The debate, of course, is about more than a beauty queen's free speech battle; it's about the very soul of America, as the First Amendment hangs in the balance.

CHAPTER 17

RELIGIOUS FREEDOM BATTLES ABOUND

WE'VE EXPLORED THE potential impact of media, entertainment, and universities as well as some of the free speech battles that have unfolded. I've also pondered whether people's perspectives are being altered by progressive ideals, with an unfair representation of the issues unfolding throughout the nation's three education veins—but is this all really so dangerous?

Many faithful who believe fervently in a higher truth would certainly waste little time in answering affirmatively, arguing that the triangular dominance of the press, Hollywood, and universities is helping to transform popular opinion and cultural norms. It's interesting to consider what *Duck Dynasty* star Phil Robertson recently had to say on the matter.

"God very eloquently and very plainly spells out exactly what the current situation is—and it's been that way since human beings have been on planet Earth," Robertson told former *Breitbart News Daily* host Stephen K. Bannon in a 2016 interview.[1]

Robertson, who regularly speaks out about his Christian faith, went on to say there is "organized evil" in the world and that "it is headed up by the evil one—Satan." And he even went a bit further, ironically invoking some of the themes espoused in this book: "Satan controls our news media, Satan controls our institutions of higher learning, and he controls what goes on in Hollywood."[2]

And while not everyone believes in a theological paradigm that would lead them to blame Satan for the state of each of these venues, there are many who would, at the least, recognize the collective bias problems existing within each.

THE STATE OF CULTURE IN AMERICA

Christian apologist Ravi Zacharias went much deeper in analyzing the current cultural dynamic in a statement published to his website just two days before America celebrated Independence Day on July 4, 2016. "Whatever happened to the American soul?" he asked, lamenting the current state of cultural affairs.[3]

"We are truly at the cliff's precipitous edge and the fall could be long and deadly," Zacharias wrote. "Why? We have a deep crisis of the soul that is killing us morally and we have no recourse. We have no recourse because the only cure has been disparaged and mocked by the elite and the powerful."[4]

"Reason," he continued, "bleeds to death before our eyes." Pointing to the violence and chaos that the nation has seen, the apologist asked how many more families will be harmed and "offered up at the altar of our foolishness." Throughout the piece Zacharias lamented the "the death of morality, the death of truth, and the death of reason." There is a war within our culture and within our souls, he argued.[5]

After sharing some quotes from famed O. J. Simpson lawyer Robert Shapiro, who once said that there is "legal justice and moral justice" and that in the case of Simpson, "legal justice" had been served, Zacharias lamented.[6]

"When justice is decapitated and something can be legal but immoral, we know we have already killed the heart of what it means to be human," he said, adding, "Our society is being dragged towards the morgue because the law has held the gun to the heart of morality." Going on to speak about the failure to label Islamic extremism what it is, among other issues, Zacharias heralded the importance of appealing to the Almighty to discern right from wrong.[7]

"True freedom is not in doing whatever we wish but in doing what we ought. That has been buried in America," he wrote. "And only one who knows the way out of the grave can give us a second chance to live: Jesus, the way, the truth, and the life that sets us free from within first, before we learn to deal with the lies around us."[8]

Some might scoff at these theological ideas and proclamations, though I would argue that they brilliantly speak to the place we are in as a culture. We're fostering environments that are failing to educate young people about the full range of available views, and beyond that, we are potentially neglecting our history and sacrificing the First Amendment all at the altar of political correctness. One can't help but ask: Are we putting at risk the very values that once made our nation incredibly unique?

That latter question is one that author and speaker Eric Metaxas tackled in his 2016 book *If You Can Keep It*, a treatise that offers a "review of America's uniqueness," with a description warning that the nation can't continue "unless we truly understand what our founding fathers meant for us to be."[9]

Metaxas told me he wrote the book after getting "freaked out" by an important realization about the nation's founding fabric: "America is not an ethnic group, it is not like an island where everybody is the same. It is an idea founded, or put into the world, by the founders in 1776." On the surface, this isn't all that surprising and is an idea that is deeply rooted in the nation's historical narrative. But Metaxas's fear is that people are no longer aware of the country's history, nor its founding values.[10]

"It dawned on me that really to be an American, if America is an idea, you need to understand the idea," he said. "You need to know the various ideas that make up the idea. You need to know the histories and the stories." Metaxas continued, "In other words, to be an American requires something, because it is an idea. Self-government requires something."[11]

His fear is that, over the past forty to fifty years, people have not been taking seriously the idea of America's profound greatness and uniqueness, something that he said many citizens haven't been learning in US schools. It's the "ideas behind what makes us who we are" that he said are being entirely overlooked.[12]

After these thoughts struck him a few years back, Metaxas said he felt it was tragic that so many had lost touch with the elements that shaped America, warning of the potential impact of the nation continuing on its current trajectory.[13]

"This is a crisis....We are at the edge of the abyss as a nation," he said. "If we don't wake up and start teaching our kids these things and start reminding ourselves of what these things are, it is game over for the United States of America. I believe that firmly."[14]

And when it comes to his belief about how we got here, Metaxas held little back, placing blame on some of the nation's main educational veins. "If you want to know why we are where we are, it is precisely because we have stopped teaching these things in schools," he said. "We have stopped teaching them and celebrating them in the media."[15]

Considering America's historical devotion to the First Amendment, Metaxas said it's essential that the public be educated about civics and, in particular, the importance of liberty and religious freedom. He emphasized the importance of "the role that faith and virtue play in the republic," but said that these are elements that people won't regularly hear in public schools and "will definitely never hear it in college, and you will never hear it in the media." Religious liberty, he said, was foundational to the creation and formation of the United States.[16]

"Every one of the founders—Benjamin Franklin, Thomas Jefferson—every one of the founders understood the utterly crucial role of faith and virtue with regard to American freedom," he said, going on to urge Americans to learn more about their history and the stories that underpin it. "You cannot really be a people unless you know your stories, your myths, your legends, your songs, what to celebrate, about why we are proud to be Americans."[17]

Circling back to the religious freedom front, Metaxas also commented on some of the battles raging as society grapples with finding a balance between the religious freedom of business owners and the rights of gays and lesbians in the wake of the June 2015 *Obergefell v. Hodges* Supreme Court case that legalized same-sex nuptials across the nation.[18]

As noted in previous chapters, some Christians have faced hurdles when they've tried to live out their faith in education settings and professional capacities. This too has unfolded in a variety of cases surrounding Christian business owners. Just consider what happened to Aaron and Melissa Klein, Oregon bakers who were forced by state officials to pay $135,000 for their refusal to bake a wedding cake for a lesbian couple. Yes, you read that correctly: one single, solitary cake. The natural question is: How in the world did we get here? Speaking more generally about a variety of ongoing religious liberty battles, Metaxas seemingly answered: "The fact that we could get here tells me that we have neglected the basics."[19]

"It is like, 'How did you get an F on this report card?' Well, you did not go to class for six months," he continued. "That is basically how we got here."[20]

Understanding religious liberty is essential, Metaxas said, calling it "the absolute nonnegotiable heart of all of our liberties." It's so essential, in fact, that he said Americans cannot understand their own country as it has existed for more than two centuries unless they truly comprehend it. "There is nothing as important," he said. "If you talk about freedom of conscience, you cannot have liberty without that." [21]

We are a nation that clamors on about the separation of church and state with little regard for what an obsessive carrying out of such a measure does to a society. Within this context, Metaxas went on to connect faith and freedom in a truly profound way, saying that the former is actually dependent upon the latter, specifically when it comes to citizens' conscience rights. [22]

"Faith requires freedom to flourish," he said. "If you have the faith forced by the government, if the government takes a step in and says, 'We are going to decide on these big issues. We are not going to allow you to believe what your conscience teaches you, what your faith teaches you. We are going to force you,' that kills faith." [23]

But he argued this isn't just an isolated casualty, as he believes that terminating faith also kills both virtue and freedom. [24] It's this very idea that has some conservative activists fearful about what's to come.

THE FIGHT FOR FREEDOM

In fact, Kristen K. Waggoner, an attorney with Alliance Defending Freedom, told me she believes the biggest freedom issue the nation faces involves the right for citizens to live in accordance with their religious beliefs and conscience. [25]

"I would say the biggest internal threat to freedom right now is whether Americans will continue to have the right to peacefully live and work consistent with their religious beliefs, without the fear of government punishment," she said. "We see this freedom threatened in a variety of contexts, including whether health care professionals will have the right to practice in the healing profession consistent with their beliefs, whether creative artists will have to create art and promote messages that violate their consciences, whether counselors will have to counsel patients in ways that violate their religious and ethical convictions." [26]

Waggoner, who is among the attorneys on the forefront of the ever-emerging cultural battles, said that these cases are impacting "many professions and nearly every business that requires any sort of license" and that most Americans are having their freedom threatened due to a political agenda that she framed as "patently dangerous."[27]

While some would argue that forcing a bakery or a photographer to serve a same-sex wedding is appropriate and keeps gay couples from experiencing discrimination, Waggoner takes a different stand on the issue. She warns that there is a push to ensure that "those who don't embrace the government's ideology on certain positions will be silenced and forced from the marketplace." She added, "A government that can fine or force the painter or florist out of the market can use that same power against anyone who disagrees with the current government policy."[28]

But not everyone paints with so broad a brush, and if we're being honest, some of these conversations are complex and difficult, including the Kleins' cake battle. After all, there's a big difference— or at least a large enough one to merit discussion—between turning a same-sex couple away from a restaurant due to their sexuality and a baker or wedding photographer declining to serve a same-sex wedding.

Attorneys and legal experts differ when it comes to what sort of opt-outs and protections Christian businesses should be afforded under the law. Volokh, for instance, told me he believes "anti-discrimination law has gone too far" and that the federal Civil Rights Act limits public accommodation discrimination bans to specific businesses like hotels and restaurants.[29]

In discussing this issue, Volokh mentioned the idea of interfaith marriage. If someone who is ethnically Jewish were to marry a Christian, some business owners might not want to provide their services, and that idea doesn't bother Volokh. If he were in this situation, Volokh would say, "That's OK. Fine. I'll go to somebody else. Lots of people will sell me cakes."[30]

But Volokh said there could be some important caveats when it comes to protections for Christian business owners. The debate really might center more on whether the product or service being rendered can reasonably be seen as free speech. "I think photographers count, maybe bakers who [are] asked to write something on the cake count, but bakers who are just asked to bake the cake don't count," he said. "I don't think baking a cake is speech, but creating a photograph is speech or at least a First Amendment–protected activity."[31]

He continued, "I believe that there should be a defense under the Free Speech Clause for photographers, for wedding singers, for press release writers, for printers, and for others from having to produce speech that they don't want to produce, including when they just don't want [to] approve of it because of sexual orientation or religion or race or whatever else." [32]

Bakers, florists, and others who simply don't want to be complicit but who aren't necessarily engaging in free speech, in his view, would need to look for protections in religious exemptions under state law. This is a dynamic that currently differs depending on the state in which an individual is living. For other businesses such as florists, bakers, and limousine drivers, Volokh said the question at hand is whether a state's religious freedom provision, which in some locations is a matter of the state's constitution or a state's Religious Freedom Restoration Act, could potentially offer a defense to these businesses. "People are only beginning to litigate that," he said. "It's unpredictable." [33]

SOME ARE FIGHTING FOR FREEDOM, OTHERS ARE SWITCHING SIDES

Again, not everyone will agree with Volokh on the matter, though it's certain that these disputes will continue to emerge, especially considering the rapid transformation that has unfolded on the gay marriage front. In 2009 the majority opposed same-sex nuptials, but by 2015 the majority opinion had flipped. And consider that many of the politicians who have helped the public change its overall views on the matter were, not that long ago, the very same people driving—or at least participating in—opposition to same-sex nuptials.

Consider the fact that President Barack Obama—who famously endorsed same-sex nuptials just months before the 2012 presidential election—has quite a curious personal history in addressing the topic. In 2008 he said he was a Christian who believed in the sanctity of traditional marriage, proclaiming during a campaign forum: "I believe that marriage is the union between a man and a woman. Now, for me as a Christian…it is also a sacred union." That said, there were murmurings and claims that he had previously expressed support for gay marriage in 1996, purportedly volleying back and forth depending on the election cycle in which he was running.[34]

And those rumors were given even more life when Obama's former political strategist David Axelrod wrote a book claiming that the president intentionally misled the public into believing he opposed gay marriage during his 2008 campaign. Axelrod wrote: "Opposition to gay marriage was particularly strong in the black church, and as he ran for higher office, he grudgingly accepted the counsel of more pragmatic folks like me, and modified his position to support civil unions rather than marriage, which he would term a 'sacred union.'"[35]

Then there's Hillary Clinton, who has been heavily criticized for changing her views on gay marriage as well—a transformation and evolution that appeared to flow right along with public opinion polling. Clinton defended her ideological transition on the issue during a 2014 NPR interview by saying "it's been one of the fastest, most sweeping transformations" and that she, along with many other Americans, simply changed her mind.[36]

Do people frequently change their minds on contentious issues? Absolutely. But when it comes to politicians, an extra level of scrutiny and questioning on such matters is prudent. And on the gay marriage front, in particular, it's patently bizarre that many of the politicians who ended up pushing the legalization of gay marriage once publicly appealed to their own Christian faith to denounce it. Now, many of these same people—leaders who have flip-flopped on the issue as the public has become more favorable of it—oppose efforts to exempt business owners from being forced to participate in same-sex nuptials. Defending marriage based on faith values is apparently no longer politically prudent, nor is a true devotion to religious liberty.

Let's briefly take a deeper look at Clinton, who has been seemingly positioning herself as a beacon for the gay rights movement, though her history on the matter is quite murky. First, remember that it was her husband, former President Bill Clinton, who signed the Defense of Marriage Act in 1996, which said that marriage, under federal law, was restricted to one man and one woman. Clinton was also behind the "Don't Ask, Don't Tell" military policy, signing it into law a bit earlier back in 1993.

Of course, Hillary and Bill Clinton are two separate individuals who have the right to cling to divergent ideals. So what's the real problem, in my view? Over the years Hillary Clinton repeatedly and openly voiced her own disagreement with same-sex marriage—until something suddenly changed. "[Hillary] Clinton came out in support of same-sex marriage in 2013 after more than a decade of opposing it," PolitiFact reported back in 2015, noting that Hillary's change of mind coincided nicely with the change in opinion of a majority of Americans.[37]

But to put it in Clinton's own words, consider what she said in January 2000 about the historic nature of marriage:

> Marriage has got historic, religious and moral content that goes back to the beginning of time, and I think a marriage is as a marriage has always been, between a man and a woman. But I also believe that people in committed gay marriages, as they believe them to be, should be given rights under the law that recognize and respect their relationship.[38]

While Clinton had maintained that she was a supporter of civil unions throughout her political career, she pivoted in the run-up of her 2016 election run, announcing in March 2013 that she fully supported gay marriage. Suddenly her religiously rooted opposition became a thing of the past.

"I support it personally and as a matter of policy and law, embedded in a broader effort to advance equality and opportunity for LGBT Americans and all Americans," she said, joining many others in her party in going the same route.[39]

Months later Bill and Hillary Clinton released a joint statement expressing support for the 2013 Supreme Court decisions that struck down provisions in the Defense of Marriage Act—the very law that Bill Clinton had signed into law as president. But, bizarrely, their public comments on the matter read as though the Clintons had no involvement in the gay marriage debate whatsoever.[40]

"By overturning the Defense of Marriage Act, the Court recognized that discrimination towards any group holds us all back in our efforts to form a more perfect union," the statement read. "We are also encouraged that marriage equality may soon return to California. We applaud the hard work of the advocates who have fought so relentlessly for this day, and congratulate [lesbian activist] Edie Windsor on her historic victory."[41]

Again, it's a stark contrast to Bill Clinton's 1996 comments to *The Advocate* in which he said, "I believe marriage is an institution for the union of a man and a woman. This has been my long-standing position, and it is not being reviewed or considered." By 2009 he too was saying that it was wrong for people to stop gays from marrying.[42]

At this point it's probably important to again clarify that this chapter is not intended to be a treatise against gay marriage. The point, however, is to show that some of the very politicians who have no interest in protecting the religious conscience rights of Christian business owners are some of the same people who had seemingly maneuvered and politically postured themselves on a highly complex issue, appealing to their own Christian faith to oppose same-sex marriage—until it seemingly became no longer politically expedient to do so.

These changes have unfolded among Democrats and Republicans alike, and aren't limited to the political arena, as some denominations such as the Episcopal Church, Presbyterian Church (USA), and United Church of Christ have embraced same-sex nuptials, parting ways with denominations that take a traditional stand.[43]

CHALLENGES TO RELIGIOUS FREEDOM ARE INCREASING

These changes of opinion on gay marriage show evolving cultural tides, but they also present a challenge to those who continue to maintain a traditional view on marriage—people who appeal to the Bible and their faith in doing so. Let's circle back to Waggoner's concerns about the current religious freedom threats that she says are emerging in "many professions."[44]

"There are a number of cases that are deeply disturbing," she told me. "We represent quite a few individuals—painters, bakers, florists, counselors, photographers, government employees—where the government is seeking to force them out of the marketplace because of their beliefs about human sexuality and marriage." One of those cases, she said, surrounds Blaine Adamson, owner of Hands on Originals, a Kentucky-based printing company.[45] Adamson, a Christian, has been locked in a legal battle since early 2012 after declining to design and print T-shirts for a gay pride festival. He didn't "want to convey the

messages printed on the shirts," and offered to connect festival orga-
nizers with another printing company. But they ended up filing a
complaint with the Lexington-Fayette Urban County Human Rights
Commission, beginning what has now been four and a half years of
legal battle.[46]

"Much of the work Blaine does is custom design. He believes that he
is accountable to God for what he creates," said Waggoner, who represents Adamson. "His very livelihood is being threatened because he
won't express certain ideas."[47]

The central issue, Waggoner said, is that the government is trying
to force Adamson, who creates custom work, to express messages
with which he disagrees. His case has been volleying back and forth
in the courts. And while Adamson has certainly had his critics who
deride his referral to another designer, he has also had some unexpected allies. Lesbian business owners Kathy Trautvetter and Diane
DiGeloromo came to Adamson's defense in the wake of the case. The
couple, who own BMP T-shirts, a company in New Jersey that prints
and carries LGBT merchandise and apparel, told me in 2014 why they
believed Adamson's refusal was entirely appropriate.[48]

"The idea is that when you own your own business, it's your own
art and creation—it's very personal…it takes a long time to build
a business," said Trautvetter. "When someone wants to force you to
go against it—that's what stuck me right in the heart. I really felt for
Blaine."[49]

Waggoner also pointed to a separate case surrounding Ruth Neely,
a judge in Wyoming who holds two separate judicial positions, one
of which she has held for over fifteen years and the other for twenty-
two. In the former, Judge Neely has served as a part-time state circuit
court magistrate, which gives her the authority—but does not require
her—to perform wedding ceremonies; in the latter position, where
she has served as a municipal judge, she is reportedly not authorized
to solemnize marriages.[50]

In late 2014, after a federal court decision changed Wyoming's law
on marriage, a local reporter, who had suspected that Judge Neely
"would not perform a ceremony for [same-sex] couple," called her and
asked whether she was "excited" to start performing same-sex marriages. Answering truthfully, Neely indicated that her religious belief
precludes her from performing them. She also noted that there are

other nearby judges who will perform any requested ceremonies. It was that statement alone that Waggoner said led Neely to be brought up on ethics charges in the state—even though no citizen complaint was filed and she'd never been asked to solemnize a same-sex wedding.[51]

"They are attempting to take both of her positions from her, not just the one where she had the authority, but not the responsibility, to do weddings, but even the one that doesn't have any responsibility or authority for weddings. They claim that she's too biased to serve as a judge in both positions," Waggoner said. "[This] is frightening. It's essentially imposing a religious test for office and declaring people of faith ineligible for such positions."[52]

Neely's comments to the reporter came in 2014—one year before gay nuptials were legalized across the land. The magistrate was quoted as saying, "When law and religion conflict, choices have to be made." Not long after, the Wyoming Commission on Judicial Conduct and Ethics began investigating Neely, claiming she had violated the rules of judicial conduct, the *Casper Star Tribune* reported.[53]

Neely was reportedly told by the commission that she would not face a continued battle if she admitted wrongdoing and agreed to resign her positions and pledge not to seek judicial office again in the state—terms that she refused. For now, she's battling on in an effort to keep her positions and ensure that people of faith are not disqualified for positions just because they affirm the millennia-old belief that marriage is between one man and one woman.[54]

And these cases barely scratch the surface. It should again be noted that every legal battle is unique and that there is not a blanket answer to the ongoing challenges surrounding the balance between legal rights for gays and lesbians and religious liberty rights of individuals, businesses, and institutions; the same goes for other issues in which secular-religious clashes unfold, such as abortion and birth control. The answers aren't easy—and the issues are multifaceted.

Clearly these conversations desperately need to be had, as the situation is surely poised to worsen. With Hollywood, universities, and media already holding biases that ofttimes fail to properly frame the role of faith both in people's lives and in the public square more broadly, many people might not realize the importance of viable protection rights that are measured and fair-minded, taking into account both the rights of gays and lesbians to marry as well as the rights of wedding vendors who have qualms about being forced to perform services for same-sex nuptials.

Our collective understanding of religious freedom is seemingly diminishing, as the nation risks losing its very identity as well as the respect for individual rights that have traditionally distinguished our country as a beacon of hope throughout the world. And don't just take my word for it.

"There continues to be a real allergy to religion in public, and I think in the last eight to ten years that has really intensified," Jeremy Dys, an attorney with First Liberty Institute, told me in an interview for this book. "You see just a general frustration by some with any exercise of religion in public." [55]

He pointed to the case surrounding Oregon bakers Aaron and Melissa Klein, who, as mentioned, were forced to pay out $135,000 to a lesbian couple after citing their Christian faith in declining to bake them a wedding cake. Dys said that the couple is being made to "follow the religious opinions of the government." If they refuse, they're punished with stiff penalties. But while I've spent some time speaking here about some of the broader cases that have gained a plethora of media attention, Dys said that it's many of the smaller, less bombastic cases that can really add up to show that there could be a broader societal problem at play. [56]

"It's remarkable that those lesser-known cases over seemingly insignificant matters are almost forgettable...but in the aggregate those cases really become a major problem to our freedom" he said. [57]

As society secularizes, the attorney warns that many Christians are "being driven back into the four walls of the church" and that "even what they say within those four walls can be a problem." [58] There was the 2014 hoopla, of course, over government officials in Houston, Texas, subpoenaing sermons and church communications amid a heated battle over a proposed nondiscrimination ordinance—a bid that Mayor Annise Parker and the city attorney dropped after the case went viral and outrage over First Amendment violations ensued. [59]

One pastor, in fact, had received a subpoena asking for "all speeches, presentations, or sermons related to [the equal rights ordinance], the petition, Mayor Annise Parker, homosexuality, or gender identity." The goal was for the government to see how church leaders

spoke to congregants about efforts to derail the equal rights ordinance; many Christians opposed it due to provisions allowing for
transgender individuals to use the bathroom that comported with
the gender they most associated with.[60]

Parker later admitted that the wording was "overly broad" but
said that there was also "deliberate misinterpretation" on the other
side.[61] Still, few can ignore the fact that the optics of the government
requesting sermons is the stuff of *1984*, a novel by George Orwell,
sparking free speech fears across the board.

With battles heating up over transgender bathroom bills, Dys said
he has some worries about where these free-speech battles will eventually end up. "What's the next thing here?" he said. "If we go after
places of public accommodation, I think the next avenue you're going
to see are churches facing a problem."[62]

Some of these battles have already started to take form, though
many critics question whether any of this will really ever start to
impact churches. Consider, though, the debate that touched off in the
summer of 2016 in Iowa after churches in the state noticed that a long-
standing document published by the Iowa Civil Rights Commission
included some potentially problematic language.[63]

The government brochure titled "Sexual Orientation and Gender
Identity" serves as a guide for public accommodations and notes that
gender identity and sexual orientation are protected classes under
Iowa law. It was a section about churches, though, that caught the ire
of some houses of worship. Titled "Does This Law Apply to Churches?"
the section proclaimed that churches are "sometimes" held accountable under anti-discrimination law:

> Iowa law provides that these protections do not apply to reli-
> gious institutions with respect to any religion-based quali-
> fications when such qualifications are related to a bona fide
> religious purpose. Where qualifications are not related to a
> bona fide religious purpose, churches are still subject to the
> law's provisions.[64]

The document then offered up some examples in which this would
be the case. For example, "a child care facility operated at a church or
a church service open to the public" would not necessarily be a "bona
fide religious purpose." It was that line that led at least one church-led

lawsuit and a separate complaint from another house of worship, as *Deseret News* reported at the time.[65]

The government quickly moved to temper controversy by amending the document to clarify that "religious activities by a church are exempt from the Iowa Civil Rights Act," and expressed regret over the "confusion" that resulted from the original language.[66]

This controversy aside, Dys said the government's role in many cases flies in the face of what the nation's founders would have wanted.[67]

"In our country we afford people the free exercise of religion," he said. "Our founding fathers didn't put together a Constitution that said, 'You can run your organization or freely exercise your religion as long as we say it's OK.' That's what we rebelled against from England."[68]

Dys went on to warn of the importance of passing down the values of freedom to the next generation—a quest that is astonishingly difficult amid the intense bias that is embedded in our nation's educational veins.[69]

"Freedom is...something you've got to personally, daily recommit yourself to [in order to transmit it to the next generation]," Dys said. "And if [we] don't transmit that to our children, our future is a very not-free future."[70]

He continued, "It's essential for each and every one of us...to be teaching our children about what it means to have religious liberty.... There's a real hope for the future here...when people start standing up."[71]

And as we'll discuss as *Fault Line* comes to a close, "standing up" isn't simply stating a political view or defending one's faith; it's also taking an active role in trying to be part of the solution by entering into some of the very arenas in which conservatives and Christians have been absent for far too long.

CHAPTER 18

THE SOLUTION

I T'S OUR FAULT."[1]
Scott Baker's answer to the media bias question really got me thinking. So many conservatives and Christians spend a fair amount of time complaining about the denigration of their world-view or theology in popular media, entertainment, and university classrooms—and, to a degree, understandably so. But complaining doesn't accomplish much, does it?

I know what you're thinking, and it's true: much of this book has focused on the problem of triangular dominance—the idea that the messages and environments espoused in Hollywood, the mainstream media, and universities tend not to favor Christian and conservative ideals and, at moments, actually denigrate faith and traditional values. I wholeheartedly believe this is an ongoing problem, and one that actually does a disservice to free speech and dialogue, as I've extensively outlined.

Not only does it deprive individuals of proper representation in those venues, but it also prevents liberals and those who reject Christian or conservative ideals from gaining enriching learning opportunities by understanding more about those with divergent ideals.

But to Baker's point, are Christians and conservatives to blame for the state of media, entertainment, and education?

If we're being honest, many of us have retreated from the afore-mentioned realms entirely, and that retreat has had some dire conse-quences. Sure, we can sit in our ivory towers and complain and whine about the mean bullies who are refusing to allow us a place at the table. Or we can politely walk up to the table, smile, pull up a chair, and insert ourselves into the discussion. Too many of us have simply recused ourselves from having any viable responsibility or presence. And our ignorance has yielded anything but bliss.

While many of us have thrown our hands up and concluded,

"Whatever; the world is going to hell in a handbasket, anyway," our culture has changed at a rapid rate. Personally, as a Christian, I know the Bible and the gospel are powerful enough to speak for themselves, breaking through the static and noise of cultural chaos, though I also believe we have a responsibility to do our very best to ensure the floodgates for that message can be as open as possible. And as for political representation, conservatives also owe it to the public discourse to have a presence in these realms.

Plainly stated, we need to quit complaining, stand up, and engage the culture. Think about it: if Christians and conservatives don't become professors, reporters, cameramen, producers, actors, and studio heads, then having substantial influence in the realms of entertainment, media, and higher education is a virtual impossibility. Is it tougher to make it in media, entertainment, or university culture based on worldview? Possibly, though there are shining examples of people who have set out to make a real and viable difference in those realms. Baker, for instance, is among those who helped to revolutionize online news, cocreating *TheBlaze* as a media outlet that, in its first few years of existence, captured widespread attention by focusing on news that conservatives—and to a large degree, Christians—were interested in. In many ways, the outlet served as a disruptive force in media, taking on subjects in a fair-minded way and forcing the mainstream media to pay attention in the process.

HOLLYWOOD AND ENTERTAINMENT

While there are plenty of examples in media and academia of individuals and institutions stepping up to the plate to make an impact, perhaps Hollywood has the strongest showing of Christians who are reentering the fray to try and turn the cultural ship around. Among those whom I've admired most in this space has been DeVon Franklin, an author, producer, and the movie-making head of Franklin Entertainment.

In recent years Franklin has been involved in some major faith films, including *Heaven Is For Real* and *Miracles From Heaven*. Both feature films fall in the top ten when it comes to the highest-grossing Christian movies in the modern era.[2] Franklin, who worked at Sony Pictures for ten years, left to form Franklin Entertainment and proceeded to work on *Miracles From Heaven*. In doing so, he took a leap of faith that clearly paid off.[3]

Considering his success in Hollywood, I asked Franklin a candid question in an interview for this book: "Is it tough being a Christian in Hollywood?"

"I don't think so," he responded. "It's probably harder being black." Then he proceeded to explain that he has found Tinseltown to be a place that is "very embracing" of his faith, reiterating that he believes it has been harder from a racial standpoint than a religious one. "I think that I have had to work harder for people not to see me based upon my skin color than my religious beliefs," Franklin said.[4]

With faith films on the increase and audiences—many of whom have been complaining about negative content for years—wanting more, Franklin said he's had quite a positive experience in the entertainment industry. "My faith has actually been the thing that has helped me find success in Hollywood. I don't know that I would be as successful without it," he said. "From that standpoint, it has really been awesome."[5]

And while Franklin has had success with bigger studio films, there have also been some major independent hits from other filmmakers as well, such as *God's Not Dead* and *God's Not Dead 2*, among many others. Let's also not forget that Hollywood and media were simultaneously shocked when the Christian film *War Room* shot to the number one box office slot after its 2015 release, proving yet again that there is a market for Christian and faith-themed movies.[6]

What's even more remarkable is that rather than making the movie to appeal more broadly to the public at large, filmmaking brothers Stephen and Alex Kendrick told me the movie was intended to specifically meet the needs of Christian audiences; clearly its success proves it did just that.

"We are making movies that are overt, specifically and first for a Christian audience, and we are being very guarded concerning the values and ethics that are being communicated," Stephen Kendrick told *TheBlaze*. "We're making the kind of movies we want to see. I don't like to see movies that trample on my faith."[7]

When I asked Franklin why he thinks it's taken Hollywood so long to come back around to bringing faith themes more fervently into the fold, he said he believes "the business is maturing."[8]

"Now studios are saying, 'Oh, OK, so we understand that if we make a movie for this amount, we can get this kind of return, and there is an audience that wants to see it, and here's how you'll get them,'" he said. "Because it's been tried over and over and over and over again recently, the studios are more open to trying to tap into it." [9]

Franklin also noted that there is currently a dearth of faith-based content on the small screen—something he's hoping to change one day.[10]

All of this in mind, there's something incredibly important to emphasize: if filmmakers like the Kendrick brothers, Franklin, the Erwin brothers (*Moms' Night Out*), Pure Flix Entertainment (*God's Not Dead*), Mark Burnett and Roma Downey (*The Bible* and *AD*), and others didn't take chances on making these films, this resurgence wouldn't be happening. They've engaged the culture to varying degrees, and it's had an impact; that's a lesson for us all.

And with those efforts, there appears to be some turnaround.

"Now you've seen a steady march toward a different world," Movieguide founder Dr. Ted Baehr told me of the changing tides in Hollywood, saying that he sees an "incredible turnaround for the industry." [11]

Again, all that was possible because people were willing to take a chance and produce independent as well as bigger budget movies that had a profound purpose: instilling faith, hope, and values in audiences. So far, not too many faith films have come through the big studio system, though there's hope that more will in the near future.

As for Franklin, he also shared some of the lessons he learned through the successes of *Heaven Is For Real* and *Miracles From Heaven*.

"You have to treat faith movies as big movies. I go back to this," he said. "I try to look at the Bible. God didn't write a faith-based gospel. He wrote a book to help everybody. I try to go into [my films] making my films as universal, as appealing as possible, without watering down the message." [12]

Franklin said he believes this approach works and that the stories that accompany it "can really impact people and touch people." The filmmaker also had a message for his fellow Christians who might criticize Hollywood.[13]

"The person that feels Hollywood is hostile to them...I have not seen that. I haven't experienced that," he said. "But I would say to that person, 'Come be a part of the solution. Don't keep people away from the industry. Help get more people in the industry that are really good at their craft that can be successful.'"[14]

Baehr too offered up his advice to Christians, encouraging them to support good films when they come to theaters and proclaiming that "we need more Christians in Hollywood and less Hollywood in the Christians." But Baehr's advice extended well beyond Tinseltown, as he encouraged parents to "train up the children" well and implored the faithful to have a cultural impact.[15]

"We need to be able to do what you're doing," he told me. "Write books, do accurate reporting, actually expose the fruitless works of darkness, and commend the good. There's a lot of good out there."[16]

There are other shining examples of people who have entered into Hollywood and have had a big impact in the process. Take, for instance, the Robertsons, stars of A&E's *Duck Dynasty*. Their willingness to invite cameras into their lives has brought their beliefs into the mainstream entertainment culture.

In a 2015 interview Korie and Willie Robertson talked to me about fame, faith, and plenty more. At the time they were speaking about their now-defunct *Duck Commander Musical*, which focused on their family's personal story, though the family's broader aim at engaging Hollywood and culture was made clear.

"It's just looking at all these forks in the roads that we came to…and we took the right ones to end up where we are today," Willie said of the musical. "For us, it was just another way to continue to tell our story to try to help people…it's more about glorifying God, and our family will give him the credit for everything we've done."[17]

And it's not only the Robertsons. Famed actress Patricia Heaton, from *Everybody Loves Raymond* and *The Middle*, is a Christian who has used her platform to spread her faith and values. First and foremost, *The Middle* is perhaps the most family friendly show on TV— it's a clean comedy that people can watch with their kids. That's clearly a rarity these days, especially during prime time.

In a 2014 interview Heaton opened up to me about her faith and why she speaks out so passionately against issues such as abortion. The actress said that while she's vocal about her views, it's important for people to pick their battles. "I think you really have to pick your battles and I think you can do so much more as an actor through your creative work than just spouting off your opinions," she said.[18]

But on the abortion front, she said she's among the few people in Tinseltown who discuss the subject, and said she believes she's supposed to do so. "It just bothers me so much. It's almost a natural, it's almost a reflex now," she said. "Once you have kids and you know what it feels like to be pregnant and you know what it feels like to have that person growing inside of you, and the beauty of it, it's just not a holistic thing to do."[19]

There's also Candace Cameron Bure, star of *Full House* and *Fuller House*—a Christian who often shares her views on faith and politics, having had a presence acting on TV and in films, as well as a previous cohosting gig in *The View*. And the list goes on.

HIGHER EDUCATION

As with media and entertainment, universities also need conservatives and Christians to enter classrooms and educate young adults. It's not about imparting or forcing political views, of course; rather it's about engagement and presence—equalizing efforts that offer up a fair and balanced representation. This is the exact point that University of North Texas Professor George Yancey spoke to in an interview for this book after I asked if he believes Christians have contributed in some ways to their lack of influence in Hollywood, media, and university settings.

He cited "cultural institutions, media, academia, arts, entertainment" and noted that Christians have set up "alternate forms" of these paradigms, including Christian entertainment, media, colleges, and the like.[20]

"That's fine and that plays a role, but they've not been willing to—in sufficient numbers, I believe—engage the culture in mainstream media, mainstream academia, mainstream arts, and things of this nature," he said. "Simply having a presence...in my experience, my presence, I think, tapers some of this down."[21]

Citing his own experience in academia, he said his presence makes it harder for people there to ignore their impact on Christians, seeing as he is one. On a broader scale, he said culture drives politics and that this should also be a point of concern for believers, seeing as so many aren't engaged in culture.[22]

"We can't just try to get short-term gains in political power," he said. "We also have to be willing to get some people in there to have an impact on the culture."[23]

With colleges and universities serving as such a powerful cultural battleground, it's important that conservatives and Christians have a presence at religious and secular institutions, alike. Again, this isn't about pushing some sort of indoctrination agenda; it's about having a seat at the table to help balance out the information and to ensure that young students have people from all walks of life helping to educate them.

MEDIA

As is the case with Hollywood and universities, Christians and conservatives have also tragically retreated from media. While we've already discussed some of the resulting pitfalls, there are those who do have a powerful presence in the industry. Among them? Megan Alexander, a correspondent for *Inside Edition*. She's a Christian who frequently and openly talks about her faith, while having a wildly successful career in secular media.

Alexander told me in an interview for this book that she's a passionate storyteller who enjoys meeting new people, relishes in deadlines, and as a result sees media as a viable way to exhibit her skills. "Working in media really gives you a 'front row seat to the world,'" she said.[24]

Alexander has worked for more than a decade in the industry— an informational sphere that doesn't necessarily put a high value on faith—and she said the experience truly "becomes what you make of it."[25]

"Conversation in the secular media does not naturally reflect a lot of the topics that interest me. But I don't find that negative. I appreciate all viewpoints and all religions," she told me. "I just don't think that conversation is naturally going to reflect Christianity. But that does not mean that my experience has been negative."[26]

Alexander acknowledged that her values are different from the beliefs espoused by many of her peers in media, explaining that different ways of looking at the world—and at faith—create a natural divide. "Very few people that I work with consider religion or faith a big part of their life," she continued. "The industry is dominated by folks who no longer go to church, or simply don't see a need for it. Therefore, it becomes difficult to discuss issues of the day through a religious lens, simply because there are fewer people who can relate to this conversation." [27]

But Alexander offered up a message for Christians who feel frustrated and underrepresented in media, entertainment, and university settings: "Do excellent work." She encouraged young people to get out, train hard, and join these venues in an effort to have a broader impact. "Go to the best college possible, and then start working," she said. "People love to 'preach' about changing Hollywood and the media, but few people get involved and work in the industry and try to effect change from the inside." [28]

As for her own career, Alexander sees her platform as an opportunity to have a positive impact on media. "Even though people often believe things are doom and gloom, I see little sparks of life," she said. "I have several friends in high positions of influence in the media who are good people of faith, and like me, they are trying to do their part—relationship by relationship. We have a seat at the table, and that is important. And all we can do is our best." [29]

Over the years Alexander has put her words into action, using her platform at *Inside Edition* to speak on important topics such as abstinence and the challenge of holding on to one's values while working in the secular world. It was in 2014 that Alexander first shared her personal decision to wait until she was married to have sex—a story that immediately sparked intrigue and widespread attention. "It was considered very strange that a national personality would believe in abstinence. So when I shared my story, that got a lot of attention," Alexander said. "It simply is not a common stance anymore. I was proud to speak up because I want young people to know there is another option—that it is perfectly fine to weigh that choice carefully and wait." [30]

She continued, "It worked for me, and I wanted them to know it could work for them. And it was interesting that shows like *Inside Edition* and *Fox News* found the story of abstinence compelling and aired the story; this shows people are still interested in this topic." [31]

But Alexander went above and beyond merely sharing her personal abstinence story, as she also penned a book in 2016 titled *Faith in the Spotlight*—a book that offers people practical advice about how to achieve their dreams while holding on to their faith and values. "There wasn't a book for the young, ambitious woman of faith, (who) has...those big career desires in the secular world, in the corporate world—but still wants to figure out how she can make her family proud and hold true to her faith," Alexander has said of her reasoning for penning the book.[32]

The TV personality also takes some personal steps to live out her values, making it clear that she believes there are some dire cultural issues in media and entertainment. With that in mind, she makes personal and concerted decisions to avoid negative and violent content if possible. "I cringe at how lightly we take morals, values, and faith. People trade their principles and decency for ratings and clicks," she said. "For example, many people love shows like *Game of Thrones* or *House of Cards*, but I personally decided I won't watch them because I think they push the envelope. And I believe people vote with the remote control and the dollar in this country. Even though [*Game of Thrones*] has incredible acting and art and certainly has the fan base (and is) the highest rated show on HBO, they also air graphic nudity and sexual content that I just don't need my eyes to see."[33]

Alexander continued, "It's just not beneficial to my spirit. And not watching sends a message to the producers that it is too much. If enough people did not watch and voiced their opinion, would they make the show more family friendly?"[34]

She said this is one other way she takes a stand for her values, encouraging others to also stand on their own laurels. "I realize my view is not the norm, but one has to take a stand somewhere," she said. "You have to decide what you stand for and be willing to not budge to make a statement. As a journalist, it is my job to report the story, regardless of my personal beliefs. But in my leisure time, I can decide what channel that remote is on and what my eyes will take in."[35]

HOW TO IMPROVE THE SITUATION

With all this in mind, it's clear we have a major cultural problem, as our three main educational spheres are dominated by values that run counter to Christianity and that ofttimes diminish or ignore conservative ideals. So, what's the solution?

In addition to the aforementioned advice other experts offered up, famed Christian apologist Josh McDowell presented a series of steps and parameters he believes people must take seriously if they actually wish to understand and come to grips with the problems we face in modern society.

"One, you've got to be informed," he said before quoting Scripture. "You shall know the truth, and the truth shall set you free" (John 8:32). "Second, you need to come to understand what are rational, physical, sound solutions, answers." [36]

McDowell continued, "See, most Christians can tell me what they believe, but 95 percent can't give me any intelligent reason why they believe it." [37]

He said this dynamic will no longer suffice because people need to be fully aware and cognizant of not only what their values and beliefs are, but why, in fact, they subscribe to such ideals. [38]

"Then, third, we've got to live it," McDowell said. "If we do not live out our faith in our own personal lives, in our marriages, with our children, in our business, in our ministry, whatever—if we don't live out Christ in a vibrant way—then no one is going to believe whatever we say, and they shouldn't." [39]

The fourth and final solution that McDowell offered up is for people to truly learn to listen without interrupting or being judgmental. It's after listening to what people think and feel—particularly nonbelievers—that he said it's possible to more appropriately engage. [40]

It is through these steps that we can begin to understand and fix the problem—or, at the least, have an impact by having a presence in the culture. Being informed, of course, is the first step, as McDowell noted; learning and discerning truth is key.

The evangelist is also right to note that we must recognize and come to grips with the proper answers to fix the problem. Many of the wonderful individuals interviewed for this book advocated becoming journalists, actors, producers, professors, and the like—and I agree. But not all of you are interested in joining those fields, and that's OK.

Either way, one practical solution is for all of us to become more aware of what we're consuming, and to make a concerted effort—like Alexander expressed—to avoid certain forms of negative content; not only are we then protecting our hearts and minds, but we can also send a collective message about what we're willing to tolerate.

At the least, we should all think deeper about the media, entertainment, and university messages we're consuming, and ask some key questions: What am I really being told? What do these themes say about the current state of our society and culture?

I'd argue, perhaps most importantly, we should ask what information is being left out of the equation.

All too often we take in and process messages without considering the information that has perhaps intentionally been left out; it's easy to become so consumed with what is in text or being uttered that we fail or forget to read between the lines. Remembering this can truly help us better judge what it is we're seeing and hearing, and what messages are intentionally being altered and tailored.

Taking these simple steps will help us to "live" our faith and values, as McDowell said. After all, we need to be the shining examples of what we claim to espouse. We can't simply say we're Christians; we need to show it in the way we live, the decisions we make, and the content we choose to consume. Our lives should speak volumes without needing any actual words to convey the powerful message of what we stand for. Personally I've often fallen in this area, as I'm sure we all have. But the stakes are high. Now more than ever we must take a stand, regardless of the uphill ideological battle.

And, finally, I agree with McDowell that we need to listen and engage with others. Rather than battle it out over values, again, show people what it means to live out the truth you espouse.

Don't give up. Make your voices heard, but do so with peace, love, and understanding. The future of free speech—and our nation— depends on it.

NOTES

INTRODUCTION

1. Michael Lipka, "Millennials Increasingly Are Driving Growth of 'Nones,'" Pew Research Center, May 12, 2015, accessed September 7, 2016, http://www.pewresearch.org/fact-tank/2015/05/12/millennials-increasingly-are-driving-growth-of-nones/.

2. Michael Lipka, "Religious 'Nones' Are Not Only Growing, They're Becoming More Secular," Pew Research Center, November 11, 2015, accessed September 7, 2016, http://www.pewresearch.org/fact-tank/2015/11/11/religious-nones-are-not-only-growing-theyre-becoming-more-secular/.

3. "The End of Absolutes: America's New Moral Code," Barna, May 25, 2016, accessed September 7, 2016, https://www.barna.com/research/the-end-of-absolutes-americas-new-moral-code/#.V9AWuZgrLct.

CHAPTER 1: AMERICA'S MORAL MELTDOWN

1. Josh McDowell, in discussion with the author, June 28, 2016.

2. Frank Newport, "Americans Continue to Shift Left on Key Moral Issues," Gallup, May 26, 2015, accessed September 7, 2016, http://www.gallup.com/poll/183413/americans-continue-shift-left-key-moral-issues.aspx?utm_source=liberal&utm_medium=search&utm_campaign=tiles.

3. J. M. Twenge, R. A. Sherman, B. E. Wells, "Changes in American Adults' Sexual Behavior and Attitudes, 1972–2012," Abstract, *Archives of Sexual Behavior* 44, no. 8 (November 2015).

4. "Moral Issues," Gallup, accessed October 24, 2016, http://www.gallup.com/poll/1681/moral-issues.aspx.

5. Newport, "Americans Continue to Shift Left."

6. Ibid.

7. *Merriam-Webster OnLine*, s.v. "tolerance," accessed September 7, 2016, http://www.merriam-webster.com/dictionary/tolerance?utm_campaign=sd&utm_medium=serp&utm_source=jsonld.

8. *Merriam-Webster OnLine*, s.v. "relativism," accessed September 7, 2016, http://www.merriam-webster.com/dictionary/relativism.

9. McDowell, discussion.

10. Ibid.

11. Ibid.

12. Ibid.

13. Ibid.

14. Ibid.

15. Ibid.

16. Newport, "Americans Continue to Shift Left."

17. "The End of Absolutes: America's New Moral Code," Barna, May 25, 2016, accessed September 7, 2016, https://www.barna.com/research/the-end-of-absolutes-americas-new-moral-code/. Used with permission.

18. Ibid.

19. Ibid.

20. Ibid.

21. Ibid.

22. Ibid.

23. Ibid.

24. Betsy Cooper, Daniel Cox, E. J. Dionne Jr., Rachel Lienesch, Robert Jones, and William Galston, "How Immigration and Concerns about Cultural Change Are Shaping the 2016 Election," PRRI, June 23, 2016, accessed September 7, 2016, http://www.prri.org/research/prri-brookings-immigration-report/.

25. Ibid.

CHAPTER 2: WHAT'S REALLY GOING ON WITH OUR CULTURE?

1. "America's Changing Religious Landscape," Pew Research Center, May 12, 2015, accessed September 8, 2016, http://www.pewforum.org/2015/05/12/americas-changing-religious-landscape/.

2. "Real Time With Bill Maher: Christianity Under Attack? – June 5, 2015," YouTube video, 6:07, from a show televised on HBO, accessed September 8, 2016, https://www.youtube.com/watch?v=ybH66U72xd0.

3. Ibid.

4. Ibid.

5. "America's Changing Religious Landscape."

6. George Yancey, in discussion with the author, June 15, 2016.

7. Ibid.

CHAPTER 3: MILLENNIALS: A COMPLEX GENERATION

1. Cooper et al., "Immigration and Concerns about Cultural Change."

2. Richard Fry, "Millennials Overtake Baby Boomers as America's Largest Generation," Pew Research Center, April 25, 2016, accessed September 8, 2016, http://www.pewresearch.org/fact-tank/2016/04/25/millennials-overtake-baby-boomers/; "Millennials: Big Career Goals, Limited Job Prospects," Barna, June 10, 2014, accessed September 8, 2016, http://www.barna.com/research/millennials-big-career-goals-limited-job-prospects/#.V9GLpZgrLcs.

3. "The End of Absolutes."

4. Emily Shire, "Millennials Are Very Mixed up About Sex," *The Daily Beast*, May 6, 2015, accessed September 8, 2016, http://www.thedailybeast .com/articles/2015/05/06/why-aren-t-millennials-sleeping-around.html.

5. Ibid.

6. Ibid; Karen Kaplan, "The Paradox of Millennial Sex: More Casual Hookups, Fewer Partners," *Los Angeles Times*, May 9, 2015, accessed October 25, 2016, http://www.latimes.com/science/sciencenow/la-sci-sn -millennials-sex-attitudes-20150508-story.html.

7. Kaplan, "The Paradox of Millennial Sex"; Beth Downing Chee, "Changing Attitudes About Sex," San Diego State University News Center, May 5, 2015, accessed September 8, 2016, http://newcenter.sdsu.edu/sdsu _newscenter/news_story.aspx?sid=75592.

8. Newport, "Americans Continue to Shift Left."

9. Kaplan, "The Paradox of Millennial Sex."

10. Ibid.

11. Ibid.

12. J. M. Twenge, R. A. Sherman, and B. E. Wells, "Sexual Inactivity During Young Adulthood Is More Common Among U.S. Millennials and iGen: Age, Period, and Cohort Effects on Having No Sexual Partners After Age 18," Abstract, *Archives of Sexual Behavior* (August 2016).

13. Tara Bahrampour, "'There Isn't Really Anything Magical About It': Why More Millennials Are Avoiding Sex," *Washington Post*, August 2, 2016, accessed September 8, 2016, https://www.washingtonpost.com/local /social-issues/there-isnt-really-anything-magical-about-it-why-more -millennials-are-putting-off-sex/2016/08/02/e7b73d6e-37f4-11e6-8f7c -d4c723a2becb_story.html#comments.

14. Ibid.

15. Dave Simpson, "Why Millennials Aren't [Expletive]," Vice, April 27, 2016, accessed September 8, 2016, http://tinyurl.com/gur2r2l.

16. Chrissy Gordon, "Key Findings in Landmark Pornography Study Released," Josh McDowell Ministry, January 19, 2016, accessed September 8, 2016, http://www.josh.org/key-findings-in-landmark-pornography-study -released/.

17. Ibid.

18. Peg Streep, "What Porn Does to Intimacy," Psychology Today, July 16, 2014, accessed September 8, 2016, https://www.psychologytoday.com/blog /tech-support/201407/what-porn-does-intimacy.

19. "Sexual Risk Behaviors: HIV, STD, and Teen Pregnancy Preven-tion," Centers for Disease Control and Prevention, updated July 18, 2016, accessed September 8, 2016, http://www.cdc.gov/healthyyouth/sexual behaviors/; "CDC Fact Sheet: Sexual Risk Behaviors Among U.S. High School Students," CDC, July 2014, accessed October 24, 2016, https://www .cdc.gov/nchhstp/newsroom/docs/factsheets/yrbs-fact-sheet-final-508.pdf.

20. "The End of Absolutes."

21. Richard Fry, "For First Time in Modern Era, Living with Parents Edges Out Other Living Arrangements for 18- to 34-Year-Olds," Pew Research Center, May 24, 2016, accessed September 8, 2016, http://www .pewsocialtrends.org/2016/05/24/for-first-time-in-modern-era-living-with -parents-edges-out-other-living-arrangements-for-18-to-34-year-olds/.

22. Ibid.

23. Ibid.

24. Ibid.

25. Ibid.

26. Ibid.

CHAPTER 4: MILLENNIALS: LOSING THEIR FAITH AND RELIGION

1. "America's Changing Religious Landscape"; Billy Hallowell, "The Most Surprising Statistic in Pew's Massive Study About Americans' Religious Beliefs," TheBlaze, May 13, 2015, accessed September 8, 2016, http:// www.theblaze.com/stories/2015/05/13/researcher-reveals-the-most -surprising-find-in-pews-massive-study-about-americans-religious-beliefs/.

2. "America's Changing Religious Landscape."

3. Ibid.

4. Ibid.

5. Betsy Cooper, Daniel Cox, Rachel Lienesch, and Robert P. Jones, "Exodus: Why Americans Are Leaving Religion—and Why They're Unlikely to Come Back," PRRI, September 22, 2016, accessed October 24, 2016, http://www.prri.org/research/prri-rns-2016-religiously-unaffiliated -americans/.

6. Ibid.

7. Michael Lipka, "Why America's 'Nones' Left Religion Behind," Pew Research Center, August 24, 2016, accessed September 8, 2016, http://www .pewresearch.org/fact-tank/2016/08/24/why-americas-nones-left-religion -behind/.

8. Ibid.

9. Ibid.

10. Hallowell, "The Most Surprising Statistic."

11. Ibid.

12. Ibid.

13. Ed Stetzer, in discussion with the author, June 2016.

14. "America's Changing Religious Landscape."

15. Hallowell, "The Most Surprising Statistic."

16. Ibid.; "The Future of World Religions: Population Growth Projections, 2010–2050," Pew Research Center, April 2, 2015, accessed September 9, 2016, http://www.pewforum.org/2015/04/02/religious-projections-2010 -2050/?utm_source=Pew+Research+Center&utm_campaign=442a1a28e0

-Religion_Weekly_April_2_2015&utm_medium=email&utm_term
=0_3e953b9b70-442a1a28e0-399913745.

17. Cooper, Cox, Lienesch, and Jones, "Exodus."

18. Ibid.

19. Ibid.

20. Stetzer, discussion.

21. Ibid.

22. Ibid.

23. Ibid.

24. Ibid.

25. Ibid.

26. "Millennials and the Bible: 3 Surprising Insights," Barna, October 21, 2014, accessed September 9, 2016, https://www.barna.com/research /millennials-and-the-bible-3-surprising-insights/#.V9LDuZgrLct.

27. Ibid.

CHAPTER 5: TV THEN AND NOW:
HOW THE TIDES HAVE CHANGED

1. Sarah Begley, "90 Percent of Hollywood Political Donations Are Going to Clinton," *TIME*, October 23, 2015, accessed September 9, 2016, http://time.com/4084807/hollywood-political-donors-hillary-clinton/.

2. Barna Group, "What Is Your Opinion of Hollywood's Treatment of Christianity?" survey commissioned by Pure Flix Entertainment, January 28 to February 4, 2016; Billy Hallowell, "Does Hollywood Demean—or Misrepresent—Christianity?" *Deseret News*, July 22, 2016, accessed September 9, 2016, http://www.deseretnews.com/article/865658611/Does -Hollywood-demean-2-or-misrepresent-2-Christianity.html?pg=all.

3. Ibid.

4. Ibid.

5. Erik Adams, Donna Bowman, Phil Dyess-Nugent, Genevieve Koski, Ryan McGee, and Todd VanDerWerff, "More Than 60 Years Ago, a Pregnant Lucille Ball Couldn't Call Herself 'Pregnant,'" AV Club, July 24, 2013, accessed September 9, 2016, http://www.avclub.com/article/more-than-60 -years-ago-a-pregnant-lucille-ball-cou-100629.

6. Michael O'Malley, "Regulating Television," Exploring US History, George Mason University, updated April 2004, accessed September 9, 2016, http://chnm.gmu.edu/exploring/20thcentury/regulatingtelevision/.

7. "'I Love Lucy,' 'Lucy Is Enceinte' More Than 60 Years Later and More Talked About TV Pregnancies," *Huffington Post*, July 25, 2013, accessed September 9, 2016, http://www.huffingtonpost.com/2013/07/25/i-love-lucy -lucy-is-enceinte_n_3652507.html.

8. Kevin Fallon, "How to Get Away With Gayness: Shonda Rhimes Kills TV's Sex Stereotypes," *The Daily Beast*, September 25, 2014, accessed September 9, 2016, http://www.thedailybeast.com/articles/2014/09/25/

how-to-get-away-with-gayness-shonda-rhimes-kills-tv-s-sex-stereotypes
.html.

9. Avery Stone, "Look: Shonda Rhimes Shuts Down Tweeter Who's
Upset With Gay Sex Scenes," *Huffington Post*, October 20, 2014, accessed
September 9, 2016, http://www.huffingtonpost.com/2014/10/20/shonda
-rhimes-shuts-down-anti-gay-tweeter_n_6014902.html.

10. O'Malley, "Regulating Television."

11. "'The Shadow of Incipient Censorship': The Creation of the Television
Code of 1952," History Matters, accessed September 9, 2016, http://
historymatters.gmu.edu/d/6558/.

12. Encyclopedia.com, s.v. "Minow, Newton N.," accessed November 10,
2016, http://www.encyclopedia.com/article-1G2-2687300070/minow
-newton-n.html; "Shadow of Incipient Censorship."

13. "The Television Code of The National Association of Broadcasters,"
fifth edition, The National Association of Broadcasters, March 1959,
accessed September 9, 2016, http://www.tv-signoffs.com/1959_NAB
_Television_Code.pdf.

14. Alessandra Stanley, "The TV Watch; It's a Fact of Life: Prime-Time
Shows Are Getting Sexier," *New York Times*, February 5, 2003, accessed
September 9, 2016, http://www.nytimes.com/2003/02/05/arts/the-tv-watch
-it-s-a-fact-of-life-prime-time-shows-are-getting-sexier.html.

15. Dale Kunkel, Keren Eyal, Keli Finnerty, Erica Biely, and Edward Don-
nerstein, "Sex on TV 4: Introduction," Kaiser Family Foundation, 2005,
accessed September 9, 2016, https://kaiserfamilyfoundation.files.wordpress
.com/2013/01/sex-on-tv-4-full-report.pdf.

16. Billy Hallowell, "Hollywood Critic Issues Warning About What's
Happening With Sex, Violence and Profanity in Entertainment," *TheBlaze*,
November 13, 2014, accessed September 9, 2016, http://www.theblaze.com
/stories/2014/11/13/hollywood-critic-issues-warning-about-whats
-happening-with-sex-violence-and-profanity-in-entertainment/.

17. Kunkel et al., "Sex on TV."

18. Cynthia Littleton, "TV Sex Studies Sparse in Recent Years," *Variety*,
October 8, 2013, accessed September 9, 2016, http://variety.com/2013/biz
/news/tv-sex-studies-sparse-in-recent-years-1200703706/.

19. Hallowell, "Hollywood Critic Issues Warning."

20. Ibid.

21. Ibid.

22. Rebecca Collins, Marc Elliott, Sandra Berry, David Kanouse, Dale
Kunkel, Sarah Hunter, and Angela Miu, "Does Watching Sex on Television
Influence Teens' Sexual Activity?" RAND Corporation, 2004, accessed Sep-
tember 9, 2016, http://www.rand.org/pubs/research_briefs/RB9068.html;
Rebecca Collins, Marc Elliott, Sandra Berry, David Kanouse, Dale Kunkel,
Sarah Hunter, and Angela Miu, "Watching Sex on Television Predicts Ado-
lescent Initiation of Sexual Behavior," *Pediatrics* 114, no. 3 (September

2004): E280–E289, accessed October 24, 2016, http://www.rand.org/pubs
/external_publications/EP20040913.html.

23. Collins et al., "Watching Sex on Television."

24. Elizabeth Landau, "Study Links Sexual Content on TV to Teen Pregnancy," CNN, November 3, 2008, accessed September 9, 2016, http://www
.cnn.com/2008/HEALTH/11/03/teen.pregnancy/.

25. Collins et al., "Watching Sex on Television."

26. "Parents Become Less Sensitive to Violence and Sex in Movies: Study," Annenberg Public Policy Center, October 20, 2014, accessed September 9, 2016, http://www.annenbergpublicpolicycenter.org/parents-become
-desensitized-to-violence-and-sex-in-movies-study-finds/.

27. Ibid.

28. Ibid.

29. Tim Winter, in discussion with the author, June 2016.

30. Ibid.

31. Ibid.

CHAPTER 6: SCRIPTING CULTURE: DRIVING HOME AN AGENDA

1. Robert Lopez and Kristen Anderson-Lopez, "Songwriters Behind 'Frozen' Let Go of the Princess Mythology," transcript of interview by Terry Gross, NPR, April 10, 2014, accessed September 13, 2016, http://www.npr
.org/templates/transcript/transcript.php?storyId=301420227.

2. Ibid.

3. Aly Weisman, "'Frozen' Songwriters Deny that Disney Banned the Word 'God'—Here's the Real Story," *Business Insider*, April 30, 2014, accessed September 13, 2016, http://www.businessinsider.com/frozen
-songwriters-deny-disney-banned-the-word-god-2014-4.

4. Ibid.

5. Victor Luckerson, "Fewer People Than Ever Are Watching TV," *Time*, December 3, 2014, accessed September 13, 2016, http://time.com/3615387
/tv-viewership-declining-nielsen/.

6. Billy Hallowell, "Actor on One of TV's Most Popular Shows Reveals Why He Refused to Take a Picture with Rick Santorum," *TheBlaze*, July 25, 2014, accessed September 13, 2016, http://www.theblaze.com/stories/2014
/07/25/actor-on-one-of-tvs-most-popular-shows-explains-why-he-refused
-to-take-a-picture-with-rick-santorum/.

7. Greg Hernandez, "Modern Family Creator Reluctant to Take Credit for Gay Characters on Other Shows," *Gay Star News*, August 1, 2012, accessed September 13, 2016, http://www.gaystarnews.com/article/modern
-family-creator-reluctant-take-credit-gay-characters-other-shows010812/#gs
.jCwPZZw.

8. Rob Lowman, "Gay-Themed Sitcoms on NBC, CBS Aim for Ratings and Laughs, Not Controversy and Protests," *Los Angeles Daily News*,

August 26, 2012, accessed September 13, 2016, http://www.dailynews.com /arts-and-entertainment/20120826/gay-themed-sitcoms-on-nbc-cbs-aim -for-ratings-and-laughs-not-controversy-and-protests.

9. Winter, discussion.

10. Ibid.

11. Ibid.

12. Ibid.

13. Phil Cooke, in discussion with the author, 2015.

14. Ibid.

15. Ibid.

16. Ted Johnson, "Hollywood Liberals Admit Hollywood Is Liberal," *Variety*, June 1, 2011, accessed September 22, 2016, http://variety.com/2011 /biz/opinion/hollywood-liberals-admit-hollywood-is-liberal-37649/.

17. Primetime Propaganda: Kauffman Says 'Friends" a [Expletive] to the Right Wing," YouTube video, May 28, 2011, accessed October 24, 2016, https://www.youtube.com/watch?v=w5A8VHTyMzg.

18. Winter, discussion.

19. Ibid.

20. Billy Hallowell, "'Moms' Night Out' Director Blasts 'Alarming' Media Reviews Calling Film 'Unabashedly Anti-Feminist' and 'Borderline Dangerous,'" *TheBlaze*, May 13, 2014, accessed September October 24, 2016, http://www.theblaze.com/stories/2014/05/13/director-blasts-alarming -media-reviews-calling-moms-night-out-unabashedly-anti-feminist-and -borderline-dangerous/.

21. Christy Lemire, "Reviews: Moms' Night Out," Roger Ebert, May 9, 2014, accessed September 14, 2016, http://www.rogerebert.com/reviews /moms-night-out-2014.

22. Ibid.

23. Christy Lemire, "Nymphomaniac: Volume I," March 26, 2014, accessed September 14, 2016, http://christylemire.com/nymphomaniac -vol-1/.

24. Abid Rahman, "Lars von Trier: 'I Don't Know if I Can Make Any More Films,'" *Hollywood Reporter*, November 28, 2014, accessed September 14, 2016, http://www.hollywoodreporter.com/news/lars-von-trier-i-dont -752797.

25. Lemire, "Nymphomaniac."

26. Inkoo Kang, "'Moms' Night Out' Review: Unfunny and Anti-Feminist," *The Wrap*, May 5, 2014, accessed September 14, 2016, http:// www.thewrap.com/moms-night-review-unfunny-anti-feminist/.

27. Hallowell, "'Moms' Night Out.'"

28. Ibid.

29. Billy Hallowell, "Something Bizarre Is Going On with This Movie's Rotten Tomatoes Page that Has Stunned Filmmakers Speaking Out," *TheBlaze*, April 28, 2015, accessed October 24, 2016, http://www.theblaze

.com/stories/2015/04/28/theres-something-bizarre-going-on-with-this-faith
-based-movies-rotten-tomatoes-page-that-has-stunned-filmmakers
-speaking-out/.

30. Ibid.

31. Alan Scherstuhl, "Clement's Masterpiece *Forbidden Games* Shows
How Far Films of Faith Have Fallen," *Village Voice*, April 22, 2015,
accessed September 14, 2016, http://www.villagevoice.com/film/clements
-masterpiece-forbidden-games-shows-how-far-films-of-faith-have-fallen
-6444171.

32. Hallowell, "Something Bizarre Is Going On."

CHAPTER 7: MOVIES THEN AND NOW: THE PARADIGM SHIFT

1. *Encyclopaedia Britannica Online*, s.v. "Hays Office," accessed September 12, 2016, https://www.britannica.com/topic/Hays-Office; *Encyclopaedia Britannica Online*, s.v. "Will H. Hays," accessed September 12, 2016, https://www.britannica.com/biography/Will-H-Hays.

2. Bob Mondello, "Remembering Hollywood's Hays Code, 40 Years On,"
NPR, August 8, 2008, accessed September 12, 2016, http://www.npr.org
/templates/story/story.php?storyId=93301189; "Hollywood Censored: The
Production Code," PBS, accessed September 12, 2016, http://www.pbs.org
/wgbh/cultureshock/beyond/hollywood.html.

3. Thomas Doherty, in discussion with the author, August 31, 2016.

4. "Mutual Film Corp. v. Industrial Comm'n of Ohio," Justia, accessed
October 24, 2016, https://supreme.justia.com/cases/federal/us/236/230/.

5. Samantha Barbas, "How the Movies Became Speech," *Rutgers Law
Review* 64, no. 3 (November 2011): 665–745, http://www.rutgerslawreview
.com/wp-content/uploads/archive/vol64/issue3/Barbas.pdf.

6. "Hollywood Censored."

7. Doherty, discussion.

8. Sister Rose, "'Censoring the Silver Screen' a History of the Legion of
Decency," *Patheos*, February 29, 2016, accessed September 12, 2016, http://
www.patheos.com/blogs/sisterrosemovies/2016/02/censoring-the-silver
-screen-a-history-of-the-legion-of-decency/.

9. *Encyclopaedia Britannica Online*, s.v. "Will H. Hays."

10. "Hollywood Censored."

11. "'Complete Nudity Is Never Permitted': The Motion Picture Production Code of 1930," History Matters, accessed September 12, 2016, http://
historymatters.gmu.edu/d/5099/.

12. Sister Rose, "Censoring the Silver Screen."

13. Doherty, discussion.

14. Ibid.

15. Ibid.

16. "Hollywood Censored."

17. Ted Baehr, in discussion with the author, August 5, 2016.

18. Ibid.

19. Jennifer LeClaire, "How a God-Inspired Ministry Helped Redeem Hollywood Movies," Charisma News, May 20, 2014, accessed September 13, 2016, http://www.charismanews.com/culture/43920-how-a-god-inspired -ministry-helped-redeem-hollywood-movies.

20. "National Legion of Decency Collection," Academy of Motion Picture Arts and Sciences, accessed November 11, 2016, http://web.archive .org/web/20070611011921/http://www.oscars.org/mhl/sc/nationall_122.html, quoted in Robert K. Johnston, ed., *Reframing Theology and Film* (Grand Rapids, MI: Baker, 2007), 275. Viewed at Google Books.

21. Doherty, discussion.

22. LeClaire, "God-Inspired Ministry."

23. Baehr, discussion.

24. Ibid.

25. Doherty, discussion.

26. Ibid.

27. Baehr, discussion.

28. Ibid.

29. Ibid.

30. Ibid.

31. Andrew Romano, "Hollywood Declares 2014 the Year of the Bible," *Daily Beast*, January 9, 2014, accessed September 13, 2016, http://www.the dailybeast.com/articles/2014/01/09/hollywood-declares-2014-the-year-of -the-bible.html.

32. Billy Hallowell, "'Some of You, You're Going to Cringe': Honest Assessment of New 'Noah' Movie," *TheBlaze*, February 26, 2014, accessed September 13, 2016, http://www.theblaze.com/stories/2014/02/26/some-of -you-youre-going-to-cringe-insiders-unveil-theological-themes-in-noah -movie/.

33. Ibid.

34. Erica Ritz, "Glenn Beck Saw 'Noah' Over the Weekend, and He's Calling It the 'Babylonian Chainsaw Massacre,'" *TheBlaze*, March 24, 2014, accessed September 13, 2016, http://www.theblaze.com/stories/2014/03/24 /beck-saw-noah-over-the-weekend-and-hes-calling-it-the-babylonian -chainsaw-massacre/.

35. Ibid.

36. "Noah," Paramount Pictures, February 27, 2014, accessed September 13, 2016, http://www.paramount.com/news-and-social-media/news-and -press-releases/noah.

37. Dave Urbanski, "After 'Exodus' Lead Actor Calls Moses 'Schizo- phrenic' and 'Barbaric,' Doubts Loom About Movie's Biblical Message," *TheBlaze*, October 25, 2014, accessed September 13, 2016, http://www

.theblaze.com/stories/2014/10/25/after-exodus-lead-actor-calls-moses
-schizophrenic-and-barbaric-doubts-loom-about-movies-biblical-message/.

38. Erica Ritz, "Beck: New 'Exodus' Movie Makes Moses 'Arrogant'
Before Turning Him Into a 'Terrorist,'" *TheBlaze*, December 15, 2014,
accessed September 13, 2016, http://www.theblaze.com/stories/2014/12/15
/did-exodus-gods-and-kings-turn-moses-into-a-terrorist-glenn-beck
-certainly-thinks-so/.

39. Cooke, in discussion with the author.

40. Ibid.

CHAPTER 8: LYRICAL CONUNDRUM:
MUSIC'S DEVOLVING STATE

1. Madeleine Morgenstern, "There Is Really Nothing *TheBlaze* Can Say
About the Miley Cyrus Performance on MTV Last Night That Will Smith's
Family Didn't Already Say (Update: Actually...)," *TheBlaze*, August 26,
2013, accessed September 14, 2016, http://www.theblaze.com/stories/2013
/08/26/there-is-really-nothing-theblaze-can-say-about-the-miley-cyrus
-performance-on-mtv-last-night-that-will-smiths-family-didnt-already-say/.

2. Bill O'Reilly, "Bill O'Reilly: Miley's 'Act' Demonstrates Bad Parenting
Is Rampant,' *SunSentinel*, August 31, 2013, http://articles.sun-sentinel.com
/2013-08-31/news/fl-bocol-miley-cyrus-oped0831-20130831_1_bad
-parenting-miley-singer-billy-ray-cyrus.

3. Ibid.

4. Kim Keller, "Dear Daughter, Let Miley Cyrus Be a Lesson to You,"
Roadkill Goldfish, accessed September 14, 2016, http://roadkillgoldfish
.com/dear-daughter-let-miley-cyrus-be-a-lesson-to-you/.

5. Ibid.

6. Robert Pace, "Joan Rivers on Miley: 'She Went One Step Too Far,'"
Entertainment Tonight, August 27, 2013, accessed September 14, 2016,
http://www.etonline.com/news/137728_Joan_Rivers_Reacts_to_Miley
_Cyrus_VMAs_Performance/.

7. Pamela LiVecchi, "Why the VMA's Do Matter," PsychCentral,
accessed September 14, 2016, http://blogs.psychcentral.com/resilient-youth
/2013/08/why-the-vmas-do-matter/.

8. Ibid.

9. Ibid.

10. Azadeh Aalai, "Twerk Heard 'Round the World: Miley Cyrus VMA
Goes Too Far," *Psychology Today*, August 27, 2013, accessed September 14,
2016, https://www.psychologytoday.com/blog/the-first-impression/201308
/twerk-heard-round-the-world-miley-cyrus-vma-goes-too-far.

11. Ibid.

12. Sarah Bull, "'It's a Sad Day When Our Kids Can't Even Watch the
Grammys': Beyoncé Slammed By Parents After VERY Risqué Performance,"
Daily Mail, January 27, 2014, accessed September 14, 2016, http://www

.dailymail.co.uk/news/article-2546569/Grammy-Awards-2014-Beyonce
-slammed-concerned-parents-VERY-risque-performance-airs-8pm.html.

13. Ibid.

14. Ibid.

15. Hollie McKay, "Grammys Say 'We Do,' Get Political with Mass Wedding," Fox News, January 27, 2014, accessed September 14, 2016, http://
www.foxnews.com/entertainment/2014/01/27/grammys-get-political-with
-mass-wedding-to-support-same-sex-marriage.html.

16. "Fascinating Graphs Trace How Music Lyrics Have Changed Over the Past 50 Years," *Huffington Post*, February 27, 2014, accessed September 14, 2016, http://www.huffingtonpost.com/2014/02/27/nickolay-lamm_n_4855787.html.

17. Ibid.

18. Ibid.

19. Shane Snow, "This Analysis of the Last 50 Years of Pop Music Reveals Just How Much America Has Changed," Contently, May 7, 2015, accessed September 14, 2016, https://contently.com/strategist/2015/05/07/this
-analysis-of-the-last-50-years-of-pop-music-reveals-just-how-much-america
-has-changed/.

20. Ibid.

21. Ibid.

22. Ibid.

23. "Violent Music Lyrics Increase Aggressive Thoughts and Feelings, According to New Study," American Psychological Association, May 4, 2003, accessed September 15, 2016, http://www.apa.org/news/press/releases
/2003/05/violent-songs.aspx.

24. Tara Parker-Pope, "Under the Influence of…Music?" *New York Times*, February 5, 2008, accessed September 15, 2016, http://well.blogs
.nytimes.com/2008/02/05/under-the-influence-ofmusic/?_r=2&mtrref
=undefined.

25. Ibid.

26. Council on Communications and Media, "Policy Statement—Impact of Music, Music Lyrics, and Music Videos on Children and Youth," *Pediatrics* 124, no. 5 (November 2009): 1488–1494, http://pediatrics.aap
publications.org/content/pediatrics/early/2009/10/19/peds.2009-2145.1.full
.pdf.

27. Ibid.

28. Ibid., 1491.

29. Council on Communications and Media, "Children, Adolescents, and the Media," *Pediatrics* 132, no. 5 (November 2013): 958–961, http://
pediatrics.aappublications.org/content/132/5/958.

30. Council on Communications and Media, "Sexuality, Contraception, and the Media," *Pediatrics* 126, no. 3 (September 2010): 576–582, http://
pediatrics.aappublications.org/content/126/3/576.full.

CHAPTER 9: THE GREATEST IRONY OF OUR AGE

1. Yancey, discussion.
2. Ibid.
3. Ibid.
4. Ibid.
5. Ibid.
6. Ibid.
7. Kevin Eagan, Ellen Bara Stolzenberg, Jennifer Berdan Lozano, Melissa C. Aragon, Maria Ramirez Suchard, and Sylvia Hurtado, "Undergraduate Teaching Faculty: The 2013–2014 HERI Faculty Survey," Higher Education Research Institute at UCLA, 2014, accessed September 15, 2016, http://heri.ucla.edu/monographs/HERI-FAC2014-monograph.pdf.
8. Alexander W. Astin, William S. Korn, and Eric L. Dey, "The American College Teacher: National Norms for the 1989–90 HERI Faculty Survey," Higher Education Research Institute, March 1991, accessed September 15, 2016, http://www.heri.ucla.edu/PDFs/pubs/FAC/Norms/Monographs/TheAmericanCollegeTeacher1989To1990.pdf.
9. Eagan et al., "Undergraduate Teaching Faculty," 39.
10. Nicholas Kristof, "A Confession of Liberal Intolerance," *New York Times*, May 7, 2016, accessed September 15, 2016, http://www.nytimes.com/2016/05/08/opinion/sunday/a-confession-of-liberal-intolerance.html?_r=1.
11. Ibid.
12. Ibid.
13. Ibid.
14. Kevin Eagan, Ellen Bara Stolzenberg, Abigail K. Bates, Melissa C. Aragon, Maria Ramirez Suchard, and Cecilia Rios-Aguilar, "The American Freshman: National Norms Fall 2015," Cooperative Institutional Research Program, 2016, accessed September 15, 2016, http://www.heri.ucla.edu/monographs/TheAmericanFreshman2015.pdf.
15. Ibid.
16. Ibid.
17. Ibid.
18. Ibid.

CHAPTER 10: CAMPUS CHAOS RAGES

1. Meghan Holden, "Safe Space vs. Free-Speech Debate Continues," *Lafayette Journal & Courier*, August 29, 2016, accessed September 15, 2016, http://www.jconline.com/story/news/college/2016/08/27/safe-spaces-vs-free-speech-debate-continues/89404294/.
2. Colleen Flaherty, "Trigger Warning Skepticism," Inside Higher Ed, December 2, 2015, accessed September 15, 2016, https://www.insidehighered.com/news/2015/12/02/survey-sheds-new-light-faculty-attitudes-and-experiences-toward-trigger-warnings.

3. Alan Levinovitz, "How Trigger Warnings Silence Religious Students," *Atlantic*, August 30, 2016, accessed September 15, 2016, http://www.theatlantic.com/politics/archive/2016/08/silencing-religious-students-on-campus/497951/.

4. Ibid.

5. Ibid.

6. Ibid.

7. Holden, "Safe Space."

8. German Lopez, "What the Conservative Caricature of 'Safe Spaces' Gets Wrong," Vox, updated August 29, 2016, accessed September 15, 2016, http://www.vox.com/2016/8/29/12684042/safe-spaces-college-university.

9. Kevin Gannon's Twitter page, August 28, 2016, accessed September 15, 2016, https://twitter.com/TheTattooedProf/status/769901373760516097.

10. Nina Burleigh, "The Battle Against 'Hate Speech' on College Campuses Gives Rise to a Generation that Hates Speech," *Newsweek*, May 26, 2016, accessed September 15, 2016, http://www.newsweek.com/2016/06/03/college-campus-free-speech-thought-police-463536.html.

11. Ibid.

12. Derald Wing Sue, *Psychology Today*, November 17, 2010, accessed September 15, 2016, https://www.psychologytoday.com/blog/microaggressions-in-everyday-life/201011/microaggressions-more-just-race.

13. Eugene Volokh, "The University of California, 'Microaggressions,' and Supposedly Anti-Semitic Criticism of Israel," *Washington Post*, August 31, 2015, accessed September 15, 2016, https://www.washingtonpost.com/news/volokh-conspiracy/wp/2015/08/31/the-university-of-california-microaggressions-and-supposedly-anti-semitic-criticism-of-israel/?utm_term=.077225880d12.

14. Eugene Volokh, "UC Teaching Faculty Members not to Criticize Race-Based Affirmative Action, Call America 'Melting Pot,' and More," *Washington Post*, June 16, 2015, accessed September 15, 2016, https://www.washingtonpost.com/news/volokh-conspiracy/wp/2015/06/16/uc-teaching-faculty-members-not-to-criticize-race-based-affirmative-action-call-america-melting-pot-and-more/?utm_term=.59501030219d.

15. Jason Howerton, "University of North Carolina Releases List of 'Hostile' So-Called 'Microaggressions'—Check Out the No. 4 Category," *TheBlaze*, June 25, 2016, accessed September 15, 2016, http://www.theblaze.com/stories/2016/06/25/university-of-north-carolina-releases-list-of-hostile-so-called-microaggressions-check-out-the-no-4-category/.

16. L. V. Anderson, "U. Chicago Sent Incoming Freshmen a Letter Decrying Safe Spaces and Trigger Warnings," *Slate*, August 25, 2016, accessed September 23, 2016, http://www.slate.com/blogs/xx_factor/2016/08/25/the_university_of_chicago_sent_incoming_freshmen_a_letter_decrying_safe.html.

17. Ibid.

18. "Liberals to Outnumber Conservative Graduation Speakers 4-to-1," Campus Reform, May 5, 2016, accessed September 15, 2016, http://www.campusreform.org/?ID=7554.

19. Josh Logue, "Another Speaker Blocked," Inside Higher Ed, February 24, 2016, accessed September 15, 2016, https://www.insidehighered.com/news/2016/02/24/cal-state-los-angeles-cancels-conservative-speakers-appearance.

20. Ibid.

21. Josh Logue, "Cal State LA Ends Ban on Speaker's Appearance," Inside Higher Ed, February 26, 2016, accessed September 15, 2016, https://www.insidehighered.com/quicktakes/2016/02/26/cal-state-la-ends-ban-speakers-appearance.

22. Ben Shapiro, in discussion with the author, August 31, 2016.

23. Emily Zanotti, "University of Michigan Cancels Plan to Help Students 'Cope' With Trump Using Coloring Books, Play-Doh and Bubbles," HeatStreet, November 14, 2016, accessed November 28, 2016, http://heatst.com/culture-wars/u-of-michigan-cancels-plan-to-help-students-cope-with-trump-using-coloring-books-play-doh-and-bubbles/.

24. Melissa Korn and Douglas Belkin, "Colleges Try to Comfort Students Upset by Trump Victory," *Wall Street Journal*, November 9, 2016, accessed November 28, 2016, http://blogs.wsj.com/washwire/2016/11/09/colleges-try-to-comfort-students-upset-by-trump-victory/.

25. Catherine Rampell, "Liberal Intolerance Is on the Rise on America's College Campuses," *Washington Post,* February 11, 2016, accessed September 15, 2016, https://www.washingtonpost.com/opinions/liberal-but-not-tolerant-on-the-nations-college-campuses/2016/02/11/0f79e8e8-d101-11e5-88cd-753e80cd29ad_story.html?utm_term=.47870a811e63.

26. Rampell, "Liberal Intolerance"; Eagan et al., "The American Freshman."

27. Rampell, "Liberal Intolerance."

CHAPTER 11: THE RISE OF COLLEGES' ALL-COMERS POLICIES

1. "Nondiscrimination FAQ," Vanderbilt University, accessed September 16, 2016, http://vanderbilt.edu/about/nondiscrimination/faq.php.

2. Ibid.

3. Ibid.

4. Billy Hallowell, "Is Vanderbilt University Denying Religious Freedom to Christian Groups on Campus?" *TheBlaze*, September 26, 2011, accessed September 16, 2016, http://www.theblaze.com/stories/2011/09/26/is-vanderbilt-university-denying-religious-freedom-to-christian-groups-on-campus/.

5. Ed Stetzer, "InterVarsity 'Derecognized' at California State University's 23 Campuses: Some Analysis and Reflections," *Christianity Today,*

September 6, 2014, accessed September 16, 2016, http://www.christianity-today.com/edstetzer/2014/september/intervarsity-now-derecognized-in-california-state-universit.html.

6. Stetzer, discussion.

7. Ibid.

8. John Inazu, "The Perverse Effects of the 'All Comers' Requirement," September 15, 2014, accessed September 16 2016, http://www.libertylawsite.org/2014/09/15/the-perverse-effects-of-the-all-comers-requirement/.

9. Lyle Denniston, "Analysis: A Fatal Stipulation," SCOTUSblog, June 28, 2010, accessed September 16, 2016, http://www.scotusblog.com/2010/06/analysis-a-fatal-stipulation/.

10. Ibid.; "Campus Challenges," InterVarsity, accessed September 16, 2016, http://intervarsity.org/page/campus-challenges.

11. Memorandum from Charles B. Reed, Chancellor, to CSU Presidents, December 21, 2011, https://www.calstate.edu/eo/EO-1068.html.

12. Kaitlyn Schallhorn, "Christian Club Finally Allowed on California State College Campuses Again," *TheBlaze*, June 20, 2015, accessed September 16, 2016, http://www.theblaze.com/stories/2015/06/20/christian-club-finally-allowed-on-college-campuses-again/.

13. Gregory Jao, in discussion with the author, 2015.

14. Ibid.

15. Ibid.

16. "California State University System," InterVarsity, updated June 19, 2015, accessed September 16, 2016, http://intervarsity.org/page/california-state-university-system.

17. Jao, discussion.

18. Ibid.

19. Ibid.

20. Jeremy Weber, "InterVarsity Regains Access to Cal State Campuses," *Christianity Today*, June 19, 2015, accessed September 16, 2016, http://www.christianitytoday.com/gleanings/2015/june/intervarsity-regains-access-cal-state-campuses.html?start=2.

21. Jao, discussion.

22. Ibid.

23. Ibid.

24. Ibid.

25. Ibid.

26. Yancey, discussion.

27. Ibid.; "Disparate Impact," Legal Information Institute, Cornell University Law School, accessed October 25, 2016, https://www.law.cornell.edu/wex/disparate_impact.

28. Yancey, discussion.

29. David French, in discussion with the author, July 9, 2015.

30. Ibid.

31. Ibid.

32. Ibid.

33. Ibid.

34. Ibid.

35. Billy Hallowell, "See Christian Students Slamming Vanderbilt's Religious Crackdown: 'They're…Asking Us to Deny Our Faith,'" *TheBlaze*, February 3, 2012, accessed September 16, 2016, http://www.theblaze.com /stories/2012/02/03/see-christian-students-slamming-vanderbilts-religious -crackdown-theyre-asking-us-to-deny-our-faith/.

36. Tennessee General Assembly HB0534, accessed November 13, 2016, http://wapp.capitol.tn.gov/apps/BillInfo/Default.aspx?BillNumber =HB0534&ga=108.

37. Associated Press, "Haslam to Veto College Discrimination Policy Bill," NBC12, accessed October 25, 2016, http://www.nbc12.com/story/18065735 /haslam-to-veto-college-discrimination-policy-bill.

38. Annalisa Musarra, "Vanderbilt Christian Groups, Citing Religious Freedom, Follow Catholics Off Campus," *Huffington Post*, April 10, 2012, accessed September 16, 2016, http://www.huffingtonpost.com/2012/04/10 /vanderbilt-religious-groups_n_1416561.html.

39. French, discussion.

40. Ibid.

41. Ibid.

42. Yancey, discussion.

43. Ibid.

44. Ibid.

45. Ibid.

CHAPTER 12: THE TRUE IMPACT ON ACADEMIA

1. David French, discussion.

2. Heather Rudow, "Resolution of EMU Case Confirms ACA Code of Ethics, Counseling Profession's Stance Against Client Discrimination," *Counseling Today*, January 9, 2013, accessed September 16, 2016, http:// ct.counseling.org/2013/01/resolution-of-emu-case-confirms-aca-code-of -ethics-counseling-professions-stance-against-client-discrimination/.

3. Oppenheimer, "A Counselor's Convictions Put Her Profession on Trial," *New York Times*, February 3, 2012, accessed September 16, 2016, http://www.nytimes.com/2012/02/04/us/when-counseling-and-conviction -collide-beliefs.html?_r=1.

4. Rudow, "Resolution of EMU Case."

5. Katrease Stafford, "EMU Resolves Case of Julea Ward, Former Student Kicked Out of Program for Declining to Counsel Gay Client, *Ann Arbor News*, December 10, 2012, accessed September 16, 2016, http://www .annarbor.com/news/ypsilanti/emu-resolves-case-of-julea-ward-former -student-kicked-out-of-program-for-declining-to-counsel-gay-cl/;

Oppenheimer, "A Counselor's Convictions"; "Ward v. Polite," Alliance Defending Freedom, accessed September 16, 2016, http://www.adflegal.org /detailspages/case-details/ward-v.-polite#Alliance+Defending+Freedom %2C.

6. Walter Kraft, "Resolution of Julea Ward Case Leaves Programs, Policies Intact at Eastern Michigan University," Eastern Michigan University, December 10, 2012, accessed September 16, 2016, http://www.emich.edu /univcomm/releases/release.php?id=1355161741.

7. Ibid.

8. Jeremy Tedesco, "The Julea Ward Settlement: A Win for Religious Liberty," Townhall, January 4, 2013, accessed September 16, 2016, http:// townhall.com/columnists/jeremytedesco/2013/01/04/the-julea-ward -settlement—a-win-for-religious-liberty-n1478423.

9. Ibid.

10. Ibid.

11. CNN Wire Staff, "Student: University Wants Her to Change 'Biblical Views' on Gays, CNN, July 28, 2010, accessed September 16, 2016, http:// www.cnn.com/2010/US/07/28/georgia.gay.sensitivity.training/.

12. Ibid; Joshua Rhett Miller, "Lawsuit Claims College Ordered Student to Alter Religious Views on Homosexuality, Or Be Dismissed," Fox News, July 27, 2010, accessed October 25, 2016, http://www.foxnews.com/us/2010 /07/27/georgia-university-tells-student-lose-religion-lawsuit-claims.html.

13. "Jennifer Keeton," Alliance Defending Freedom," accessed October 25, 2016, https://www.adflegal.org/detailspages/client-stories-details/jen-keeton.

14. CNN Wire Staff, "Student: University Wants Her to Change 'Biblical Views' on Gays"; Scott Jaschik, "New Loss for Anti-Gay Student," Inside Higher Ed, June 27, 2012, accessed September 16, 2016, https://www.inside highered.com/news/2012/06/27/judge-rejects-anti-gay-students-suit-against -augusta-state.

15. CNN Wire Staff, "Student: University Wants Her to Change 'Biblical Views' on Gays."

16. Stoyan Zaimov, "Georgia Student Counselor Fired for Religious Views on Homosexuality Loses Case," Christian Post, June 28, 2012, http:// www.christianpost.com/news/ga-student-counselor-fired-for-religious -views-on-homosexuality-loses-case-77377/.

17. French, discussion.

18. Julea Ward v. Roy Wilbanks et al., No. 10-2100, 2011, http://www .counseling.org/resources/pdfs/EMUamicusbrief.pdf.

19. "An Explanation of Gordon College's Policy on Homosexuality," Gordon College, accessed September 16, 2016, http://www.gordon.edu /download/galleries/An%20Explanation%20of%20Gordon%20College's%20 Policy%20on%20Homosexuality1.pdf.

20. Michael Gryboski, "Massachusetts City Terminates Contract With Christian College Over Its Stance on Homosexuality," Christian Post, July

14, 2014, accessed September 16, 2016, http://www.christianpost.com/news /massachusetts-city-ends-contract-with-christian-college-over-its-stance -on-homosexuality-123220/.

21. Ibid.

22. Ibid.

23. D. Michael Lindsay, interview by Billy Hallowell, "Ep. 9: Way, Way, Way Too Much Time on Our Hands," *The Church Boys*, *TheBlaze*, podcast audio, March 16, 2015, accessed October 26, 2016, https://soundcloud.com /thechurchboys/ep-9-way-way-way-too-much-time-on-our-hands.

24. Ibid.

25. Ibid.

26. Ibid.

27. Ibid.

28. Ibid.

29. Ibid.

30. "Behavioral Standards," Gordon College, accessed September 16, 2016, http://www.gordon.edu/page.cfm?iPageID=380&About&Behavioral _Expectations.

31. D. Michael Lindsay, interview by Billy Hallowell; John Hanc, "Gay Issues Enter the World of Philanthropy," *New York Times*, November 2, 2015, http://www.nytimes.com/2015/11/08/giving/gay-issues-enter-the -world-of-philanthropy.html.

32. D. Michael Lindsay, interview by Billy Hallowell.

33. "Joint Statement by Gordon College and the Commission on Institutions of Higher Education, NEASC," New England Association of Schools & Colleges, Inc. Commission on Institutions of Higher Education, April 25, 2015, accessed September 16, 2016, https://cihe.neasc.org/sites/cihe.neasc .org/files/downloads/Public_Statement/Joint_Statement_by_Gordon _College_and_CIHE.pdf.

34. French, discussion.

35. Ibid.

36. Samuel Smith, "Christian Colleges' Right to Deny Married Housing for Gay Couples Is 'on the Edge of the Indefensible,' Barry Lynn Asserts," *Christian Post*, July 7, 2015, accessed September 19, 2016, http://www .christianpost.com/news/christian-colleges-right-to-deny-married-housing -for-gay-couples-is-on-the-edge-of-the-indefensible-barry-lynn-asserts -141265/.

37. Bob Jones University v. United States, 461 U.S. 574 (1983), Legal Information Institute, Cornell University Law School, accessed September 19, 2016, https://www.law.cornell.edu/supremecourt/text/461/574#writing -USSC_CR_0461_0574_ZO.

38. Brian McVicar, "How Gay Marriage Ruling May Impact Christian Colleges," *Grand Rapids Press*, July 2, 2015, accessed September 19, 2016, http://www.mlive.com/news/grand-rapids/index.ssf/2015/07/how_gay

_marriage_ruling_may_im.html; Billy Hallowell, "Are Christian Colleges Activists' Next Target Following Gay Marriage Legalization?," *TheBlaze*, July 8, 2015, accessed September 19, 2016, http://www.theblaze.com /stories/2015/07/08/are-christian-colleges-activists-next-target-following -gay-marriage-legalization/.

39. Billy Hallowell, "'We Are Entering a Cultural Civil War': Lawyer's Warning About 'Assault Against Christians'—and His Message for the Supreme Court," *TheBlaze*, July 14, 2015, accessed September 19, 2016, http://www.theblaze.com/stories/2015/07/14/we-are-entering-a-cultural -civil-war-lawyer-warns-about-assault-against-christians-and-he-has-a -message-for-the-supreme-court/.

CHAPTER 13: THE MEDIA PARADOX: IGNORANCE VERSUS INTENTIONALITY

1. Nick Wing, "Sarah Palin Goes on Offense Against Lamestream Media: 'Reload Or White Flag?'" *Huffington Post*, May 25, 2011, accessed September 19, 2016, http://www.huffingtonpost.com/2011/03/25/sarah-palin -reloads-lamestream-media_n_840490.html.

2. "Lamestream Media: Reload or White Flag?" Sarah Palin's Facebook page, March 24, 2011, accessed September 19, 2016, https://www.facebook .com/note.php?note_id=10150119801048435.

3. Dylan Byers, "2016 Republicans vs. the Media," CNN, October 29, 2015, accessed September 19, 2016, http://www.cnn.com/2015/10/28/politics /republican-debate-media/.

4. Ibid.

5. Susan Jones, "Rubio Critical of 'Bias that Exists in the American Media Today," CNSNews.com, October 29, 2015, accessed September 19, 2016, http://www.cnsnews.com/news/article/susan-jones/rubio-critical-bias -exists-american-media-today.

6. Jordan Chariton, "Carly Fiorina Blasts 'Liberal Media' Double Standard over Hillary Clinton Supporter Threatening to Strangle Her," *The Wrap*, November 12, 2015, accessed September 19, 2016, http://www .thewrap.com/carly-fiorina-blasts-liberal-media-double-standard-over -hillary-clinton-supporter-threatening-to-strangle-her-video/.

7. Dylan Byers, "Fiorina Takes On the Washington Post," CNN, October 6, 2015, accessed September 19, 2016, http://www.cnn.com/2015/10/06 /politics/carly-fiorina-washington-post/.

8. "MRC/YouGov Poll: Most Voters Saw, Rejected News Media Bias," NewsBusters, November 15, 2016, accessed November 28, 2016, http://www .newsbusters.org/blogs/nb/nb-staff/2016/11/15/mrcyougov-poll-most-voters -saw-rejected-news-media-bias.

9. Paul Farhi, "How Biased Are the Media, Really?" *Washington Post*, April 27, 2012, accessed September 19, 2016, https://www.washingtonpost

.com/lifestyle/style/how-biased-is-the-media-really/2012/04/27/gIQA
9jYLmT_story.html.

10. Jack Mirkinson, "Mitt Romney: 'Vast Left Wing Conspiracy' Against
Me in the Media," *Huffington Post*, April 18, 2012, accessed September 19,
2016, http://www.huffingtonpost.com/2012/04/18/mitt-romney-vast-left
-wing-conspiracy-media_n_1433913.html.

11. Rose French, "Evangelicals Say They're Not Represented in Newsrooms," *USA Today*, October 21, 2008, accessed September 19, 2016, http://
usatoday30.usatoday.com/news/religion/2008-10-20-evangelical-journalists
_N.htm.

12. "PEJ Renamed Pew Research Center's Journalism Project," Pew
Research Center, October 3, 2013, accessed September 19, 2016, http://www
.pewresearch.org/2013/10/03/pej-renamed-as-pew-research-centers
-journalism-project/.

13. "The Web: Alarming, Appealing and a Challenge to Journalistic
Values," Project for Excellence in Journalism, Pew Research Center, March
17, 2008, accessed September 19, 2016, http://www.stateofthemedia.org
/files/2011/01/Journalist-report-2008.pdf.

14. Ibid.

15. Lydia Saad, "Conservatives Hang On to Ideology Lead by a Thread,"
Gallup, January 11, 2016, accessed September 19, 2016, http://www.gallup
.com/poll/188129/conservatives-hang-ideology-lead-thread.aspx.

16. Lars Willnat and David H. Weaver, "The American Journalist in the
Digital Age: Key Findings," School of Journalism, Indiana University, 2014,
accessed September 19, 2016, http://news.indiana.edu/releases/iu/2014/05
/2013-american-journalist-key-findings.pdf.

17. Ibid.

18. French, "Evangelicals Say They're Not Represented in Newsrooms,"
USA Today.

19. "Pre-Employment Inquiries and Religious Affiliation or Beliefs," U.S.
Equal Employment Opportunity Commission, accessed September 19,
2016, https://www.eeoc.gov/laws/practices/inquiries_religious.cfm.

20. French, "Evangelicals."

21. Ibid.

22. Andrew Beaujon, "There's No Good Data on How Many Christians
Are in Newsrooms," Poynter, April 12, 2013, accessed September 19, 2016,
http://www.poynter.org/2013/theres-no-good-data-on-how-many-christians
-are-in-newsrooms/210127/.

23. Matt K. Lewis, "Why Newspapers Need to Hire More Christians,"
The Week, April 12, 2013, accessed September 19, 2016, http://theweek.com
/articles/465626/why-newspapers-need-hire-more-christians. Used with
permission.

24. Ibid.

25. Ibid.

26. Ibid.

27. David Shaw, "Journalists' Skepticism Hinders Religion Coverage," *Los Angeles Times*, February 23, 2003, accessed September 19, 2016, http://articles.latimes.com/2003/feb/23/entertainment/ca-shaw23.

28. Ibid.

29. French, "Evangelicals."

CHAPTER 14: IS THERE PROOF THE MEDIA ARE BIASED?

1. David Gregory, interview by Billy Hallowell, *The Church Boys*.

2. Ibid.; Robert Scheer, "With God on His Side...," *Los Angeles Times*, April 20, 2004, accessed September 19, 2016, http://articles.latimes.com/2004/apr/20/opinion/oe-scheer20.

3. Gregory, interview.

4. Gabriel Sherman, "Q&A: David Gregory On Losing His Dream Job, Brian Williams, and His New Book About Faith," *New York*, September 9, 2015, accessed September 19, 2016, http://nymag.com/daily/intelligencer/2015/09/david-gregory-nbc-brian-williams-faith.html.

5. Ibid.

6. David Brody, "Luke Russert Tells Brody File: Media Is Biased Against People of Faith," CBN, video, accessed September 19, 2016.

7. Ibid.

8. Ibid.

9. Keach Hagey and Nick Niedzwiadek, "CNN Enjoys Outsize Ratings Boost from Presidential Race," *Wall Street Journal*, May 1, 2016, accessed September 19, 2016, http://www.wsj.com/articles/cnn-enjoys-outsize-ratings-boost-from-presidential-race-1462126349.

10. Ibid.

11. Michael Calderone, "JournoList: Inside the Echo Chamber," Politico, March 17, 2009, accessed September 19, 2016, http://www.politico.com/story/2009/03/journolist-inside-the-echo-chamber-020086.

12. Howard Kurtz, "Washington Post Blogger David Weigel Resigns After Messages Leak," *Washington Post*, June 26, 2010, accessed September 19, 2016, http://www.washingtonpost.com/wp-dyn/content/article/2010/06/25/AR2010062504413.html.

13. Jonathan Strong, "Documents Show Media Plotting to Kill Stories About Rev. Jeremiah Wright," *The Daily Caller*, July 20, 2010, accessed January 6, 2017, http://dailycaller.com/2010/07/20/documents-show-media-plotting-to-kill-stories-about-rev-jeremiah-wright/.

14. Patrik Jonsson, "JournoList: Is 'Call Them Racists' a Liberal Media Tactic?" Christian Science Monitor, July 20, 2010, accessed September 19, 2016, http://www.csmonitor.com/USA/Politics/2010/0720/JournoList-Is-call-them-racists-a-liberal-media-tactic.

15. Ibid.

16. "Confidence in Institutions," Gallup, 2016, accessed September 19, 2016, http://www.gallup.com/poll/1597/confidence-institutions.aspx.

17. Ibid.

18. Ibid.

19. "The 2016 State of the First Amendment," Newseum Institute, 2016, accessed September 19, 2016, http://www.newseuminstitute.org/wp-content/uploads/2016/06/FAC_SOFA16_report.pdf.

20. Rebecca Riffkin, "Americans' Trust in Media Remains at Historical Low," Gallup, September 28, 2015, accessed September 19, 2016, http://www.gallup.com/poll/185927/americans-trust-media-remains-historical-low.aspx.

21. Ibid.

22. Art Swift, "Americans' Trust in Mass Media Sinks to New Low," Gallup, September 14, 2016, accessed October 25, 2016, http://www.gallup.com/poll/195542/americans-trust-mass-media-sinks-new-low.aspx.

23. "Three-Fourths of Americans Think News Organizations Keep Political Leaders in Line but Nearly the Same Portion Say News Media Are Biased," Pew Research Center, July 6, 2016, accessed September 19, 2016, http://www.journalism.org/2016/07/07/the-modern-news-consumer/pj_2016-07-07_modern-news-consumer_2-02/.

24. Riffkin, "Americans' Trust in Media"; Swift, "Trust in Mass Media."

25. Ibid.

26. Ibid.

27. Justin McCarthy, "Trust in Mass Media Returns to All-Time Low," Gallup, September 17, 2014, accessed September 19, 2016, http://www.gallup.com/poll/176042/trust-mass-media-returns-time-low.aspx.

28. Ibid.

29. Ibid.

30. Tim Groseclose, in discussion with the author, June 13, 2016.

31. Tim Groseclose, *Left Turn: How Liberal Media Bias Distorts the American Mind* (New York: St. Martin's, 2011), vii.

32. Groseclose, discussion.

33. Ibid.

34. Robert J. Barro, "Bias Beyond a Reasonable Doubt," *Weekly Standard*, December 13, 2004, accessed September 19, 2016, http://www.weeklystandard.com/bias-beyond-a-reasonable-doubt/article/6208; Tim Groseclose and Jeff Milyo, "A Measure of Media Bias," September 2003, accessed October 26, 2016, http://itre.cis.upenn.edu/~myl/GrosecloseMilyo.pdf.

35. Groseclose, *Left Turn*, vii.

36. Ibid., ix.

37. Ibid.

CHAPTER 15: HOW WE GET HERE

1. Chris Field, in discussion with the author, August 19, 2016.

2. Ibid.

3. Ibid.

4. Ibid.

5. Ibid.

6. Ibid.

7. Scott Baker, in discussion with the author, August 16, 2016.

8. Ibid.

9. Ibid.

10. Ibid.

11. Ibid.

12. Field, discussion.

13. Ibid.

14. Ibid.

15. Baker, discussion.

16. Ibid.

17. Field, discussion.

18. Baker, discussion.

19. Ibid.

20. Ibid.

21. Field, discussion.

22. Ibid.

23. Baker, discussion.

CHAPTER 16: IS FREE SPEECH UNDER ATTACK?

1. Eugene Volokh, in discussion with the author, August 15, 2016.

2. "Miss California Carrie Prejean In Your Face Perez Hilton," YouTube video, originally aired on NBC on April 19, 2009, accessed September 20, 2016, https://www.youtube.com/watch?v=OF-ZdVK69jo.

3. Ibid.

4. "Marriage," Gallup, accessed September 20, 2016, http://www.gallup.com/poll/117328/marriage.aspx.

5. Gina DiNunno, "Did Miss California's Anti-Gay Marriage Answer Cost Her the Crown?" *TV Guide*, April 21, 2009, accessed September 20, 2016, http://www.tvguide.com/news/miss-california-perez-1005266/.

6. Carrie Prejean, in discussion with the author, August 11, 2016.

7. Ibid.

8. Ibid.

9. Ibid.

10. Ibid.

11. Ibid.

12. Ibid.

13. Ibid.

14. Ibid.

15. Ibid.

16. "Perez Hilton Calls Miss California a 'Dumb [Expletive],'" YouTube Video, April 21, 2009, accessed September 20, 2016, https://www.youtube.com/watch?v=NMYP9opfMfI.

17. Luchina Fisher, "Perez Hilton 'Floored' by Miss California," ABC News, April 20, 2009, accessed September 20, 2016, http://abcnews.go.com/Entertainment/Television/story?id=7381893&page=1.

18. Prejean, discussion.

19. Ibid.

20. Roland Martin, "Commentary: Miss California, Thanks for Being Honest," CNN, April 22, 2009, accessed September 20, 2016, http://www.cnn.com/2009/POLITICS/04/22/martin.miss.california/.

21. Ibid.

22. Ibid.

23. Prejean, discussion.

24. Ibid.

25. Ibid.

26. Volokh, discussion.

27. Ibid.

28. Ibid.

CHAPTER 17: RELIGIOUS FREEDOM BATTLES ABOUND

1. Phil Robertson, interview with Stephen Bannon, *Breitbart News Daily*, https://soundcloud.com/breitbart/sets/breitbart-news-daily-july-22.

2. Ibid.

3. Ravi Zacharias, "The Soul of America," Ravi Zacharias International Ministries, July 2, 2016, accessed September 20, 2016, http://rzim.org/global-blog/the-soul-of-america/. Used with permission.

4. Ibid.

5. Ibid.

6. Ibid.

7. Ibid.

8. Ibid.

9. "If You Can Keep It," Eric Metaxas, accessed September 20, 2016, http://ericmetaxas.com/books/if-you-can-keep-it/.

10. Eric Metaxas, interview by Billy Hallowell and Chris Field, *The Church Boys*, *TheBlaze*, podcast audio, July 20, 2016, accessed September 20, 2016, https://soundcloud.com/thechurchboys/freefall-qa-eric-metaxas.

11. Ibid.

12. Ibid.

13. Ibid.

14. Ibid.

15. Ibid.

16. Ibid.

17. Ibid.

18. Ibid.

19. Ibid.

20. Ibid.

21. Ibid.

22. Ibid.

23. Ibid.

24. Ibid.

25. Kristen Waggoner, in discussion with the author, June 15, 2016.

26. Ibid.

27. Ibid.

28. Ibid.

29. Volokh, discussion.

30. Ibid.

31. Ibid.

32. Ibid.

33. Ibid.

34. Billy Hallowell, "President Obama Has an Odd History of Flip-Flopping on Gay Marriage," *TheBlaze*, May 10, 2012, accessed September 21, 2016, http://www.theblaze.com/stories/2012/05/10/president-obama-has-an-odd-history-of-flip-flopping-on-gay-marriage/; Jason Linkins, "Obama Once Supported Same-Sex Marriage 'Unequivocally,'" *Huffington Post*, May 25, 2011, accessed September 21, 2016, http://www.huffingtonpost.com/2009/01/13/obama-once-supported-same_n_157656.html.

35. Zeke J. Miller, "Axelrod: Obama Misled Nation When He Opposed Gay Marriage in 2008," *Time*, February 10, 2015, accessed October 25, 2016, http://time.com/3702584/gay-marriage-axelrod-obama/.

36. Terry Gross, "Hillary Clinton: The Fresh Air Interview," NPR, June 12, 2014, accessed September 21, 2016, http://www.npr.org/templates/transcript/transcript.php?storyId=321313477; Amy Sherman, "Hillary Clinton's Changing Position on Same-Sex Marriage," Politifact, June 17, 2015, accessed September 21, 2016, http://www.politifact.com/truth-o-meter/statements/2015/jun/17/hillary-clinton/hillary-clinton-change-position-same-sex-marriage/.

37. Sherman, "Hillary Clinton's Changing Position."

38. Ibid.

39. Ibid.

40. "Supreme Court Defense of Marriage Act Ruling: Bill Clinton Reacts to Decision," *Huffington Post*, June 26, 2013, accessed September 21, 2016, http://www.huffingtonpost.com/2013/06/26/supreme-court-defense-of-marriage-act-ruling_n_3454798.html.

41. Ibid.

42. Alisa Wiersema, "High-Profile Politicians Who Changed Their Positions on Gay Marriage," ABC News, March 15, 2013, accessed October 25,

2016, http://abcnews.go.com/Politics/high-profile-politicians-changed
-positions-gay-marriage/story?id=18740293.

43. Billy Hallowell, "Christian Denomination Officially Embraces Gay
Marriage, Axing 'Man and a Woman' From Canon," *TheBlaze*, July 2, 2015,
accessed October 25, 2016, http://www.theblaze.com/stories/2015/07/02
/episcopal-church-changes-definition-of-marriage-to-include-same-sex
-marriage-axing-man-and-a-woman-from-canon/.

44. Waggoner, discussion.

45. Ibid.

46. "Lexington-Fayette Urban County Human Rights Commission
v. Hands on Originals," Alliance Defending Freedom, February 9, 2016,
accessed September 21, 2016, http://www.adfmedia.org/News/PRDetail
/9254.

47. Waggoner, discussion.

48. Billy Hallowell, "T-Shirt Maker Who Refused to Print Gay Pride
Shirts Is Being Punished—but These Lesbian Business Owners Reveal Why
They're Supporting Him, *TheBlaze*, November 7, 2014, accessed September
21, 2016, http://www.theblaze.com/stories/2014/11/07/lesbian-business
-owners-tell-glenn-beck-why-they-support-the-t-shirt-maker-whos-now
-being-punished-for-refusing-to-print-gay-pride-shirts/.

49. Billy Hallowell, "Why a Lesbian Business Owner Is Standing Up for a
Christian Printer's Right to Refuse Making T-Shirts for a Gay Pride Event,"
TheBlaze, November 5, 2014, accessed October 25, 2016, http://www
.theblaze.com/stories/2014/11/05/why-a-lesbian-business-owner-is-standing
-up-for-a-christian-printers-right-to-refuse-making-t-shirts-for-a-gay-pride
-event/.

50. Lillian Schrock, "Wyoming Judge Who Refuses to Marry Gay Couples Fights Removal," *Casper Star Tribune*, May 6, 2016, accessed September 21, 2016, http://trib.com/news/local/crime-and-courts/wyoming
-judge-who-refuses-to-marry-gay-couples-fights-removal/article_9b274bee
-5eeb-57b8-a72c-ff19a8cf7490.html.

51. Waggoner, discussion; Schrock, "Wyoming Judge"; Jonathan G.
Lange, "A Biblical View of Marriage Spoken Openly May Get This Judge
Fired and Disbarred," LifeSiteNews, September 7, 2016, accessed October
25, 2016, https://www.lifesitenews.com/opinion/dissent-will-not-be
-tolerated-what-the-case-of-a-wyoming-judge-means-for-al.

52. Ibid.; Schrock, "Wyoming Judge."

53. Schrock, "Wyoming Judge."

54. Ibid.

55. Jeremy Dys, in discussion with the author, June 9, 2016.

56. Ibid.

57. Ibid.

58. Ibid.

59. Josh Sanburn, "Houston's Pastors Outraged After City Subpoenas Sermons Over Transgender Bill, *Time*, October 17, 2014, accessed September 22, 2016, http://time.com/3514166/houston-pastors-sermons -subpoenaed/.

60. Ibid.

61. Ibid.

62. Dys, discussion.

63. Billy Hallowell, "Churches Say This Government Brochure 'Should Send Chills down the Spine of Every Congregation in Iowa.' Here's Why," *Deseret News*, July 5, 2016, accessed September 22, 2016, http://www .deseretnews.com/article/865657483/Churches-say-this-government -brochure-should-send-chills-down-the-spine-of-every-congregation-in .html?pg=all. Used with permission.

64. Ibid.

65. Ibid.

66. "Iowa Civil Rights Commission Releases Revised Sexual Orientation and Gender Identity Public Accommodations Brochure," Iowa Civil Rights Commission, July 8, 2016, accessed September 22, 2016, https://icrc.iowa .gov/pressrelease/iowa-civil-rights-commission-releases-revised-sexual -orientation-gender-identity-public.

67. Dys, discussion.

68. Ibid.

69. Ibid.

70. Ibid.

71. Ibid.

CHAPTER 18: THE SOLUTION

1. Baker, discussion.

2. "Christian," Box Office Mojo, accessed September 22, 2016, http:// www.boxofficemojo.com/genres/chart/?id=christian.htm.

3. Melissa Mushaka, "How Miracles From Heaven Producer DeVon Franklin Created, A Compelling Balance, Within the Film and His Own Life As Well," *Huffington Post*, March 25, 2016, accessed September 22, 2016, http://www.huffingtonpost.com/melissa-mushaka/how-miracles -from-heaven-_b_9542534.html.

4. DeVon Franklin, in discussion with the author, June 13, 2016.

5. Ibid.

6. Patrick Ryan, "'War Room' Trounces 'Compton' for No. 1," *USA Today*, September 7, 2015, accessed September 22, 2016, http://www.usa today.com/story/life/movies/2015/09/07/box-office-war-room-straight -outta-compton-transporter-refueled/71625350/.

7. Billy Hallowell, "Movie Critics 'Trash' and 'Destroy' Hit Christian Film that Shocked at the Box Office—but Wait Until You See the Stunning Audience Response," *TheBlaze*, September 1, 2015, accessed September 22,

2016, http://www.theblaze.com/stories/2015/09/01/movie-critics-trash-and
-destroy-hit-christian-film-that-shocked-at-the-box-office-but-wait-until-you
-see-the-stunning-audience-reaction/.

8. Franklin, discussion.

9. Ibid.

10. Ibid.

11. Baehr, discussion.

12. Franklin, discussion.

13. Ibid.

14. Ibid.

15. Baehr, discussion.

16. Ibid.

17. Billy Hallowell, "Willie and Korie Robertson Reveal Something You
Might Not Know About 'Duck Dynasty' and Uncle Si," *TheBlaze*, April 16,
2015, accessed September 22, 2016, http://www.theblaze.com/stories/2015
/04/16/willie-and-korie-robertson-reveal-something-you-might-not-know
-about-duck-dynasty-and-uncle-si/.

18. Billy Hallowell, "'It's Almost a Reflex Now': Actress Patricia Heaton
on Why She Speaks Out Against Abortion," *TheBlaze*, March 4, 2014,
accessed October 25, 2016, http://www.theblaze.com/stories/2014/03/04
/its-almost-a-reflex-now-actress-patricia-heaton-on-why-she-speaks-out
-against-abortion/.

19. Ibid.

20. Yancey, discussion.

21. Ibid.

22. Ibid.

23. Ibid.

24. Megan Alexander, in discussion with the author, June 28, 2016.

25. Ibid.

26. Ibid.

27. Ibid.

28. Ibid.

29. Ibid.

30. Ibid.

31. Ibid.

32. Billy Hallowell, "TV Host Reveals Why She Saved Sex Until
Marriage—and How She Lives Her 'Faith in the Spotlight,'" *Deseret News*,
October 4, 2016, accessed October 25, 2016, http://www.deseretnews.com
/article/865663994/TV-host-reveals-why-she-saved-sex-until-marriage-2
-and-how-she-lives-her-faith-in-the-spotlight.html?pg=all.

33. Alexander, discussion.

34. Ibid.

35. Ibid.

36. McDowell, interview.

37. Ibid.
38. Ibid.
39. Ibid.
40. Ibid.

ABOUT THE AUTHOR

THROUGH JOURNALISM, MEDIA, public speaking appearances, and the blogosphere, Billy Hallowell has worked as a journalist and commentator for more than a decade. He has been published and featured in political and cultural books, textbooks, articles, and websites that focus on the youth of America and their role in the future of our world.

Hallowell is the senior editor at Faithwire.com and the former faith and culture editor at *TheBlaze*. He has contributed to the *Washington Post*, *Human Events* (blog), *The Daily Caller*, *Mediaite* (blog), and *The Huffington Post*, among other news sites. He has also appeared on Fox News, FOXNews.com LIVE, and HuffPo Live, among others.

Hallowell's career in journalism and commentary began at an early age. Following the Columbine shooting in 1999, the then fifteen-year old launched Teen Web Online, a website intended to address violence, discrimination, and other social issues facing America's young generation.

In 2002 he founded Pathufind Media, an ongoing project that subcontracts affordable speakers to colleges and community groups.

In 2003 Hallowell was selected to represent the United States at the World Bank's conference on youth development in Paris, France.

Following this experience, he was honored by the International Youth Foundation with the YouthAction Net Fellowship. On the educational front, he was a Rhodes Scholar nominee in 2006 and the recipient of the prestigious Clark Fellowship during the same year. In addition to these honors, Hallowell has received a number of journalism and community awards for his work.

Hallowell was educated at the College of Mount Saint Vincent in Riverdale, New York, and graduated with a BA in communications, with concentrations in broadcasting, corporate and journalism, and a minor in writing. In June 2008 he completed his MS in social research from Hunter College in Manhattan, New York. You can follow him on Twitter (@BillyHallowell).

CONNECT WITH US!

CHARISMA HOUSE

(Spiritual Growth)

f Facebook.com/CharismaHouse

y @CharismaHouse

◉ Instagram.com/CharismaHouse

(Health)

⦿ Pinterest.com/CharismaHouse

(Bible)
www.mevbible.com

SUBSCRIBE TODAY

Exclusive Content

Inspiring Messages

Encouraging Articles

Discovering Freedom

CHARISMA MEDIA

FREE NEWSLETTERS

to experience the power of the *Holy Spirit*

 Charisma Magazine Newsletter
Get top-trending articles, Christian teachings, entertainment reviews, videos, and more.

 Charisma News Weekly
Get the latest breaking news from an evangelical perspective every Monday.

 SpiritLed Woman
Receive amazing stories, testimonies, and articles on marriage, family, prayer, and more.

 New Man
Get articles and teaching about the realities of living in the world today as a man of faith.

 3-in-1 Daily Devotionals
Find personal strength and encouragement with these devotionals, and begin your day with God's Word.

Sign up for Free at nl.charismamag.com